MAD LOVES

PRINCETON STUDIES IN OPERA

CAROLYN ABBATE AND ROGER PARKER
SERIES EDITORS

MAD LOVES

WOMEN AND MUSIC IN OFFENBACH'S
LES CONTES D'HOFFMANN

Heather Hadlock

PRINCETON UNIVERSITY PRESS   PRINCETON AND OXFORD

Library of Congress Cataloging-in-Publication Data
Hadlock, Heather
Mad loves : women and music in Offenbach's Les contes d'Hoffmann / Heather Hadlock.
p.   cm.
Includes bibliographical references and index.
ISBN 0-691-05802-4 (cl : alk. paper)
1. Offenbach, Jacques, 1819–1880. Contes d'Hoffmann.
2. Women in opera.   I. Title.
ML410.O41 H33   2000
782.1—dc21   00-023688

"Voulez-vous le récit de ces folles amours?"

Contents

Acknowledgments

THROUGHOUT THE research and writing of this book I have had many occasions to be grateful for Carolyn Abbate's discernment and skill as an advisor, critic, and mentor. I have relied on Roger Parker's critical and editorial acumen since the very early stages of this project, and his detailed commentary on the penultimate version of the manuscript did much to shape its final form. I also appreciate the encouragement I have received from my colleagues at Stanford University during that process of revision and transformation. The Opera Studies Workshop funded by the Stanford Humanities Center has provided a lively forum for discussions of opera and opera scholarship, due in large part to the ongoing involvement of Paul Robinson, Herbert Lindenberger, Karol Berger, Thomas Grey, and Stephen Hinton. John Speagle has been an indefatigable source of intellectual and moral support.

Thanks are due to the Andrew Mellon Foundation, the American Musicological Society, and the National Endowment for the Humanities Summer Stipend Program for their support of dissertation and post-dissertation research and writing. I thank the program committees of the Third Feminist Theory and Music Conference (June 1995) and of the 1995 American Musicologial Society meeting for opportunities to present portions of the chapter on music and mesmerism; the University of California–Berkeley colloquium audience for their stimulating response to my colloquium on the Venetian act in 1996; and Mary Ann Smart for inviting me to speak on *Les Contes* as a fantastical narrative in her 1999 symposium on "E.T.A. Hoffmann and Music," also at Berkeley. An earlier version of Chapter Three appeared as "Returns of the Repressed: The Prima Donna from Hoffmann's *Tales* to Offenbach's *Les Contes*," in *Cambridge Opera Journal* 6, no. 3 (November 1994): 221–43.

From the moment I began to write it, I have imagined this book as an expression of gratitude to tenor Neil Shicoff, for his performance in the Metropolitan Opera's 1988 *Contes d'Hoffmann*; and to my mother, for taping it.

MAD LOVES

Introduction

> [N]ot only a man's knowledge or wisdom, but above all his
> real life—and this is the stuff that stories are made of—
> first assumes transmissible form at the moment of his
> death. Just as the sequence of images is set in motion
> inside a man as his life comes to an end—unfolding the
> views of himself under which he has encountered himself
> without being aware of it—suddenly in his expressions and
> looks the unforgettable emerges and imparts to everything
> that concerned him that authority which even the poorest
> wretch in dying possesses for the living around him. This
> authority is at the very source of the story.
> *(Walter Benjamin, "The Story-Teller")*

BENJAMIN's characterization of the storyteller as a mediator between past and present, between life and death, and as a figure who cannot be securely located in any single condition, will serve to introduce my discussion of Offenbach's *Les Contes d'Hoffmann,* which may be interpreted on more than one level as a death-utterance. Death plays a prominent role in the plots of the opera's three tales: the death of illusions, in the story of Olympia; the death of love, in the story of Antonia; and the symbolic death of the lover himself in the story of Hoffmann's lost reflection. But the larger narrative, of which these three tales are only constituent parts, also shows us Hoffmann in a situation resembling Benjamin's moment of death: the poet is a man (even a "poor wretch") looking back over his life with the authority, perhaps for the first time, to make sense of the whole scope of his experience and to recount that experience to others. The opera is the last utterance of another dying man, its composer, for as Hoffmann reviews his three *folles amours,* so Offenbach in the course of the work reviews his own compositional past, drawing its various elements into a musico-dramatic kaleidoscope. Finally, the death of the composer left an indelible mark on the piece, which was not and never has been satisfactorily finished.

It might be more precise, then, to say that *Les Contes d'Hoffmann* and its narrator are not dying, but rather *undead.* Even after his symbolic death at the loss of his reflection, the narrator continues to live and speak; likewise, his three lost beloved women turn out not to be truly dead, but only masks worn by a prima donna who remains very much alive. And the opera, despite or perhaps because of its unfinished condition, lives and flourishes as well. Consider the conductor-scholar Antonio de Almeida's description of how he discovered a cache of new sources for the opera in the home of one of Offenbach's descendants in 1976: "Although Madame Cusset, who represented the Offenbach family, insisted they had little, if any, music . . . I was finally allowed to probe around the studio. In a very large *armoire,* I spotted two large green cartons, somewhat like the ones in which French notaries file their acts. I opened them, and it took the merest of glances to realize the real Offenbachian treasure trove I was facing."[1] This tale has all the elements of a Gothic drama in miniature: the ancestral home, the gatekeeper, the search, the casket within a casket, and finally the shock of recognition at the uncanny vitality of the casket's contents, which would provide material for a new edition by Fritz Oeser that radically altered the opera's contents and form. The opera was not laid to rest with this edition, however: rather, de Almeida's adventure was repeated in November 1984 with the emergence of another "treasure trove" and Michael Kaye's preparation in 1992 of another critical edition, equally distant from Oeser's and from the traditional version. Nor is the story ended, for Jean-Christophe Keck promised in 1993 that he would publish yet another edition, using sources to which Kaye had not had access.[2]

Thus *Les Contes d'Hoffmann* has resided and continues to reside, in Slavoj Žižek's phrase, "between two deaths"—in a liminal condition of restless incompleteness. How appropriate, then, that the opera should be populated with undead musical presences: Hoffmann, the storyteller; Dr. Miracle, the demonic violinist; Antonia, the singer suspended between life and death and between human and instrumental status; a feminine robot and a dead mother's portrait that inexplicably come to life. Indeed, *restlessness* characterized this piece from its very inception, for Offenbach conceived the idea for his "Hoffmann opera" decades before he sat down to write it, and once he began to write the work kept changing under his hands. The usually speedy and efficient composer was unable to put his project to rest, but instead kept rethinking, reshaping, and revising it, both in response to his own impulses and to external ones.

A LONG GENESIS

Offenbach's *Les Contes d'Hoffmann* is based on a five-act *drame fantastique* of the same name, which had enjoyed a reasonable success at the Théâtre de l'Odéon in March 1851. By making Hoffmann himself the narrator, the playwrights Jules Barbier and Michel Carré had contrived to stitch together three short tales, each thrilling but none substantial enough for a full evening's entertainment. E.T.A. Hoffmann's stories provided a cast of fantastical characters and four colorful settings: a tavern, a mad scientist's workshop, a parlor with its imposing portrait of Antonia's mother, and a Venetian palazzo, complete with gondolas and faro tables. This synopsis of the play will also serve as a précis of the opera's plot, despite changes Barbier made to the ending of the opera's Venetian act:

Act I. Prologue

Luther's tavern, attached to a theater where Don Giovanni is being performed. Councilor Lindorf arrives in search of the prima donna "La Stella" and learns to his disgust that she has promised to meet the poet Hoffmann. A crowd of students arrive, followed by Hoffmann and his companion Nicklausse. Hoffmann offers to tell the stories of his three "mad loves."

Act II. The Tale of Olympia
(based on E.T.A. Hoffmann's "The Sandman")

Hoffmann's first love is the daughter of Spalanzani, a mad scientist. Seen through magic spectacles provided by the sinister Coppélius, Olympia appears as a charming girl. At her debut party, Olympia sings a brilliant aria and seems to accept Hoffmann's love. But when they dance together, she flings him aside, breaking his spectacles, and runs away. Coppélius, furious at Spalanzani for cheating him out of some money, breaks Olympia into pieces—and Hoffmann realizes that she was only a robot.

Act III. The Tale of Antonia
(based on E.T.A. Hoffmann's "Counselor Krespel")

Hoffmann's second love, Antonia, has a mysterious illness that will kill her if she sings. For his sake she promises not to sing anymore, but the demonic Dr. Miracle arrives and tempts her. He brings to life a portrait of her dead mother, a great singer, and Antonia sings herself into a fatal frenzy. Hoffmann arrives just in time to see her die.

Act IV. The Tale of Giulietta
(based on E.T.A. Hoffmann's "A New Year's Eve Adventure")

Hoffmann, having renounced love, gambles at the Venetian palazzo of Giulietta, a courtesan. Her master, Dapertutto, commands Giulietta to steal Hoffmann's reflection for him in a mirror. Hoffmann succumbs to Giulietta, but must kill her current lover, Schlemil, to get the key to her room. The guests mock Hoffmann's terror at the murder and the loss of his reflection. Giulietta mistakenly drinks poison intended for Nicklausse. Dappertutto laughs.

Act V. Epilogue

Luther's tavern. Hoffmann is drunk when Stella arrives, and Stella leaves with Lindorf. Nicklausse now reveals himself as the Muse of Poetry in disguise, and claims Hoffmann for her own.

The outline of an opera libretto was, in a sense, ready-made, for many of the play's scenes already revolved around musical numbers. In Act I, the students greeted the tavern-keeper with a rousing chorus, and Act II featured Olympia's "Doll Song" (not sung, but played on an English horn) and a waltz for Spalanzani's guests. Hoffmann and Antonia sang a love-duet at the beginning of Act III, and that act ended with a fatal duet for Antonia and her mother, urged on by Dr. Miracle's violin. In Venice, Hoffmann scoffed at love in a *couplets* with chorus, "Amis, ce flot vermeil," and the students, back in the tavern, sang a final chorus.[3] Although the musical episodes attracted no critical attention, the text did provoke some raised eyebrows when its prose dialogue blossomed into rhyming hexameters at emotional and dramatic high points, including the "Vision" that interrupts Hoffmann's Kleinzach ballad; the struggle between Antonia and Dr. Miracle, which culminates in the mother's song; and the love scene between Giulietta and Hoffmann. These extended poetic passages were retained *verbatim* in the libretto.

It is not surprising that this play, with its musical episodes and musician characters, should have captured Offenbach's fancy, although more than twenty years elapsed before he suggested to Barbier and Carré that they should rework *Les Contes d'Hoffmann* as the libretto for a serious opera. His theatrical imagination had always been drawn toward the fantastical landscapes, playful humor, grotesquerie, and pathos found in these tales. Furthermore, E.T.A. Hoffmann embodied the generation of German Romanticism that Offenbach loved, not yet weighed down by what he saw as Wagnerist bombast and self-conscious modernism. This was the German style he admired in Weber's *Der Freischütz* and had tried to emulate in his own "gros Romantisch Oper" *Die Rhein-Nixen* of 1864. As recently as 1872, his failed opéra-comique *Fantasio* had featured moments of old-fashioned "Weberist" color, including a *Männerchor* from which he would later borrow a climactic phrase for the chorus of students in Luther's tavern. Indeed *Fantasio*, featuring a lovelorn jester-hero, anticipated the tone of *Les Contes* in its combination of facetious and pathetic accents. He began work on the Hoffmann subject in 1876, envisioning a five-act opéra-lyrique for performance at Vizentini's Théâtre de la Gaîté-Lyrique. This planned opéra-lyrique would have adhered closely to Barbier and Carré's play, retaining both the poetic passages and the order of the tales, with Olympia first, Antonia in the middle, and Giulietta last. As in the play, the opera's three tales would have progressed from light to darkness, from comedy to something approaching horror.

The score of *Les Contes,* as initially conceived, can be seen as a negotiation with the classic outlines of opéra-comique, which Offenbach had claimed as the model for all his previous works—not only those presented at the Salle Favart in the 1870s, but even his operettas at the Bouffes

Parisiens. In 1856, at the beginning of his career as impresario of the Bouffes, he had published a brief manifesto on the genre of opéra-comique, reminding readers of its eighteenth-century origin as a play with songs and defining its native French qualities as wit, clarity, and brevity.[4] Most elusive of all, perhaps, was the quality of *esprit*, a lightly borne confidence and melodic ease, propelled by rhythmic impulses and gestures rooted in dance. Songs, such as *couplets*, rondos, ballads, chansons, predominated in opéra-comique, and vocal style was simple and light, avoiding the excessive virtuosity of the Italian style and the strenuous style of grand opera. Melody should be the primary musical value throughout a score, and forms and accompaniments should never become so complex as to obscure or distract from a number's songful qualities. Offenbach pledged that his new theater would uphold these values, and throughout his career he did adhere to them, even when he mingled—or some would say adulterated—them with the strains of facetiousness, parody, and farce that were equally constitutive of his operettas. Now, in his self-consciously serious opéra-lyrique, he would not leave the values and techniques of opéra-comique behind, but would extend its expressive and dramatic resources.

Although *Les Contes* was conceived as a number opera, Offenbach's musical thought was working on a larger scale. The Olympia act, for example, is largely made up of traditional *couplets*, romances, choruses, and chansons, but these are linked together to form longer, uninterrupted stretches of musical action, a procedure more typical of act finales. Thus the party scene that begins with the waltz chorus for the guests' entrance continues without a break through Spalanzani's tuneful presentation of his "daughter," Olympia's "Doll Song", a *parlando* dialogue over yet another dance theme, and finally a reprise of the waltz chorus as the guests depart.[5] Borrowing Auber's technique of constructing a scene over a continuous stream of dance music, Offenbach integrates the characters' private conversations into the musical action without having to stop and start for spoken dialogue. Elsewhere he seems to test the boundaries of individual numbers from within. The Antonia act, strikingly short of *couplets* and romances, is dominated by larger-scale dramatic ensembles. While it would have been perfectly appropriate, in the opéra-comique tradition, to present the charming "C'est une chanson d'amour" as a self-contained song, Offenbach frames it instead as the final section of a four-movement grand duet for Hoffmann and Antonia. The men's trio "Pour conjurer le danger" has the same Italianate structure, with a wonderfully suspenseful *tempo di mezzo* in which Dr. Miracle compels the absent Antonia to sing. The composer does not entirely give up his old habit of pushing his ensembles to a frenzied conclusion, but now employs it to a new and more serious dramatic purpose: instead of culminating in wild dances or hilariously inebriated exhaustion, musical frenzy proves fatal, with Olympia whirling into the malevolent grasp of Coppélius, and Antonia falling dead. The finales of the Olympia and Antonia acts unmask the latent violence beneath the old slapstick numbers.

Without abandoning his native tunefulness, Offenbach expanded it beyond the boundaries of conventional *couplets* structures, treating melody and form with unaccustomed freedom. The prologue, with only a few full-scale "numbers," seems the most modern part of the score: here Offenbach treated melodic ideas with wonderful nonchalance, and from the moment of the students' entrance the prologue bubbles along in an almost seamless flow of *arioso* fragments and musical miniatures, including the exchange of insults between Hoffmann and Lindorf, and the brief chorus "Écoutons!" The most striking formal innovation is Hoffmann's "Légende de Kleinzach," where an extended rhapsody is embedded within a traditional strophic song. In that rhapsody we also see Offenbach's melody at its most unconstrained, as the composer breaks out of his customary four-square phrases in favor of free declamation. The tenor romance "O dieu de quelle ivresse," which could have been a self-contained solo, also occurs within a larger number, the "Duo de reflet." (Perhaps this move imitates Bizet's placing of the Flower Song within Carmen and Don Jose's Act II duet). Finally, Offenbach complicated the relationship between voice and orchestra at expressive high points: at the climaxes of Hoffmann's "Vision" and his lavish "O Dieu de quelle ivresse," the orchestra takes over the melody, and the interdependence of voice and orchestra anticipates Massenet and even Puccini. At these moments of emotional excess, the melody seems to exceed the scale of individual human utterance, and to pass to a transcendent instrumental voice. All these innovations suggest that Offenbach hoped at once to retain and to transcend the conventional musical values of opéra-comique.

It is ironic, then, that *Les Contes,* conceived for a more serious venue, ended up at the Opéra-Comique after all. The bankruptcy of the Gaîté-Lyrique's impresario Vizentini, in January 1878, left Offenbach without a producer for his still-unfinished work, and Leon Carvalho, director of the Opéra-Comique, accepted the piece in May 1879. Offenbach had made several previous attempts at composing legitimate works for this venue, but had so far found it difficult to convince its audiences of his sincerity and worth; "Petrus," writing for *La Petite République,* recalled that in response to *Robinson Crusoe,* "The public had cried, 'Return to the Bouffes or the Folies-Dramatiques: the Opéra-Comique is not made for you.'"[6] The Opéra-Comique, as both an institution and a genre, was defined by its respectability, and this meant the careful maintenance of social and stylistic boundaries between opéra-comique and operetta. (Offenbach undoubtedly ran afoul of the Opéra-Comique audience's horror of *parvenus,* of joking, and of vulgarity with his first effort, *Barkouf,* which featured a singing dog.) This was, after all, the theater to which a respectable man could bring his wife and daughters without endangering their purity of mind or associations. And the institution's sociological profile translated into a vague yet powerful notion of musical respectability: a mastery of emotion, a preference for epigrams over diatribes or rhapsodies, and for sincere and well-formed expression over outbursts of raw feeling.

The Opéra-Comique itself was changing, however, and *Les Contes'* unconventional qualities were not unsuited to the institution's emerging modern profile. Carvalho, who had spent most of his career as impresario of the Théâtre-Lyrique between 1856 and 1868, defined "opéra-comique" liberally enough to accommodate those features of *Les Contes* that broke or tested the traditional limits of the genre. As both a genre and an institution the opéra-comique was moving into a new phase, which would be its last: while it remained committed to the heritage of what Hervé Lacombe has characterized as the "conversational" salon style—such hard-to-translate qualities as *élan, insouciance,* and *légèreté*—it was admitting more diverse and serious works than had been favored in the past.[7] Bizet's oft-cited cry of "Down with *La dame blanche!*" signaled that opéra-comique had entered a period of transition, and in the aesthetic turbulence of the 1870s, the Favart was becoming an "experimental theater." *Carmen,* in 1875, had broken the long-standing taboo on tragic endings, so the death of Antonia and even Hoffmann's slaying of Schlemil and Pitichinaccio in the Venetian act were acceptable, as was the progress of the dramatic tone from bright to nightmarish. Although one would be hard-pressed to claim resemblances between *Carmen* and *Les Contes,* both works show how the new opéra-comique could tolerate diminishing amounts of spoken dialogue, and a modern style of vocalism. Rather than leaving opéra-comique behind, *Les Contes d'Hoffmann* became one of its last, modern incarnations.

Despite Carvalho's acceptance of the numbers already written, and his support for the composer's overall conception, he did immediately insist upon one significant change to the score; indeed the modern *sound* of the opera probably owes as much to Carvalho as to Offenbach. Offenbach had conceived the role of Hoffmann as a baritone, but Carvalho insisted that he adapt the lead role for the Opéra-Comique's star tenor, Andre Talazac, currently enjoying a brilliant success in Gounod's *Roméo et Juliette.*[8] Talazac belonged to the first generation of tenors that broke with the opéra-comique tradition of genteel light vocalism, and in transposing the role for him, Offenbach endowed Hoffmann with that lyric urgency which also characterizes the nearly contemporary role of Don José. The role of Hoffmann thus helped to define an emerging French tenor voice and persona: the modern opéra-comique hero sang in full voice, like his colleagues in serious and tragic pieces, but in an ardent rather than bellicose strain. Fascinating though it is to imagine how the opera would sound with a baritone hero, it is hard to consider the rewriting of this role in 1879 as anything other than a fortunate change. The tenor Hoffmann's plangent tones—like those of Don José before him, and of Massenet's Chevalier Des Grieux and Werther a few years later—now seem uniquely suited to the expression of *amour fou*.

Other changes were required as well, for better and worse. Offenbach's original conception would have omitted a bright spot for modern sopranos, for Olympia was to have been a simple soubrette, and her "Doll Song," as drafted in 1877, had only a moderate tessitura and limited ornamentation. The Opéra-Comique's leading lady, Adele Isaac, was a coloratura whose recent success as Gounod's Juliette no doubt convinced her that her new role would be incomplete without a brilliant waltz aria. Isaac's talents inspired—indeed, commanded—the showpiece we know today. The double role of the Muse/Nicklausse, which Offenbach had imagined as a dramatic mezzo-soprano, was entrusted to the inexperienced *soubrette* Marguerite Ugalde, a change that proved less happy than the casting of Talazac and Isaac. In the course of rehearsals, the double role of the Muse/Nicklausse lost two substantial solos: the *couplets* for the Muse that opened the Prologue, and Nicklausse's sumptuous aria "Vois sous l'archet frémissant" in the Antonia act. The lively "Trio des yeux," in which Hoffmann and Nicklausse were to meet Coppélius and buy his magic spectacles, had to be replaced by a stretch of spoken dialogue. (These three numbers, restored to the score in Fritz Oeser's 1977 critical edition, have had various degrees of acceptance: mezzo-sopranos have embraced the *couplets* and especially the aria, but the trio, which replaces Coppélius's only solo, remains something of a novelty piece.) Ultimately Nicklausse was demoted to a *comprimaria* role, and the Muse's part cut back to a single speech in the Epilogue.

Revisions, rewrites, and cuts made to accommodate individual singers were not the only challenges Offenbach confronted as he worked to complete *Les Contes* in its opéra-comique form, and the Venetian act and epilogue had not yet been finished to everyone's satisfaction when the composer died on October 5, 1880. Carvalho, together with Ernest Guiraud, worked for several months to pull together the unfinished work, but on February 5, 1881, five days before the opera's long-delayed premiere at the Opéra-Comique, Carvalho decided to cut the troublesome fourth act altogether, eliminating the tale of the Italian courtesan Giulietta. The loss of the Venetian act was both aesthetic and material: when Talazac complained that he would lose some of Hoffmann's best music, Carvalho responded petulantly, "You may lose one lovely act, while I—I lose three sets and a hundred costumes."[9] Yet even at this point, the Venetian act was not completely eliminated; rather it was dismantled and dispersed. Carvalho, reluctant to lose the three most effective numbers, distributed them elsewhere in the opera: the Barcarole was sung by off-stage soloists and chorus during the Antonia act; Hoffmann's passionate "O Dieu de quelle ivresse," which would have been sung to Giulietta, was moved to the Epilogue, where Hoffmann addressed it to the Muse; and the *Duo de Reflet*, in which Giulietta would have stolen Hoffmann's reflection, became a "rejection duet" for Hoffmann and Stella in the epilogue. Still other numbers were stored away, and had been presumed lost until their very recent rediscovery. Thus the opera as premiered in Paris and in Vienna included only two of the intended three tales.

Within a year of the premiere, however, the tale of Giulietta had been revised and restored. The Offenbach family appointed Ernest Guiraud to reconstruct the Venetian act and to replace the spoken dialogue of the opéra-comique version with recitatives so that the opera could be performed in other theaters, and his version was published later in 1881 and in 1882. Guiraud condensed the unwieldy act from four scenes to one, retaining only four numbers: the Barcarolle, Hoffmann's *couplets,* Dapertutto's "Tournez, miroir," and the *Duo de Reflet* for Hoffmann and Giulietta. He rewrote the ending so that the courtesan did not die, but sailed away in a gondola, laughing at Hoffmann. Most significantly, Guiraud rearranged the three tales, placing the Venetian act between the Olympia and Antonia acts.[10] Like his other decisions, this was a pragmatic one: the reconstructed Venetian act, shorter and musically weaker than either "Olympia" or "Antonia," would show its flaws least if sandwiched between these two more powerful pieces.

Within a year of its first performance and publication, then, *Les Contes d'Hoffmann* already existed in a double form—one version with the Venetian act, and one without—and this initial instability only foreshadowed the proliferation to come. Guiraud's version of the Venetian act remained a magnet for editorial intervention. Three twentieth-century editions will be discussed in more detail in the pages that follow; however, a brief sketch will serve to introduce their salient features. The version published in 1907, which amounted to another recomposition, was created at the Théâtre de Monte Carlo by composer/impresario Raoul Gunsbourg, together with librettist Pierre Barbier and orchestrator André Bloch, and this version far surpassed Guiraud's efforts to repair the work's deficiencies. Gunsbourg and his collaborators removed Dapertutto's *chanson,* "Tournez, miroir," assigning it (with new text) to Coppélius in Act II, and they supplied Dapertutto with a new aria, "Scintille diamant." They were also responsible for "Italianizing" the Venetian act, for they added the *pezzo concertato* finale, a septet with chorus ("Hélas, mon coeur s'égare encore") in which Hoffmann and all the Venetian characters respond to the loss of Hoffmann's reflection. During the twenty-five years after its opening night, then, *Les Contes d'Hoffmann* had gained—or regained—an entire act, a palimpsest of music by Offenbach, music in imitation of Offenbach, and one number, the septet, that had no connection at all with Offenbach. It was in this form, already several stages removed from that of its 1881 Opéra-Comique premiere, that *Les Contes d'Hoffmann* entered the international repertory.

Despite its widespread acceptance, however, this version had certain dramatic and musical weaknesses. It lacked an aria for Giulietta; Hoffmann's spontaneous declaration, "Giulietta, je t'aime!" seemed improbable without a song or even dialogue to trigger it; and the final note of Dapertutto's new aria "Scintille, diamant" lay high in the baritone range, making the role musically inconsistent with those of Lindorf, Coppélius, and Dr. Miracle. Furthermore, anecdotes from the time of the opera's premiere suggested that spectacular things had been lost with Carvalho's initial cut; Martinet, for example, had referred not only to "three sets and one hundred costumes," but also to a shadow-play and a fantastical duel scene.[11] Behind Gunsbourg's version and the earlier versions by Guiraud and Carvalho hovered an increasingly mythologized *Urtext,* the never-performed version that Carvalho had cut and that Guiraud had decided not to publish in full.

Since the publication of Gunsbourg's version, innumerable performing versions have been assembled, and two scholarly editions have appeared. Fritz Oeser's 1976 edition drew on newly discovered manuscript sources, together with Barbier and Carré's original play and Offenbach's *Die Rhein-Nixen.* Oeser not only added previously unknown music throughout the opera, but also insisted that the Venetian act, rather than the Antonia act, should be the climax of Hoffmann's evening of storytelling.[12] Between 1992 and 1995, Michael Kaye reconstructed the opera again on the basis of sources that were unknown to Oeser, including the censor's libretto of 1881 and rehearsal materials from the period leading up to the Opéra-Comique premiere.[13] The Venetian act presented in these two editions, particularly the version prepared by Kaye, has rendered the traditional version's master plot increasingly untenable, by shifting both the distribution of national styles in the score and its balance of tragic and comic, sincere and ironic elements.

The arrangement of the chapters that follow roughly imitates the content and shape of the opera. The first chapter, like the opera's prologue, introduces the narrator-protagonist. It takes up the eternal question of how "Hoffmannesque" this opera is, contending that as a story about storytelling and an opera about singing, *Les Contes* is true in its fashion to E.T.A.

Hoffmann's self-reflexive narrative style. Chapter Two takes Dr. Miracle and his diva/patient Antonia as a case study in how the parallel nineteenth-century discourses of theater and "mental science"—including mesmerism, *magnétisme animal,* hypnosis, and other proto-psychoanalytic treatments—constructed the female voice as an object to be conjured up and manipulated by male authorities. Mesmeric performances frequently involved music, both in the theater and the clinic, for Mesmer believed that animal magnetism was "communicated, propagated and augmented by sound," and that music facilitated the magnetic trance. Both the singing of musical clairvoyants and the *speech* of mesmerized women took on a quasi-supernatural status, possessing the same uncanny presence attributed to music in the Romantic imagination. Yet the popular conception of Dr. Miracle as a proto-Svengali is not entirely convincing, and the chapter concludes with an alternative reading of Antonia's story and her fatal song, based on nineteenth-century testimony that the image of the conjurer-doctor-therapist controlling his inert trance-maiden was an elaborate deception, impossible to sustain without the "backstage" participation of the women involved. Perhaps, contrary to the interpretive tradition that began with Hanslick in 1881, Antonia's fatal song is not a helpless submission, but a choice, for in "succumbing" to Dr. Miracle, this female artist rebels against a domestic/paternal order that would silence her.

Antonia's choice between song—at the price of her own death—and silent bourgeois life thus becomes an allegory of the choices facing women musicians in nineteenth-century Europe, and the third chapter explores this conflict in more detail, introducing Antonia's artist-mother and her influence as another factor in the father's and doctor's struggle over the daughter's voice. If the spectacular elements of Antonia's story derive from stage conventions of mesmerism and magnetism, her family relations have more in common with those of nineteenth-century hysterics: Antonia is an archetype of the daughter on the brink of womanhood, unconsciously—and violently, often self-destructively—acting out her conflicts over desires that male authorities have declared off-limits. The seductive phantom song of her mother and the music of Miracle's violin manifest the disorderly and imperfectly repressed elements in Antonia's fictional psyche.

Chapter Four provides a kind of intermission before proceeding on to the Venetian act and its restoration, a pause to consider Offenbach himself as a liminal figure: a foreigner in his two home countries, both before and after his death; a converted German Jew who became the voice of Second Empire Paris; a "gifted musician who hated music," as Debussy described him. *Les Contes d'Hoffmann* has since 1881 held a privileged place within Offenbach's *oeuvre,* and its status as his most serious and sincere work, and therefore his best, invites us to meditate on the categories of "serious music" and "musical sincerity." The special status of *Les Contes* was summarized by Edouard Hanslick in his review of the Viennese premiere in 1881:

> Is this last work of Offenbach truly his best? Yes and no. His best in the sense that—to take a more elevated example—*Guillaume Tell* is Rossini's best opera. But the *Barber* is even better. *Les Contes d'Hoffmann* is musically more profound and purer than the author's earlier operettas; only its nightmarish content lacks the unique elements in which Offenbach's peculiar talent really shone forth: comic, parodistic humor and gaiety. If what makes one a master is the thing that nobody else can do as well, what is uniquely one's own, then Offenbach became Offenbach through musical jests and pranks.[14]

Les Contes was received from the very beginning as both a departure from and a culmination of Offenbach's style. But perhaps Offenbach's conflicting tendencies toward frivolity and seriousness, toward lowbrow and highbrow styles, had less influence on his last creation than did certain political and artistic prejudices in Paris after the Franco-Prussian war. As much as any artistic ideals, cultural politics pushed Offenbach to shape and promote *Les Contes* as a departure from and even a disavowal of his former style.

The final chapter, like the last of Hoffmann's three tales, turns to Giulietta's Venice, where the identities of the main character and of the opera itself dissolve and seem to become unrecoverable, as music and women pose alluring threats to the poet. Thanks to the polymorphous condition of the Venetian act, it is possible to interpret *Les Contes* itself as an undead object that challenges fantasies of and nostalgia for authentic or stable musical texts: since Offenbach's death before the opera's premiere, years of *ad hoc* performance solutions have made the plot and music of the Venetian act into a tangled web.[15] Reading this act leads to philosophical and semiotic speculations about the nature of the musical work; and to feminist analyses of identity itself as an impossible category, constructed only through repetition and imitation—that is, through performance.[16]

Les Contes d'Hoffmann, together with Gounod's *Faust* and Bizet's *Carmen,* is one of only three nineteenth-century French operas that have achieved enduring international status, and where once it would have ranked behind those two in popularity, it might now be promoted to second place. If *Faust* has grown a bit stale, its charms a bit too picturesque and unavoidably Victorian, *Carmen* and *Les Contes* remain eternally modern, the former for its sexual politics and the latter for its post-Romantic portrait of the Romantic artist. *Les Contes d'Hoffmann,* in so many ways a summation of nineteenth-century concerns, has grown younger with the passage of time, seeming more contemporary as the twentieth century gives way to the twenty-first. Like so much nineteenth-century fantastical art, this fanciful piece with its magic, illusions, and bogeymen prefigures modern psychology: are not these stories the protagonist's attempt at a "talking cure," trying to make sense of his mad loves? The episodic structure, recurring characters, and resemblances among the three plots remind us that our unfinished business, "the repressed," returns. Just as a life story is inevitably more and less than the sum of its episodes, the interior tales and their framing narrative, with its ambiguous conclusion, add up to more and less than a whole opera. As Hoffmann's mistress is really "trois maitresses . . . trio charmant d'enchanteresses," so this opera comprises three operas in miniature: three related works with characters in common, three variations on basic themes. The tales re-create the conventional elements of Romantic opera "through the looking glass," rendering the obligatory love triangles, death scenes, *diablerie,* and climactic high notes in distorted fashion. With its neurotic antihero and mechanized prima donna, it anticipates twentieth-century attitudes toward operatic plots as nonsense, operatic emotion as a set of conventional gestures, and operatic singing as extravagant and mechanical. *Les Contes* revisits and ironizes Romanticism's central themes: the place of the artist in a hostile and worldly society, the imaginary conflation of Music and Woman, and above all the artist's search for an ideal Presence, metonymized as an elusive ideal Voice.

This work's unfinished and disorderly condition have made it inexhaustibly rich for both performers and critics. Whoever wants to perform it must first resolve—at least for the duration of a performance—its inconsistencies and ambiguities. One cannot simply sit back and let this work speak for itself: it compels each new team of interpreters, even the most traditional, to decide what it means and how. Demanding reinvention every time, *Les Contes* resists ossification into a colorful museum piece. For the same reasons it challenges the critic/interpreter: how conclusively can one read an unfinished text? With the composer's authority thus compromised, half-realized intentions, fragments, revisions, and posthumous interpolations all jostle against each other with their competing claims. Reception cannot be separated from composition because the two processes were enmeshed from early in the work's genesis, and its "afterlife" of revisions, performance editions, multiple critical editions is simply its life. But if this throws us into a kind of interpretive free fall, it is also a liberation. Each generation of readers and performers brings its own concerns, obsessions, and desires to the work—which being incomplete, being undead, continues to change in response to our needs.

The unfinished masterpiece both fascinates and frustrates, its delights never untainted by thoughts of what might have been. And if the unfinished work has something elegiac about it, is this not part of the ephemeral charm of any music? The desired object vanishes before we can take hold and fix it forever; a sound barely grasped in the present instantly slips into the past. Music, always already part of the silent past, waits to be brought to life again . . . like Euridice, it waits to be called back up to the surface even for a moment. Maybe the allure of *Les Contes d'Hoffmann,* this tantalizingly partial and self-contradictory work, does not after all differ so dramatically from the allure of any piece—maybe all music sleeps in a green casket until we raise the lid and peer inside at the rich treasures that our imagination, our creative energy (as performers, readers, editors, audiences) will animate once more.

CHAPTER ONE

Telling the *Tales*

THE NINETEENTH-CENTURY librettist, at least before the advent of *Literaturoper*, was not expected to treat literary sources with any particular reverence, and among librettists Jules Barbier and Michel Carré have an unusually poor reputation in this regard. Indeed, history has generally condemned these busy men of the theater as insensitive to or unconcerned with literary values as they rummaged through world literature for plots, characters, and colorful situations. In their hands, the philosophical drama of *Faust* devolved into a picturesque romance; for Ambroise Thomas they reduced *Wilhelm Meister*'s enigmatic Mignon to a sentimental heroine, happily if improbably married off to Wilhelm himself. In the nineteenth-century French operatic milieu, at least, philosophy and enigmas did not sing, and Barbier and Carré efficiently boiled down literary masterpieces to provide opportunities for sensational situations, catchy melodies, and colorful sets.

How curious, then, that Barbier and Carré not only named their *Les Contes d'Hoffmann* after the author of its sources, but even included that author in their cast of characters. The opera, annexing E.T.A. Hoffmann's signature for its very title, might be expected to do justice to his literary achievements. The designation *opéra fantastique* also promised fidelity to Hoffmann, for the German writer's *Contes fantastiques* had set a standard of what characters, incidents, subjects, and procedures would constitute the "fantastical" ever since their French publication in 1830. This opera, at least, seems to declare an intention of living up to its model. How does *Les Contes d'Hoffmann*—catchy and colorful as it is—manage to do more than travesty its literary sources?

We might frame the question another way and ask, What sort of *fantastique* piece is this opera? The designation promised marvelous images and stage pictures, for *fantastique* scenarios, like dreams and fairy tales, involve the transformation and transcendence of everyday physical reality: mirrors and lenses show images that are not there, portraits speak, toys and machines come to life, reflections and shadows may be lost or stolen. *Les Contes* has always received full marks on this score. Even contemporary critics who doubted the music's quality lavished praise on the mise-en-scène, and the piece, apparently able to support even the most extravagant visual fantasies, has always presented a fabulous opportunity for stage designers. The ultimate example must be the Powell-Pressberger film, *The Tales of Hoff-*

mann (1951), in which cinematic technology removed every possible barrier to the directors' visual imagination. Spalanzani's guests appear both as
marionettes and human beings, and the magic spectacles cause living figures to appear in place of line drawings. The film's Venice is a city of illusions, where Giulietta watches her own reflection sing the Barcarole and
Dapertutto's "diamant" is a necklace of wax that looks like jewels so long
as Giulietta cooperates with him. Antonia follows the wraith of her mother
through a shadowy forest and finds herself on an infernal stage, accompanied by endless multiplications of Dr. Miracle with his violin. Visual
extravagance, as epitomized in this film and attempted in most stage productions—brilliant colors, magical transformations, fanciful images tend-
ing toward the super- or surreal—is one important aspect of the *fantas-*
tique imagination.

Yet while Hoffmann's stories had been fantastical in this picturesque
sense—on what we might call the level of content—they were also fantastical in a deeper, more elusive sense, one defined not by a tale's content but
rather by its form and structure. This would seem harder for an opera to
emulate. The truly fantastical essence of the tales resides less in their sub-
stance than in the manner of their telling—in their elaborate presentations
of stories within stories, their manipulations of the reader's perception, and
their ambiguity as to the reality of the events they present. As a writer,
E.T.A. Hoffmann continually blurred the lines between waking life and
dreaming life, experience and hallucination, real event and fantasy. And a
still subtler aspect of Hoffmann's fantastical narratives is their author's
complicated relationship to his own creation: his ironical presentation of
events, his apparent need to distance himself from their bizarre, incredible,
absurd, and at times frightening content. The ambiguity of perception and
the process of authorial distancing or disavowal are the subtlest and most
individual elements of Hoffmann's *fantastique,* and they surely posed the
greatest challenge to his theatrical imitators and adaptors. That the libretto
alone could not achieve this genuine *fantastique* was already proved by the
indifferent quality and reception of the play on which it was based, a play
we now remember only as a spur to Offenbach's own fantastical imagination. The opera's true *Hoffmannisme* lies in Offenbach's music, which im-
bues the poet-narrator with a mixture of Romantic sensibility and ironic
distance. The narrator's musical discourse, not his words, render him at
once engaging and unreliable. And Olympia, Antonia, and Giulietta, the
three singers whose performances enthrall him in turn, become *charmantes*
enchanteresses through the siren songs Offenbach wrote for them.

———————

When Théophile Gautier reviewed Barbier and Carré's new *drame fantas-*
tique, Les Contes d'Hoffmann, in 1851, he paid the playwrights a rather

back-handed compliment. "The idea of putting some of Hoffmann's characters on stage," he conceded, "is . . . not so eccentric as it might initially appear."[1] Gautier, one of Hoffmann's most ardent advocates in Paris, surely did not doubt the worthiness or interest of these characters—on the contrary, he wrote essays in their praise and published stories of his own with characters similar to Hoffmann's. Not the vapors and delusions of Hoffmann's protagonists, but the idea of embodying them in objective reality on the stage, seemed eccentric. What Hanslick called "the wild, captivating dreamworld of Hoffmann's fantasy-pieces" seemed unlikely to survive its transplantation from the realm of a reader's imagination to the more brightly lit and material realm of the theater.[2]

Let me demonstrate the difficulty of such a transplantation with one of E.T.A. Hoffmann's own stories—not one of the three actually adapted in the opera (which will be discussed in later chapters) but another tale whose subject and ambience seem to have exercised an indirect influence on *Les Contes*. Both E.T.A. Hoffmann's "Don Juan: A Strange Episode in the Life of a Music Fanatic" and *Les Contes d'Hoffmann* engage in a kind of intertextual play with Mozart's *Don Giovanni*. While the plot of *Les Contes* does not follow that of "Don Juan," both works take place next door, as it were, to Mozart's opera: like the tavern in which the protagonist of "Don Juan" finds himself, the tavern of the opera's prologue connects directly to a theater in which *Don Giovanni* is being performed. Most importantly, the opera takes up the tale's characteristically Hoffmannesque concerns with storytelling, with female singers, and with events that teeter between dream and reality.

"Don Juan" exemplifies E.T.A. Hoffmann's fantastical narrative style and techniques. The story's first characteristic feature is its dramatic focus on a narrator-protagonist. This is the anonymous "Enthusiast," perhaps a student; apparently an aesthete, connoisseur, and amateur composer; certainly a bohemian, judging from his wry surprise at being mistaken for an aristocrat by the hosts of the provincial inn where he pauses in his travels. The host surprises him with the information that there is a theater connected to the inn, and that Mozart's *Don Giovanni* is to be played that very night by a troupe of Italian singers, adding that Mein Herr's chamber is unique and special in offering private access to a theater-box, where he may watch the opera in absolute solitude, unseen by the rest of the audience. The Enthusiast's meticulous descriptions of the singers, costumes, and musical numbers that pass before him create a realistic backdrop for the implausible turn the story takes at intermission: a visitor has silently entered the private box during the first act, and the Enthusiast discovers that she is none other than "Donna Anna in person."[3] The use of realistic detail as a foil for supernatural events is characteristic, as Gautier explains, of fantastical narratives: "a series of ordinary things, of objects minutely detailed, an accumulation of believable little circumstances serve to mask the essential improbability."[4]

At this point in his tale, the Enthusiast demonstrates yet another characteristic of fantastical narrators—he becomes acutely self-conscious about his role, and about the status of his tale. This self-consciousness is signaled with such apostrophes to the reader as "you will scarcely believe . . .," and "How can I describe . . .," and with repeated apologies that his own powers are insufficient to his task. Thus the Enthusiast begins with an admission of defeat: "I would dearly love . . . to set down every single word of the extraordinary conversation that now followed between the Signora and myself, but in recording it all in German I find the words wooden and lifeless" ("Don Giovanni," 109). The content of their conversation need not concern us now, though we will return to it later in this chapter; for the moment it suffices to note how the narrator apologizes for the strangeness of his story, how he warns his reader in advance and assures us with all his powers that he is not lying, dreaming, or drunk. He knows that what he is about to say will strain our credulity—and this is not only the Enthusiast's apologia, but the author's as well. It is E.T.A. Hoffmann himself who begs our indulgence through the persona of his narrator-protagonist, and who bolsters his fiction with the apparatus of truth.

Donna Anna leaves at the end of the intermission, and, his understanding of the opera illuminated by their discussion, the Enthusiast turns to the second act with almost preternatural attention. The performance transports him into a dreamworld that he cannot bear to leave for the chit-chat of the other guests in the hotel, and rather than talk to them, he retreats to his room. The night-scene that follows demonstrates Hoffmann's practice of clouding the reader's perceptions as to whether the events described are real or illusory, an ambiguity that is the single most distinguishing feature of the literary-fantastic. It seems to the Enthusiast that he hears music coming from the theater adjacent to his bedroom, and once again he goes through the little passageway which proved to be the gateway to that barely credible encounter with Donna Anna. All is silent, but he feels a presence; although there is nothing to see, he feels sure that someone is there. "I cried out 'Donna Anna!' The name echoed round the empty theater, then died away, but the spirits of the instrument in the orchestra awoke" ("Don Giovanni," 112) and "from the distance, as the sounds of an orchestra were wafted towards me on billowing waves of harmony, I seemed to hear Donna Anna's voice: *Non mi dir, bell' idol mio*" (ibid., 116).

Was this visionary encounter a dream, or did it really happen? What does the narrator want us to believe?

The question does not admit of an answer, and in that uncertainty lies both the fantastical essence of the tale and the difficulty of translating Hoffmann's stories to the stage. A tale like this *Don Juan* could not be made into a play without a sacrifice of ambiguity: no longer would the narrator be able to take refuge in indirect discourse, for his companion's untranscribable insights, like her ghostly voice, would have to be put into words and spoken aloud. The hypothetical problem of staging the Signora's speech may stand for the problems attendant on making audible any of the powerful and enigmatic female singers in E.T.A. Hoffmann's tales: Olympia, the voice of mechanical perfection; Antonia, the fatal power of music; Giulietta, the seductive music of Italy. Hoffmann's narrators convince us of these singers' charms without our being able to hear them, and indeed the narrator's rhetoric endows their songs with power that mere live performance would be hard-pressed to equal. But in the theater, audiences would hear Donna Anna's quasi-magical discourse just as the Enthusiast does and form their own judgments about her words. In short, a theatrical adaptation of "Don Juan" or of any of Hoffmann's tales would seem bound to compromise the narrator's privileged status, weakening the nearly absolute authority he wields over his readers' imaginations. Deprived of his power to channel our perceptions through his own point of view, to select what details shall command our attention, and to interpret their meaning, the Traveling Enthusiast would become one character among all the others. The adaptation of Hoffmann's fantastical tales for the stage thus carries two potential costs: the shift from description to enactment might diminish the effect of a story's characters and events, and must inevitably loosen the narrator's grasp on the tale that has been so entirely his.

––––––––––

Despite these challenges, *Les Contes d'Hoffmann* does prove itself a "Hoffmannesque" opera. The prologue focuses our attention on a forthcoming act of *narration,* and establishes the protagonist's primary identity as a story-teller. Indeed the first thing we learn about Hoffmann is that he is a *raconteur;* only in the three narrated episodes, a series of flashbacks, will we get to know him as a student, a lover, a traveler. Rather than being plunged into a scene of action, we find ourselves next door to action—having come to see an opera, we find ourselves backstage. While in most operas action precedes narrative (in that dramatic action provides the frame in which narrative happens and temporarily comes to a halt while a story is told), the Prologue to *Les Contes* reverses those terms: here in Luther's tavern, storytelling is the action, and all the events that we see will be understood as part of a story being told.

Hoffmann's three tales of amorous folly, which constitute the action, develop themes introduced in this prologue: persecution by a nemesis; the inadequacy and unreliability of women; and the dream of an Ideal Woman who could embody the contradictory aspects of "Artiste, jeune fille, et courtisane!"[5] Barbier and Carré's fourfold nemesis figure, variously appearing as Lindorf, Coppélius, Miracle, and Dapertutto, resembles the Sand-Man/Coppola/Coppélius who brings a new disaster to Nathanael in each episode of "The Sand-Man." The tales-within-tales of "A New Year's Eve Adventure" provides the model for the opera as a whole, for Hoffmann's "three women in one woman" resemble that tale's multiplications of Julia/Giulietta, who appears first as a cold bourgeoise and later as a demonic courtesan.[6] As in the play of 1851, whose antagonists had been played by a single actor and heroines by a single actress, the opera originally featured one baritone as the villains and one soprano playing Olympia, Antonia, Giulietta, and Stella. Finally, the telling of Hoffmann's three "folles amours" is embedded within a fourth enactment of the basic plot as Lindorf, the villain's present-day manifestation, takes Stella away from Hoffmann at the play's end. No matter where Hoffmann travels— Paris, Germany, Venice—he meets the same array of people, the singing beloved, the villain, even the comic servant, and thus the three tales that comprise the opera are at once independent stories and retellings of a single plot.

Yet although this plot is presented and re-presented, its meaning is never explicated, and perhaps the opera's *Hoffmannisme* resides precisely in this enigmatic quality: one senses that there is a meaning to be interpreted from this welter of strange events, yet the text refuses to supply a single or clear conclusion. Starting from the observation that fantastical narrators fixate on details which become invested with occult meaning, Deborah Harter has argued that fantastical literature, as a genre, is obsessed with fragments and partial objects.[7] In *Bodies in Pieces: Fantastic Narrative and the Poetics of the Fragment,* Harter proposes that the apparently opposite modes of fantastic and realist fiction represent opposite solutions to the same narrative crisis: how can a complete story be told? Realism attacks the problem with exhaustive descriptions and meticulous analysis of characters' backgrounds, motivations, and behavior, in artistic structures that present themselves as organic wholes. Fantastical narrative, by contrast, abandons all pretense of wholeness, instead constructing tales driven by the fascination of partial objects: Gautier's *Le Pied de Momie,* the teeth of Poe's Berenice, Olympia's eyes, the painted foot of Balzac's *belle noiseuse.* The opera's Olympia act stages that fantastical topos literally, even farcically, with its obsession with Olympia's "yeux vivants" and the ultimate revelation of the woman as "un automate!"—a fabricated whole, assembled from pieces. Even the relatively wholesome Antonia is a broken subject, fatally divided between allegiance to the past and the present; between life and death; between the claims of mother and lover. The tale of Giulietta complements the other two, this time making the woman an agent of fragmentation, who divides Schlemihl from his shadow and Hoffmann from his reflection.

Les Contes d'Hoffmann, with its fragmented structure and refusal to synthesize a unified or coherent meaning, conforms to a fantastical taste for the episodic and disjunct. Fantastical fiction pathologizes narrative itself in stories riddled with temporal and spatial dislocations: moments, hours, days unaccounted for; amnesia; inexplicable removals from one place to another. Stories are often cobbled together from smaller, incomplete stories such as dreams, letters broken off in mid-sentence, plots left unresolved. Similarly the opera's story emerges only in pieces, with each internal episode refracting the structural elements differently. The narrative puzzle that is Hoffmann's life story admits of multiple interpretations: Hoffmann himself presents it in the prologue as a tale of diabolical persecution, but the Muse, in the epilogue, suggests that the apparently evil force has been an instrument of the artist's *Bildung,* propelling him away from destructive human desire into the nourishing embrace of Poetry. It has even become popular, in recent years, to stage the entire plot, like that of Gautier's short story "Onuphrius," as a series of hallucinations culminating in madness. Although the Muse vows to shield the poet from the temptations of the inauthentic-feminine as personified in the three women, David Rissin has argued that the "maternal consoler" who reveals herself behind the masculine costume "is in reality a castrating and possessive character," subtly aligned with the Devil to prevent Hoffmann's success with women.[8] E. F. Bleiler's comment on "A New Year's Eve Adventure" seems equally appropriate to the opera: "Whether Hoffmann was completely successful in telling his story in this way is open to dispute; at worst he tells two repetitive stories, at best his method offers a strange parallelism and fusion of experience."[9] In both the structure and the content of his stories, the opera's protagonist qualifies as an authentically *fantastical* narrator.

The opera's portrait of Hoffmann as a narrator-protagonist conforms closely to depictions of the historical author's personality, appearance, manner, and discourse in earlier French essays and fiction. The first French translation of E.T.A. Hoffmann's famous essay on Beethoven in 1830, for example, bears a footnote warning readers that the German author has a "free and capricious spirit, little disposed to submit to the rules of taste."[10] This thumbnail sketch of his character, derived from his stories and from biographical essays by F. J. Fétis and Sir Walter Scott, captures the essence of the fictional "Hoffmann" imagined in Hoffmannist literature.[11] This fictionalized Hoffmann first appeared in Jules Janin's "Hoffmann, conte fantastique," which describes the eccentric German genius in terms that were already stereotypical, and that testify to the self-perpetuating function of the stereotype: "I recognized our poet Hoffmann without ever having seen Hoffmann."[12] Janin imagines Hoffmann as verbally extravagant and self-absorbed, claiming that "Hoffmann always talked to himself . . . he already thought me far away."[13] Subsequent fictionalizations of Hoffmann exaggerated these qualities, culminating in the visionary digression within the opera's *Légende de Kleinzach.*

The strophic form of this number and the choral response to its first two verses make it clear that one should hear the *Légende* as a well-known comic song, but Hoffmann's outburst at the beginning of the third verse transforms the familiar ballad into something new, establishing his poetic energy and emotion as forces that cannot be contained in a closed form and must spill out of formal boundaries. Enumerating the dwarf Kleinzach's grotesque features—his bow legs, bulging stomach, and blackened nose—Hoffmann reaches the "traits de sa figure," and that simple word arrests his attention: he repeats his jaunty line *très lentement* and on the word "figure" he sings a wrong note, lingering on his B rather than proceeding down to the tonic A that should end the phrase (Example 1.1).

Nothing more than the single word and that wrong-note B precipitate the astonishing middle section of the number, the *Vision* that introduces both the narrator's inner being and the dramatic kernel of his three forthcoming tales. Declaimed over a restless, upward-pressing harmonic progression, Hoffmann's fragmentary first-person narrative describes the futile pursuit of an evasive beloved, and its vertiginous vocal lines and rhapsodic melody define his musical rhetoric. He thus shows himself to be at home in the markedly different idioms of sardonic patter and rhapsody, yet barely in control of either: while the *Vision* that disrupts the ballad's conventional strophic form is a deliberate and highly effective shattering of the comic frame, the poet's shift from mockery of poor "Kleinzach" to first-person pathos seems almost involuntary, as if his vision of that beautiful, longed-for face were drawing him along convoluted paths not of his own making. This episode also signals Hoffmann's alienation, for by the end of his rhapsody, he has lost his on-stage listeners, who greet his self-disclosure with, "o bizarre cervelle! que diable parles-tu là? Klein-zach?"

Hoffmann's unconscious slip from the third-person voice of his narrative ballad to first-person reverie and self-revelation shows the double nature of his character in the opera: although he would appear to be the opera's only "unitary" character, the only one who does not appear in multiple incarnations and who remains the same in every setting and through every adventure, this Hoffmann is "multiple" after all.[14] Just as the beloved woman has four aspects, and the antagonist four manifestations, so are there two Hoffmanns. The younger self, described and performed in the *Vision,* is the one familiar from the three tales: ardent and restless, seeking to grasp securely a beauty that repeatedly evades him. This "narrated" Hoffmann, the lyric tenor protagonist, inevitably dominates the opera, but

Example 1.1 The visionary digression within Hoffmann's "Kleinzach" ballad

Example 1.1, cont.

Je la vois, bel - le, bel - le com-me le jour où cou-rant a - près el - le Je quit - tai comme un fou la mai - son pa - ter - nel - le Et m'en - fui à tra - vers les val - lons et les bois!

he has a double in the "narrator" Hoffmann of the prologue, the older and more calculating figure who can look back and emplot his experiences—rendered as disjunct fragments in the *Vision*—into three comprehensible stories. Peter Brooks has suggested, in a discussion of autobiographical (and pseudo-autobiographical) plots, that the heroes of such plots must always be double, for it is necessary for "the narrating *I* to objectify and look back at the narrated *I*."[15]

The narrator-Hoffmann of the prologue must (logically) be older than his narrated younger self, and his distinguishing traits are older in historical terms as well. The ardent and hysterical qualities of the younger Hoffmann that dominated French representations of Hoffmann by 1850 had been anticipated in the 1830s, but that early period of French *Hoffmannisme* had even more strongly emphasized other, contrasting traits. The standard biographical essay by F. J. Fétis, like Janin's story, had represented Hoffmann as nearly diabolical, with "his fixed and savage gaze that let flashes of flame escape through a forest of black hair."[16] This Hoffmann opposed himself to bourgeois norms and could turn his painful emotions into sarcastic jibes, satirizing the artist's suffering even as he evoked it. The smoke that surrounded him seemed more infernal than convivial, and he appeared more mad than merely eccentric. To quote Fétis again, "His temper was brusque, irritable, and excessive. Sometimes he was somber and taciturn; sometimes he would indulge himself in excesses of mad gaiety" (Fétis, "Hoffmann," 327). This is the narrator-Hoffmann we meet in the prologue, who is rude to his companion, insults his friends' sweethearts, and habitually calls for tobacco and punch to drown his disappointments. Curiously, the "brusque, irritable, and excessive" narrator-Hoffmann has certain features in common with the sinister nemesis on whom Hoffmann blames all his disappointments and failures.

By splitting its complex narrator-protagonist into halves, the opera follows the example of E.T.A. Hoffmann's French admirers between 1830 and 1850. In their adaptation and emulations of Hoffmann's stories, writers like Gautier and Dumas underplayed the diabolic aspects of his character—those emphasized by Janin and Fétis—and represented him instead primarily as a youthful victim of hysteria and madness. This second generation of Hoffmannists confined their German hero, as it were, "inside" his own tales. Yet if the hysterical young poet-hero of the three interior tales reflects the influence of Dumas and Gautier, the protagonist introduced in the prologue more strongly resembles the cynical adult imagined by Janin and Fétis. When Offenbach rewrote his baritone lead role for the lyric tenor Talazac, in 1879, the necessary transpositions and revisions mitigated the demonic elements of Hoffmann's personality. Prior to that change, and without his now-characteristic plangent high notes, Hoffmann had sounded closer to the bass villain: thus a reviewer who heard excerpts from the work-in-progress *before* the 1879 revision remarked that, "[Hoffmann's] ballad of Klein Zach, a fantastical composition full of humor and originality, recalls the derisive laughter and diabolical verve of Mephistopheles."[17] We may recover another trace of lost *diablerie* in Offenbach's early conception of Hoffmann if we recall that his swaggering *couplets* in the Venice act, "Amis, l'amour tendre et rêveur, Erreur!" was first assigned to the villain Dapertutto and had originally been composed as a drinking song for the bass villain of *Die Rhein-Nixen* (1864). Thus the ardent young tenor Hoffmann of the finished opera has an older, subtextual double in the diabolical baritone Hoffmann of the abandoned *opéra-lyrique* version.

Although the final version of the opera seems to propose an absolute dissimilarity between the tenor protagonist and his nemesis, the prologue allows us to imagine this dissimilarity as the result of a sorting out and ordering of contradictory elements within a single dramatic character, the "Hoffmann" understood by French *Hoffmannistes* as both devilish and bedeviled, young poetic genius and cruel old cynic. Any similarity between Hoffmann and his nemesis has to be repressed in the plot, for the protagonist's narrative of his life as a series of persecutions could not be sustained if he were to recognize himself in the demonic presence that shadows him. Much of the prologue is devoted to establishing Lindorf and Hoffmann as mutually hostile, with one as the poet and the other the cynic; one repeatedly thwarted while the other always gets his way; one who adores the Ideal woman and the other planning to buy her favors. Their opposing musical styles make audible the opposition of their characters: one a tenor and the other a bass; one hysterical and the other suave; one whose expressions exceed conventional forms and the other perfectly at home in old-style *couplets*. Only near the end of the prologue do we witness a moment of mutual recognition and confrontation between them. Their diminutive Duetto lasts no more than a minute, but nonetheless it is a privileged moment, the one time in the opera when these two characters have each other's full attention. In the three tales, some literal or metaphorical barrier—an eyeglass, a curtain, a mirror—always obscures Hoffmann's view of his nemesis. Hoffmann ignores Coppélius in the "Trio des Yeux" in order to gaze at Olympia, whom he sees for the first time through the magic spectacles; later he peers at Dr. Miracle from behind a curtain, never meeting him or comprehending what he has seen. In the Venetian act, the poet's nemesis dogs his footsteps more closely, but Hoffmann cannot truly see him until after the theft of his reflection.[18] Only the grown-up, narrator-Hoffmann can look the devil in the eye, and the prologue stages the most substantial exchange between the protagonist and his nemesis, who will pursue each other through the opera, scrutinize and remark upon each other's appearance, desires, and actions, without confronting each other face to face.

Example 1.2 An ironic exchange of compliments between Hoffmann and Lindorf

Example 1.2, cont.

Example 1.2, cont.

Although the text of this encounter, an elaborate exchange of insults, foregrounds the characters' mutual antagonism, its music suggests a buried affinity between them. If the "narrated Hoffmann" of the interior tales is not allowed to recognize his opponent as a double, the narrator-Hoffmann of the prologue does so when he adopts Lindorf's own ironic discourse in their exchange. Hoffmann's mannered exchange with Lindorf suggests a social dance, as if the two rivals were performing an ironic bourée, and his orderly melodic lines contrast with his previous out-of-control utterances in the *Vision* of the "Kleinzach" ballad, the rhapsodic idiom in which he will sing for the rest of the opera. Their courtly music matches such stylized epithets as "Cher oiseau de malheur," "cher suppôt de Lucifer," and "Cher orateur du tripôt" (Example 1.2).

In this duet, as in the insults Hoffmann later hurls at his friends, we hear the older Hoffmann of French imagination, the narrator who not only recognizes his antagonist but is almost as fluent as the devil himself in the language of old-fashioned *diablerie*.

THE DEVIL, THE DOUBLE, AND DON JUAN

Diablerie was, by the late nineteenth century, a set of well-known mannerisms and markers, imitable through external signs, and thus Lindorf and the other antagonists in *Les Contes* have features in common with earlier fantastical devils such as Gounod's Mephistopheles, Meyerbeer's Bertram, and the sinister doctor in Dumas's *La Femme aux colliers du velour*. These French devils are worldly, suave, and cynical; they wield power over women;

they wear black garments and drive black horses; their sudden appearances and disappearances are accompanied by smoke and/or sinister music. When appearing in operas, they are bass-baritones and older than their tenor costars. *Les Contes d'Hoffmann* contains frequent references to Lindorf as "le diable" or "Lucifer," together with numerous puns and clichés such as "may the devil take me" if I do such and such a thing, or "Speak of the devil and he appears." Hoffmann even claims to see horns on Lindorf's head—though Nicklausse reassures him that they are only the horns of a cuckold.

The conventional and joking *diablerie* of the libretto, however, is not enough to account for the four villains' genuinely sinister effect. The "diabolic" antagonist is a secular, or psychological, threat in that he personifies the hero's dark side, and thus the villains of E.T.A. Hoffmann's stories do not precisely oppose the protagonist's "true" self, but rather embody certain disavowed aspects of that self.[19] In "A New Year's Eve Adventure," for example, Erasmus Spikher is appalled at Dapertutto's suggestion that he should kill his friend, his wife, and his child in order to remain with Giulietta—appalled not so much because this sacrifice is unthinkable as because it would literalize the ways in which he has already abandoned and betrayed them by loving her. Similarly, Hoffmann's loss of his reflection in the opera ostensibly satisfies Dapertutto's desire, but it also satisfies Hoffmann's own covert desire to lose himself, to give up his soul. Dr. Miracle, in urging Antonia to sing to and beyond the limits of her voice's power, even at the cost of her own life, acts out Hoffmann's selfish, suppressed wish to hear her. The antagonist perversely embodies the hero's own forbidden desires, and their "rivalry" screens the resemblance between them. An interpretation of Lindorf as Hoffmann's destructive "alter-ego" as well as his demonic antagonist, however, cannot override the larger action of Hoffmann's defeat at the villain's hands. Offenbach does not depict Hoffmann as one who has mastered his sinister double, but rather as one who repeatedly falls short of that double's example, culminating in the closing scene when Lindorf escorts Stella off the stage, as he had vowed to do at the beginning of the opera. The sinister double serves as both an ego-ideal, in that he has done and can do what Hoffmann dreams of doing, and an implacable enemy, in that he prohibits the fulfillment of Hoffmann's desire.

The relationship of fear, envy, and identification between the operatic Hoffman and his nemesis can also be compared to that of E.T.A. Hoffmann's "Traveling Enthusiast" and Mozart's Don Giovanni, as described in the short story "Don Juan" with which this chapter began. The Enthusiast's admiration for the almost diabolical antihero of *Don Giovanni* distinguishes this fantastical tale from tales like "The Sand-Man" and "The New Year's Eve Adventure," whose dark and cruel male figures inspire terror rather than identification. For Hoffmann, Mozart's Don Giovanni embodies "the qualities that destine a man to conquer and to rule" ("Don Giovanni," 113), a figure of insatiable desire and rebellion against the secular and sacred authority personified in both the mortal and immortal father figures of the Commendatore. He is a cynic for whom "when he takes a woman it is now no longer an act of sensual gratification but a wanton affront to God and Nature" (114). He is therefore irresistible to women, even the heavenly Donna Anna, for when she saw him, "she [became] filled with a burning sensual desire which rendered all resistance pointless" (115). The narrator ascribes fatal power over Donna Anna to Don Juan and thus to Mozart, declaring that the character "will not survive her year of mourning" (115) and interpreting the prima donna's sudden death after the performance as a tribute to the potency of the music she sings. It is Mozart's music that endows Don Giovanni with his unique power; it is the role of Donna Anna that overwhelms the singer, bringing on her collapse and death. The narrator imaginatively partakes of Mozart/Don Juan's irresistible fascination when he describes Donna Anna seeking him out to declare that her whole life is music—*his* music—"it was of you I was singing, and your melodies were *me!*" (109). Thus the story is the Enthusiast's fantasy of sharing the omnipotence of his two heroes, "Don Juan" the character and Mozart the composer.

If Hoffmann, the opera's own Traveling Enthusiast, stands in relation to his antagonists as E.T.A. Hoffmann's original Enthusiast stood to Don Juan, perhaps Offenbach's opera has a similar relation to Mozart's. *Don Giovanni* haunts the details, the sources, and the structure of *Les Contes d'Hoffmann,* and like the older work *Les Contes* has a curiously mixed effect; its mixture of farce, pathos, and the supernatural make it a latter-day *dramma giocoso.* Like the Don, the opera's Hoffmann pursues three women of markedly different voice and character types—Olympia, a mechanical Zerlina; Giulietta, with the suspect intensity of Elvira; Antonia, aspiring to the tragic nobility of Donna Anna. *Don Giovanni* structures the temporal and geographic space of *Les Contes,* as the action of Offenbach's opera occurs "backstage," next door to an imaginary theater where Mozart's masterpiece is being played. Although Mozart's opera remains unheard and unseen, its progress frames the action of *Les Contes d'Hoffmann,* for Hoffmann's three stories are told during *Don Giovanni's* second act, and his last tale is followed by a burst of applause from the unseen opera-house. These references in *Les Contes d'Hoffmann* to *Don Giovanni* seem playfully to acknowledge its composer's status as "the little Mozart of the Champs-Elysée."

Yet although *Les Contes d'Hoffmann* begins by suggesting that Hoffmann is another Don Juan (with the revelation that the Donna Anna on-stage loves the poet and is on her way to meet him), and although Nicklausse acknowledges his own Leporello-like status with his wry citation of "Notte e giorno faticar," Offenbach indicates at once that these parallels will be complicated. Hoffmann brusquely silences Nicklausse's joking tribute, and the sturdy "notte e giorno" figure darkens into a restless chromatic sequence (Example 1.3).

This introduction of the morbid and neurotic Hoffmann with a transformation of Mozart's motif foreshadows the opera's systematic inversion of each characteristic of E.T.A. Hoffmann's sublime antihero. Lindorf, by acquiring Stella's key, bans the promised rendezvous between "Anna" and Hoffmann, signaling that this old man will interfere more effectively than the Commendatore, the mortal father whom Don Juan had easily dispatched. *Les Contes d'Hoffmann's* four villains comprise a demonic father-figure too suave and slippery for outright defiance, a protean father who cannot be compelled to cede his women to the next generation: "Je suis vieux, mais je suis vif!," as Counselor Lindorf repeats with malicious good humor.[20] Mozart's martyred Commendatore, the righteous "Name-of-the-Father" incarnate, becomes, in *Les Contes d'Hoffmann's* four villains, an "obscene figure of the Father-of-Enjoyment"—a sadistic, possessive, and murderous "Lucifer" who more strongly resembles E.T.A. Hoffmann's diabolical vision of Don Giovanni.[21]

Having proposed Hoffmann as a second Don Juan, the opera undoes him, exposing him in each tale as a dupe. The demonic power of Mozart's Don is invested instead in the antagonists, with the narrator always a step behind. *Les Contes d'Hoffmann* consistently consigns its protagonist to the position of Don Ottavio and "the vulgar masses . . . the common creatures" (113). E.T.A. Hoffmann had imagined that Don Giovanni could compel women's very souls: "He seemed to possess a magnetic power like that of a rattlesnake, as though, once caught in his gaze, women were unable to avert their eyes from him and, mesmerized by his uncanny power, became willing accomplices in their own ruin" (106). But the opera's Olympia act makes the would-be seducer an ineffectual figure of fun, flung to and fro by Olympia in their dance—lacking eyes, she is invulnerable to the serpent's gaze. Olympia is ruined not by Hoffmann but by her cruel "father" Coppélius. Similarly, Hoffmann watches in helpless fascination as Dr. Miracle demonstrates his uncanny power over Antonia: "Am I caught in a dream? Is he a ghost?"[22] Offenbach's depiction of Hoffmann systematically inverts each characteristic of the sublimely antiheroic "Don Juan," as the poet-narrator is by stages deluded, hysterical, and symbolically castrated by the theft of his reflection. Musically, these reversals are made audible in the contrast between Don Giovanni's cry of final "No!" and Hoffmann's precarious, almost hysterical high B on the final "Voilà Kleinzach!" in the Epilogue.[23]

How can we trust, or why *should* we trust, this wild-eyed neurotic as a

Example 1.3 Nicklausse as Leporello

narrator? In undoing its protagonist to this extent, the opera creates potential problems for itself. While we might give ourselves over to the absurd and colorful pleasures of Hoffmann's tales, they would not touch us if he—the narrator—did not also convince us (at least for the duration of the piece) that his stories are more than deluded ramblings, paranoid daydreams, or opium dreams. Some grain of truth captures our sympathy, draw us into that "wild, captivating dream world." What narrative devices make these tales captivating rather than simply ridiculous?

MUSIC AND THE "PHYSIOGNOMY OF THINGS"

Fantastical narrators as a class are not very reliable, their perceptions being clouded by any number of characteristic afflictions—madness, drunkenness, magnetism, somnambulism, delusion, bewilderment, and paranoia. A defining element of fantastical narrative, in fact, is the distortion of perception. But another, equally definitive element of the genre is the way in which narrators try continually to compensate for their own unreliability, bolstering their narratives with apologias, proofs, and evidence of the implausible events they recount. The self-conscious design of fantastical narrative results from the author's urge to distance himself from his material; the narrator's apparent compulsion to show that he's not making this up, to render the bizarre and implausible as plausibly as possible. Gautier had explained that the writer who hoped to emulate Hoffmann must be "able to depict the physiognomy of things and to give the appearance of reality to the most incredible creations."[24] Music—whether described in stories, inserted in spoken plays, or performed within an opera—is part of this physiognomy of things, and *Les Contes'* single most important device for grounding fantastical events in a real and tangible world is the score's abundance of realistic music, or performed song.

Edward T. Cone has suggested that characters in opera "go around singing all the time," but that they do not know it—the inhabitants of "the world of opera" do not experience their world as made of music. Although all the characters in an opera are played by performers, only a few will *be* performers within the drama they act out. (A few such characters come immediately to mind—Carmen, for example, with her insinuating gypsy songs, or Cherubino, with his love poems.) Given the relative scarcity of "heard music" in operas, it is striking that the inhabitants of *Les Contes d'Hoffmann's* world perform, and hear each other's performances, almost continually. The score of *Les Contes* comprises a catalogue of types of performed song in nineteenth-century opera: drinking songs, a narrative ballad, an oracular voice, a serenade, festive choruses, and a music lesson scene.[25] Nicklausse's warning about the doll in Act II and Giulietta's seduction song in Act IV exemplify another convention, the narrative song that carries a message; in these cases, an older ballad tradition is translated into *couplets* in the *opéra-comique* style.[26] Indeed, approximately half the opera's music is presented as music that the characters are consciously *singing*, and that they and others on-stage can *hear*.

The unusual abundance of musical performance within the opera is in part due to its literary sources. Scenes of music-making, particularly those involving violins and sopranos, were essential ingredients of Hoffmannist literature, thanks to the prominence of such scenes in E.T.A. Hoffmann's fiction and to his fame as a music critic. In both fiction and criticism Hoffmann seems to struggle toward a prose that could adequately describe musical sounds and even reproduce their impact on the listener, breaking through the frustrating silence of writing.[27] His musical stories often feature a strange mix of technical detail and breathless description. Several short stories, including "Rat Krespel," "Don Juan," and "Ritter Gluck," oscillate between fictional narrative and music criticism, with detailed celebrations of venerable composers, works, or repertoires. When Antonia sings in *Rat Krespel*, Hoffmann specifies that her repertoire includes "Leonardo Leo's beautiful soul-stirring songs" and "Padre Martini's motets." We see this particular strain of *Hoffmannisme* in Dumas's *La Femme au Collier du Velours*, where the description of Antonia's singing flagrantly imitates its model in "Rat Krespel." Dumas's heroine (also called Antonia) sings another example of antique Italian sacred music, "that marvelous composition of Stradella's which had saved the life of its composer, the 'Pietà, signore.'"[28] Indeed Dumas outdoes Hoffmann's own blend of affective language and technical precision: "The accompaniment prayed at [Antonia's] side, begged, groaned, climbed with her toward the *fa*, descended with her to the *ut*" (Dumas, *La Femme*, 33). Dumas ladles on the clichés of sublimity, declaring Antonia's voice "not the voice of a woman, but that of an *angel*," and both technical detail and sublime transport reach their peak at the aria's conclusion: "when the motif 'Pietà, signore' returned . . . Antonia attacked with all her voice's power the *fa* of 'volgi,' a shudder passed old Gottlieb's veins, and a cry escaped from the mouth of Hoffmann" (ibid., 34). Only in an opera, however, could Hoffmann's French emulators fully realize his goal of making music *audible*. Instead of being confined to verbal accounts of Antonia's angelic tones, Olympia's crystalline sounds, or Giulietta's seductive incantations, *Les Contes d'Hoffmann* could try to inspire those soul-stirring effects—that shudder of delight, that astonished cry—directly in the audience.

Other scenes of music-making in the opera serve another and subtler function that we might call "documentary," being used to establish the authenticity of fantastical events. The use of performed songs and dances to provide local color has a long pedigree, and *Les Contes d'Hoffmann* needs music to "locate" each act in a national and social space. Characteristic music reorients the audience each time the curtain rises on a new scene: the all-male chorales and festive choruses in the prologue and epilogue establish the tavern's German setting; the waltz sung and danced by Spalanzani's guests sets a Parisian tone for Act I; Antonia's song at the piano sets the scene of the Biedermeier parlor; and Giulietta's Barcarole moves us to Venice, where Hoffmann's drinking song reinforces the hedonistic ambience. These numbers do more than merely indulge a theatrical impulse toward the picturesque; rather, they are essential to the opera's mixture of the vividly familiar and the bizarre.

A few of the opera's scenes of musical performance are even more precisely analogous to E.T.A. Hoffmann's use of realistic textual "objects" such as letters and documents to authenticate his antirealistic stories of dreams, hallucinations, and hauntings. Hoffmann's narrators typically distance themselves from the implausible events they describe by presenting them in what we might call documentary form, ostensibly unmediated by the narrating voice and uninflected by the narrator's (or the author's) own imagination. In "Don Juan," the climactic news of the prima donna's death is not presented by the Traveling Enthusiast, but rather in the form of an "addendum," a brief transcript at the end of the tale:

> *Clever man with snuffbox:* What a tragedy that we are not going to hear a decent opera again for such a long time! That's what comes from all these frightful exaggerations!
>
> *Mulatto:* Quite right—and I told her so time and again. The part of Donna Anna always affected her deeply and yesterday she was like a woman possessed. They say she lay in a swoon throughout the interval and that at times during the scene in the second act her nerves gave way.
>
> . . . .
>
> *I:* How terrible!—the attacks were not serious, I trust? Shall we be hearing her again soon?
>
> *Clever man with snuffbox, taking a pinch:* I hardly think so. She died in the night at exactly two o'clock. (Hoffmann, "Don Juan," 117).

There the story ends, and the Enthusiast neither tells the reader directly that "Anna" died, nor interprets her death. Rather he puts the reader in a position to hear the news with him, to greet it with the same stunned silence that he does, and to arrive independently at the uncanny conclusion that his intermission encounter with "Donna Anna in person" had happened while the "Signora" lay exhausted, and that her ghostly greeting to him in the middle of the previous night, through the rustling of strings in the theater's empty orchestra pit, had coincided with the moment of her death. Similarly, "Rat Krespel" is driven by the narrator's obsession with Antonia's voice, but because he never heard this voice, he introduces it into his own story on the authority of another character who did hear it. Rather than describe it himself, the narrator reports someone else's description of Antonia's "surpassingly beautiful female voice" and its "peculiar, deep, soul-stirring impression."[29] The narrator tells the reader only what he himself was told, and cannot be accused of exaggeration or excessive fancy in his extravagant conclusion that "nobody but Antonia knows how to sing" (Hoffmann, "Rat Krespel," 221). Finally, the Traveling Enthusiast of "A New Year's Eve Adventure" does not tell the tale of the Lost Reflection directly; rather, he says, "upon the table where I had seen [Erasmus Spikher] sitting and writing I found a fresh manuscript, whose content I am sharing with you."[30] He then reproduces this manuscript so that the reader reads it along with him. This presentation leaves no room for readerly skepticism because reader and narrator become coterminous, both receiving Spikher's bizarre story in an apparently unmediated form.

The opera contains two special scenes of musical performance that serve this "documentary" function, seeming to authenticate uncanny events by putting the listener in the same position as the narrator-protagonist. Both scenes blur the line between delusion and reality, or rather they make an acoustic "delusion" *real,* because the audience is compelled to share it with Hoffmann: what Hoffmann hears, we hear. The first such scene is Olympia's "Les oiseaux dans la charmille," an uncanny performance in that only Hoffmann, regarding Olympia through his magic spectacles, mistakes her voice for that of a human being. In "The Sand-Man," Olympia's deluded lover Nathanael had perceived her voice as human, while his friends heard it—and the narrator described it—as inhuman, like the sound of "glass bells." In their 1851 play, Barbier and Carré followed the story by making the audience hear through the un-deluded ears of Hoffmann's friends, for Olympia's song was produced by an off-stage English horn: no woman sang, and only Hoffmann heard the doll's "voice."[31] The comedy of the scene resulted from Hoffmann's being alone in his delusion, the only one on stage who could not hear the audible proof of Olympia's nonhuman status. The opera, however, complicates the situation by compelling the audience to share Hoffmann's perception of Olympia as a live woman. The skeptical listener is still present in the person of Nicklausse, who, as in the play, recognizes the inhuman whirring of "la physique" behind Olympia's coloratura. But now it is Hoffmann's *mis-hearing* of the Doll Song that is audible, and this song becomes the equivalent of a letter or quoted narrative in a story: an implausible event that we, the audience, experience together with the protagonist. There is no place for us to argue that Olympia is really or only a machine, once we have heard her sing. The performance compels the audience to accept the original, uncanny scenario of "The Sand-Man"—that one could mistake a singing doll for a live person—because we were there: like Hoffmann, we saw (and heard) Olympia through the magic spectacles. Thus the opera meets the challenge of *fantastique* narrative, drawing the audience into the narrator's deluded perceptions by presenting the musical equivalent of documentary evidence, the performed song. The opera's presentation of this particular "folle amour" compels our belief, and even more, our participation, for it is hard for the listener not to feel as delightfully infatuated with Olympia as Hoffmann himself does.

Is there ever room for skepticism? is the fantastical narrator's authority ever compromised?

The peculiar structure of E.T.A. Hoffmann's "The Sand-Man" had staged the movement beyond documentary realism into the narrator's compelling yet unreliable discourse.[32] According to Freud's famous reading, this tale's shocking effect results from the fact that, in the end, no safe distance separates the mad Nathanael and the narrator: the narrator recounts the madman's frightful thoughts and fantasies without explaining how he knows them. When he steps out from behind the shelter provided by his initial, epistolary mode—when he begins to speak directly to the reader rather than relying on documents to tell his story for him—the narrator implicates himself (and the reader) in Nathanael's delusions.[33] The narrator's own place in his story becomes increasingly ambiguous and troubling . . . how does he know all this? What is his relation to "Nathanael" or to "Coppola"? What evidence do we have that he is not after all inventing this; that the horrid fancies he attributes to Nathanael are not in fact his own? Whether the narrator of "The Sand-Man" is another madman, or a fabulous liar, he inevitably compromises himself by the adoption of that unmediated, omniscient voice in which he delivers the story of poor Nathanael's deterioration and destruction. Thus the fantastical narrative betrays itself—its elaborate narrative strategies can no longer conceal its own fictional status, its origins in the author's imagination rather than in reality.

The opera contains one such narratorial "slip-up" when it stages Antonia's death by singing, another uncanny performance presented as an indisputably real event. The "impossible voice" in this scene is that of Antonia's mother, like Olympia a singer more fantastical than real. Both Olympia's waltz-song and the mother's entreaty "Chère enfant," emerging respectively from a doll and a portrait, function as signs of real presence conjured out of absence. These objects take the place of women who are dead or who, as Nicklausse warns in Act II, "have never been alive." The songs that emanate from the doll and the portrait, transmitted across the gap that separates the living from the dead, resemble Spikher's manuscript, which transmits his impossible story across the gap that separates him from people who still have their reflections. Furthermore, not only does the dead mother's portrait sing, and Antonia expire, but we (the audience) see and hear it all: this scene is unique within the opera, in that Hoffmann makes his audience witness an event to which there were no witnesses. In this sense the operatic adaptation differs greatly from its source, "Rat Krespel," for the original story had represented the death scene at several removes from reality, perhaps with no truth content at all. There the narrator had paraphrased Krespel's description of a trance in which he "fancied one night that he heard somebody playing the piano . . . he was utterly unable to move . . . he was surrounded by a dazzling brightness . . . [then] fell into a sort of dead faint."[34] On waking, he found Antonia dead, but the gap between this trance vision and Antonia's death renders the relationship between them utterly ambiguous. The opera, on the other hand, would seem to remove all uncertainty, as it makes the audience witness that death precisely as Krespel had dreamed or fantasized it: as the result of a rapturous, uncontrollable, overpowering song.

This "documentary" presentation of both the mother's music and Antonia's death, however, ultimately gives away the operatic Hoffmann's narrative strategy. As the narrator-protagonist, Hoffmann vouches for the other uncanny events of his stories by his own presence, and the rest of the opera is remarkably consistent in filtering events through Hoffmann's point of view—in the Olympia and Giulietta acts, he is on stage almost the entire time. But when Antonia's mother sings, the audience is made privy to music that no living person, including Hoffmann, actually heard. Despite the apparently unmediated representation of Antonia's singing death as an audible, visible, on-stage event, this is Krespel's dream all over again—an elaborate fiction with which Hoffmann accounts for Antonia's inexplicable death, unseen and alone in her room. The uncanny voices that seem to emerge from dead things are authorial defenses against the real absence—the fictional status—of their ostensible producer-performers. And all the realistic, performed songs in the opera, like the documentary elements in the stories, are attempts to conceal the fact that all these events, stories, and characters do, after all, come from Hoffmann's imagination. These elaborate narrative strategies, together with their ultimate failure to prove the "reality" of events represented, constitute the authentically *fantastical* quality of the opera. Neither the characters, nor the events, nor even the presence of Hoffmann "in person" suffice to make the opera Hoffmannesque; rather its *Hoffmannisme* lies in the way the music creates an appearance of reality—Gautier's "physiognomy of things"—and thus seduces the audience into believing incredible, fantastical events.

CHAPTER TWO

Mesmerizing Voices

MUSIC, MEDICINE, AND THE INVENTION OF DR. MIRACLE

WHEN THE fantastical drama *Les Contes d'Hoffmann* opened at the Théâtre de l'Odéon in March 1851, contemporary commentators did not remark on the number of liberties that playwrights Jules Barbier and Michel Carré had taken with E.T.A. Hoffmann's original stories. Indeed, in introducing Barbier and Carré's adaptation to his readers, Théophile Gautier claimed that "Hoffmann's stories take form and unscroll themselves before the eyes of the spectator," noting neither the new forms of Barbier and Carré's "tales of Hoffmann" nor the addition of a few new characters to the cast.[1] The most significant of Barbier and Carré's innovations was Dr. Miracle, the death-dealing doctor of the "Antonia" act: a diabolic intruder not only within Antonia's story, but upon its literary source, "Rat Krespel," in which the only doctor is an innocent bystander and the source of Antonia's death-music is a composer named only as "B—".[2] Yet thirty years later, Dr. Miracle was the play's best-remembered figure, as a somewhat distorted synopsis of Offenbach's opera in *Le Ménestrel* indicates: "The plot is the same as that which had such a success at the Odéon; the poet Hoffmann, aided by Doctor Miracle and his enchanted violin, pursues his three loves." Ironically, Dr. Miracle quickly became the official emblem of Hoffmann's tales in contemporary illustrations: he and Antonia dominate the frontispiece of the 1881 piano-vocal score (Figure 1), and are second in importance only to Hoffmann himself in the engraving that appeared in *Le Théâtre Illustré*. Olympia, by contrast, is sketched lightly in the upper right- and left-hand corners. Two photos from the Opéra-Comique premiere focus on him: Taskin (Miracle) brandishes his violin behind Isaac (Antonia) during the *scena* "Tu ne chanteras plus?" while in the closing tableau of Isaac stretched out on the ground with all the principals arranged around her, only Taskin looks out at the camera, and his grinning face crowns the line-up.

Thus from the time of the play's premiere in 1851, Dr. Miracle was welcomed into the Hoffmann pantheon; for all intents and purposes, he was a creation of E.T.A. Hoffmann himself. Despite this contemporary acceptance, however, Dr. Miracle does not originate in the world of Hoffmann's fantasy pieces; he is more contemporary, and specifically more Parisian, than his Hoffmann-pedigreed fellow villains, Coppélius and Dapertutto.

Figure 1. Antonia and Dr. Miracle. (Reproduced by permission of the Bibliothèque nationale de France.)

This chapter seeks to account for Barbier and Carré's departures from their Hoffmann sources: Dr. Miracle with his satanic attributes, particularly his violin; Dapertutto's magic diamond; each villain's uncanny rapport with and access to his "patient," Antonia and his "servant," Giulietta; and Miracle's conjuring of fantastical voices, first Antonia's from off-stage and then her mother's from beyond the grave.

In "Councilor Krespel," as in Barbier and Carré's play and Offenbach's opera, the young soprano Antonia Krespel has a magically beautiful voice, but the act of singing threatens her health, pushing her to the brink of feverish overexcitement and death. However, the original tale includes no straightforward villain, nor any of the demonism that the French adaptations would add; rather it features the far more ambiguous Councilor Krespel, who is at once a loving father and a half-demented grotesque, obsessed with the secret of his daughter's voice.[3] The story hints at incestuous desire sublimated through music: Krespel's dissection of antique Italian violins in search of the "secret" of their inner construction symbolizes his desire to penetrate Antonia's inner mysteries, and the coffinlike chest of broken violins in his house testifies to both his persistence and his failure. The only instrument to escape this fate is a "Cremona violin," built by "some unknown master, probably of Tartini's time."[4] Symbolically, this violin is Antonia: she recognizes her own voice when it is played, and when she wishes to "sing," her father plays the violin for her: "Scarcely had he drawn the first few notes from it than Antonia cried aloud with joy: 'Why, that's me!—now I shall sing again!' . . . She often said to the Councillor, 'I should like to sing something, father!' and Krespel would take his violin down from the wall and play her most beautiful songs. . ."[5] Krespel sequesters his daughter from the world, and particularly from other men, ostensibly out of concern for her health. His construction of marvelous violins that he plays only once, then hangs in a cabinet to be silent forever, betrays his wish to possess exclusively his virginal daughter and her music. Or perhaps he does not refrain from touching them after all: this "genuinely Hoffmannesque" antihero is a highly unreliable narrator, and the tale concludes with his ambiguous account of Antonia's death in a musical-erotic apotheosis, a dream-vision of his daughter passionately clasped in the arms of a lover while her voice continued to ring out.

Typically, however, the French adapters and their audiences ignored or suppressed the dark psychological nuances of Hoffmann's tale. Barbier and Carré instead projected the negative aspects of Councilor Krespel onto an intruder with superhuman powers, a splitting of the father figure into his protective and malignant sides that renders the bizarre tale more comprehensible and more theatrical, if more predictable. Their play, *Les Contes d'Hoffmann,* reduced "Monsieur Crespel" to a grave yet largely ineffectual father, while the newly created "Docteur Miracle" incarnated Krespel's original dark side: his abrupt temper and sudden movements, his unique access to Antonia and her singing, and his grotesquely "harsh," "grating," and "cracking voice" that would later become, in the opera, a malicious laugh.

Barbier and Carré's Dr. Miracle, with his clinking flasks of poisonous medicines and his repeated intrusions on the Crespel household, may have been modeled on Hoffmann's original Dapertutto, the villain of the story "A New Year's Eve Adventure" (and ultimately of *Les Contes d'Hoffmann's* Venetian act). In portions of that tale which Barbier and Carré omitted from their adaptation in *Les Contes d'Hoffmann,* Dapertutto had been both a poisoner and a threat to the family order with his attempts to corrupt the narrator and to steal the souls of the narrator's wife and family. A French translation of "A New Year's Eve Adventure" even suggests the origin of the newly created villain's name, for in it Dapertutto is introduced as "le docteur miracle."[6] (Having deprived Dapertutto of this epithet and of his original sinister attributes, Barbier and Carré invented for him the magic diamond, whose origins we will see shortly.) Six years after *Les Contes d'Hoffmann,* the playwrights reused the name "Dr. Miracle" in a context that again confirms its associations with poison and domestic infiltration: in 1857, they wrote a one-act libretto entitled *Le Docteur Miracle* for a composers' competition sponsored by Offenbach's Théâtre des Bouffes Parisiens.[7] The comic "Miracle Doctor" is (again) a foreigner with more potions than medical ethics, an *opera buffa*–style charlatan who doses a young girl's family with nonfatal poisons so that her lover—also disguised as a doctor—can sneak into her house and win his way into the family's good graces. Still penetrating a forbidden paternal house and playing tricks with clinking flasks, this Docteur Miracle parodies his sinister antecedent in *Les Contes d'Hoffmann,* and their mutual nominal ancestor, Hoffmann's "miracle doctor, Dapertutto."[8]

Yet none of these Hoffmannist antecedents for Dr. Miracle's name will quite account for his appearance on the French stage, and the allusions seem too subtle for the pragmatic and fast-working Barbier and Carré, whose Dr. Miracle, I believe, originates much closer to home. One textual clue does connect him to the "wild and captivating dream world" of "Rat Krespel," and that is Krespel's description of the Cremona violin that sings with his daughter's voice: "this inanimate object to which I may, when I desire, give life and words, often speaks to me in a marvelous fashion, and when I played it for the first time, it seemed to me that I was only the magnetizer who excites the somnambulist, and helps her to reveal all her hidden sensations."[9] The attributes Barbier and Carré assigned to their newly invented Dr. Miracle, and to their revised Dapertutto, reflect contemporary familiarity and fascination with mesmerism and magnetizers, self-proclaimed "doctors" of a sinister art who stood at the nexus of medical quackery, malpractice, stage magic, and sorcery in mid-nineteenth-century Paris.[10]

"SPARKLE, DIAMOND": MESMERIST PROPS AND IMAGES

When Dapertutto, in Barbier and Carré's play, summons Giulietta by holding aloft a diamond, his incantation invokes mid-century images of visual fascination:

> O diamant, d'où ruisselle
> L'ardente étincelle!
> D'où jaillit comme l'éclair
> Un feu vif et clair;
> Vers tes étoiles sans nombre,
> Attire dans l'ombre,
> L'âme de la Giulietta,
> Qui te couvoita![11]

[Oh diamond, from whence stream forth / burning sparks! / From whence shoots forth like lightning / a bright and lively fire; / To your numberless stars, / draw into the shadow / the soul of Giulietta / who covets you!]

Magnetizers of the late eighteenth and early nineteenth centuries, following Mesmer's example, had relied on "charged" objects such as iron magnets, tubs of water, iron rods, and pieces of polished glass to focus and direct the power of their personality. But these commonplace substances had to be transmuted into something more distinctive for literary and dramatic purposes, and so handbooks on mesmerism in the 1820s replaced iron bars and magnets with precious metals: an *Instruction practique sur le magnétisme* recommends that a gold coin or medallion will fix the subject's attention.[12] In mesmerist fiction and theater, sparks emanated from precious stones, descendants of Mesmer's humble chunks of glass. Thus the villain of Alexandre Dumas's *Hoffmanniste* novel, *La Femme au colliers du velour* (1850), is a "fantastical doctor [with] diamond buckles on his shoes, diamond rings upon his fingers, and his [diamond] skull on his snuffbox."[13] Arsène, the ballerina desired by Hoffmann (the novel's protagonist), wears a black velvet collar fastened with a diamond, and in a scene analogous to Dapertutto's with Giulietta, the diamond seems magnetically to bind the ballerina to the doctor watching her performance: "Hoffmann saw quite distinctly the rays that the buckle of Arsène's collar threw forth, and those which the doctor's little death's-head produced. These rays met each other half-way, in a straight line, they collided, they bounced off of and reflected one another in a veritable spray of thousands of white, red, and gold sparks."[14] But perhaps such sparks and "eye-beams," so thrillingly sinister in 1850, had come to seem old-fashioned or hackneyed by the time of the opera's conception, for Barbier's 1880 libretto neglects mesmerist imagery in favor of a different metaphor. The 1851 Dapertutto had concluded by comparing the diamond to a hunter's mirror that dazzles his prey and lures it into his net:

> Comme au miroir qui tournoie,
> Vient tomber la proie,
> Dans le filet ravisseur,
> De l'adroit chasseur!

[As in the turning mirror / the prey comes to grief / in the plunderer's net / of the clever hunter!]

In the 1880 libretto, Dappertutto begins with this image, saluting the diamond as his "turning mirror" and introducing himself in song as the "Black Hunter" who "watches and waits."[15] This more specifically diabolical persona elicited from Offenbach fast and vehement music in the style of Mephistopheles' serenade in Gounod's *Faust*. Both devils sing abrupt, angular lines, with deliberately misplaced melismas. Mephistopheles' mocking refrain of "Ha! ha! ha! ha!" set the tone for the orchestral interjections after Dappertutto's opening lines, and for the exultant "Oui!" that leads into his galloping conclusion (Example 2.1). The vigorous hunting horns that underline the peroration, "Femme, oiseau, le chasseur est là, qui vous voit et qui vous guette," remove Dappertutto conclusively from the hushed milieu of mesmerist incantation.

When in 1907 the Monte Carlo editors were casting about for a replacement aria for Dapertutto—having assigned the original "Tournez, miroir" to Coppélius with a new text, "J'ai des yeux"—they preserved the metaphor of dazzled bird and greedy woman; however, their music abandons hunting imagery to strike a hypnotic tone. Their "Scintille, diamant," a melody borrowed from Offenbach's own *Voyage dans la lune,* paints a compelling sound-portrait of the Venetian cityscape, with moonlight shimmering on the canals and glinting off the facets of the diamond Dapertutto holds aloft. More importantly, this "inauthentic" number restores the scene's original mesmerizing atmosphere with its slow waltz motion, static harmonies, shimmering tremolos, and glassy chime.

Diamonds, coins, and medallions, while theatrically impressive, were not thought absolutely necessary for controlling a patient through "animal magnetism," and Dr. Miracle's "passes magnétiques" over an empty chair as he examines the absent Antonia (during the scene that would become the trio "Pour conjurer le danger") derive from the more basic therapeutic technique of producing magnetic effects through gesture alone. A magnetizer could even induce the trance from a distance, as LaFontaine explained in 1841: "during my public seances, I often magnetized—from

Example 2.1 Dapertutto as the "Black Hunter" (1881)

Example 2.1, cont.

behind, and with a single gesture—the somnambulist Manette, who was my subject at the time. Often she would have her back turned . . . and someone would signal me to put her to sleep; at that instant she would fall as if struck."[16] Thus mesmerism transformed women themselves into entranced objects, channels for potent energies originating outside themselves. Sometimes, in this condition, they became tools that the mesmerist used to capture the souls (shadows, reflections) of men: Giulietta, in the diamond's thrall, became Dapertutto's instrument of destruction, just as Arsène was the "fantastical doctor's" instrument for entrapping Dumas's Hoffmann. A similar rapport exists between Dr. Miracle and Antonia, but the "instrumentalization" of Antonia is both more literal and more complicated, for in their case both magnetizer and magnetized woman are musicians: Dr. Miracle, wielding a violin rather than a diamond, seems to command both Antonia's body and her singing voice.

The uses of music in mesmerism and in the succeeding techniques of magnetism and hypnotism reveal these practices as metaphors of the "inside" and "outside" of the human body, psyche, family, and community. As discourses of the body, its integrity, and its signifying capacity, mesmerism and animal magnetism anticipated hysteria and Freudian psychoanalysis as condensation points for nineteenth-century ideas of gender, the body, and the psyche.[17] However, where most theorists have read these discourses as mechanisms for policing the subversive force of female sexuality, my analysis makes "sexuality" secondary to "music," intepreting music as the figure of desire, knowledge, and disorder. The entranced performer, variously referred to as a "somnambulist" or "medium," is represented as vulnerable to music's mesmerizing power, and she has both literal and figurative music inside her that only the mesmerist can access. In her trance, she stands on the border between "home" and "outside"; between order and disorder; between vulnerability to sinister forces and her own powers, to which her listeners are vulnerable. The nineteenth century provides an array of magnetizers and mediums, whose marvelous displays and demonstrations may be interpreted as fantasies about the uncanny power of musical performance, and as reflections of the desires and anxieties attached to music itself in the Romantic imagination.

THE MESMERIST PARADIGM

Questo è quel pezzo di calamita pietra Mesmerica,
ch'ebbe l'origine nell'Allemagne
che poi si celebre là in Francia fù.
(*Lorenzo DaPonte,* Così fan tutte)

Les Contes d'Hoffmann's representation of Dr. Miracle's relationship with Antonia and of his behavior in the Crespel home follows a template established by the notorious episode involving Dr. Franz Mesmer and his failed cure of the blind pianist, Maria Theresa von Paradis in Vienna, 1772. The particulars of this case matter less than the paradigm it established of the prototypical mesmeric subject and the doctor's mysterious intimacy with—

and control over—her, so it will suffice to outline them here. Indeed, the very impossibility of determining the truth of the von Paradis situation became integral to the history and discourse of mesmerism and its successor, animal magnetism; interpretations of the case varied wildly depending on the inclinations of the witnesses, and this would remain characteristic of every encounter between mesmerists, patients, and self-professed rational observers. Von Paradis, a virtuoso pianist, had been blind from the age of three, as well as suffering from fits that later decades would label "hysteric."[18] Although her musical talent and physical disability had won her an imperial stipend, they had also attracted the attention of doctors who subjected her, throughout her life, to various and fruitless "therapies," including constrictive bandages around her temples and electric shocks to her eyes.

Her parents brought von Paradis to Mesmer when she was seventeen, after Mesmer's "miraculous" cure of another young woman by means of radical magnetic therapies. Mesmer sequestered her in his home, where his treatments slowly began to restore her sight; however, an antagonism soon arose between the doctor and his patient's father. Scurrilous rumors circulated about the doctor and the young blind girl whom he treated alone in a darkened room, and Mesmer's rivals insisted that this "doctor" would not only fail to cure her blindness with his unorthodox methods, but render her imbecilic as well—a prediction that seemed to come true when von Paradis abruptly lost her musical facility. Convinced that Mesmer was restoring his daughter's sight only at the cost of her mind and livelihood, her father removed her from the clinic and publicly denounced the "doctor" as a charlatan and a ruiner of young girls. Here perhaps we have a historical model for Crespel's terrified hostility to Dr. Miracle's solicitations: "don't let him in! he wants to kill my daughter, as he killed my wife!" Subsequent developments in Mesmer's biography would only intensify the link between magnetizers and vulnerable females in the popular imagination.

The disappointed Mesmer left Vienna for Paris, where suspicions about young women's peculiar vulnerability to his powers persisted: In 1785, a Royal Commission "charged with the examination of animal magnetism, as now practised in Paris" visited the clinics of Mesmer and several of his disciples and noted that "in the number of patients in the state of crisis, there were always many women and few men";[19] while denying that the science was anything more than auto-suggestion or mass hysteria, they concluded that women made the best patients for this pseudo-medicine because of their credulous and excitable minds.[20] Mesmer and his therapies became, in DaPonte's phrase, "so famous in France" that a French magnetic science and imaginative tradition endured through the 1840s. Charles LaFontaine, the era's most dedicated proselytizer for *le magnétisme animal,* mingled scientific demonstration and feminine spectacle to an almost laughable degree, and whether understood as medicine, fakery, or sorcery, the magnetic arts always presented an alluring spectacle, as a newspaper commentary on one of LaFontaine's mediums makes clear: "this poor child who, hardly a few days before, would have inspired no reaction except perhaps that of pity, now excited much admiration through the inexpressible beauty of her face and figure and of her ecstatic poses."[21]

It is hard not to recognize the Antonia of *Les Contes d'Hoffmann* as a cousin to these professional somnambulists. Therapeutic magnetism had reached the height of its popularity by 1850, the year of Barbier and Carré's play, and LaFontaine wrote proudly in 1847 that "there is not a city in France that does not possess a good roster of magnetizers; cures of all kinds have been effected, theories (more or less clear) have appeared, practices (more or less good) have come into use."[22] In the decades that followed, magnetic medical therapies would give way to hypnotism and the hysteric theater of Charcot's Salpêtrière, while mesmeric science would flourish in theatrical entertainments and parlor tricks propagating the now-cartoonish spectacle of female medium and male manipulator. A pamphlet from the 1880s, for example, instructs schoolboys on "compelling a subject by mental influence," noting that "a woman is usually the subject from being weaker-minded." (As women were scarce in boys' schools, the chapter on "Willing a Subject into Obedience" advises the young magician to choose a subject, "as impressionable as possible; one of those fair-haired, watery-eyed, girlish boys is best.")[23] But no matter where the techniques proliferated, the gendered paradigm persisted: from Mesmer and Maria Theresa von Paradis to Charcot and his hysterics; from Svengali and Trilby to Freud and Dora. *Les Contes'* two mesmeric couples, Dr. Miracle and Antonia, and Dapertutto and Giulietta, belong in this network as well. Post-mesmerist Paris provided abundant inspiration for Barbier and Carré's versions of both "Rat Krespel" and "A New Year's Eve Adventure": black-coated doctors and sorcerers, fainting girls, fascinating gems, and entrancing melodies.

WOMAN AND INSTRUMENT

Music in mesmerist practice became an intangible correlative of the magic/magnetic objects that increased the body's receptiveness and charged the atmosphere, causing magnetism to flow more freely and inducing trance or collapse ("crisis"). The sixteenth of Mesmer's *Twenty-Seven Principles* declared that "[Animal magnetism] is communicated, propogated, and augmented by sound," and accounts of magnetic seances frequently include musicians on the scene.[24] An engraving from Mesmer's time shows two string players in an antechamber at the back of the salon, and music serves both mesmerism's benign image and the therapeutic process, as the caption explains: "All day, some Musicians in an antechamber play appropriate airs to excite gaity in the invalids."[25] In Dr. Deslon's salon in 1784, "A piano forté is placed in one corner of the apartment, and different airs are played with various degrees of rapidity; vocal music is sometimes added to the instrumental."[26] According to the Royal Commission's report of 1785, the presiding doctor in another clinic explained that "to communicate the fluid to the piano-forté, nothing more is necessary than to approach to it the iron rod; that the person who plays upon the instrument furnishes also a portion of the fluid, and that the magnetism is transmitted by the sounds to the surrounding patients."[27] The extravagant displays of somnambulist "magnetic ecstasy" offered by Charles LaFontaine, a self-proclaimed scientific magnetizer of the 1840s, turned music's mesmerizing echoes into a marketable commodity. At once a researcher, an apostle, and a showman, LaFontaine toured France demonstrating his art in lecture halls, theaters, and schools. At present we must rely on LaFontaine's own descriptions of his displays and recruitment methods; however, his accounts are best read as propagandistic conversion narratives, in which audiences become "firmly convinced by experiments which could leave them no doubt" as to the validity of what they saw.[28] According to LaFontaine's own accounts, then, he traveled with an entourage of young somnambulist-performers who might well have been models for Barbier and Carré's Antonia. They demonstrated numerous phenomena, most notably a "magnetic ecstasy," which LaFontaine describes as a sort of "magnetism and transfiguration" mediated by music.

LaFontaine begins his account of "magnetic ecstasy" by emphasizing his subjects' vulnerability and lack of boundaries: "I could approach their eyes with a lit candle, without provoking the least movement of their lids or contraction of their pupils."[29] The eye's failure to shut out candlelight with involuntary contractions is a metaphor for the subject's complete exposure, his or her lack of resistance against the harsher light of LaFontaine's and the audience's scrutiny. Furthermore, the magnetic state transforms the eye— normally able to be averted or to close out light—into an ear, the one organ that cannot resist sensory stimuli. Apparently rendered "all ears" by LaFontaine's gestures, the subjects made appropriate responses, postures, and movements to various musical cues. LaFontaine claimed that somnambulists from all backgrounds—"the assassin and the lost girl as well as the most virtuous creature"—must yield to music's power and experience its ecstasy, which in his description resembles the trances of medieval saints and mystics: each one's face was "lit with inner joy; one senses intimately that she is face to face with something sublime."[30] Nor can his pious language disguise the erotic aspects of this trance: "I have seen *ecstasy* many times, and nothing in the world is more arresting: the somnambulist . . . becomes beautiful, with a beauty that one cannot describe . . . incoherent words fall from her lips . . . she hears floods of sound that ravish and uplift her."[31]

I would like to meditate briefly on LaFontaine's characterization of the somnambulist's appearance and behavior as "arresting," the most vivid language in which he describes an audience's—and his own—response to the spectacle of magnetic ecstasy he has created. Although his project of scientific promotion requires a dispassionate tone, and in most accounts he carefully attributes *passionate* responses to magnetism only to the somnambulists on stage, his rhetoric consistently betrays how audiences and magnetizer alike were caught up in the spell of music and its demonstrated effects: like the magnetized children gazing steadily into the candle's flame, or moving like puppets in response to the sounds they hear, the spectators cannot look away or to tune out what is before them. Although LaFontaine tries to enforce boundaries between himself and his somnambulists, the ravishing power attributed to music cannot be contained; his magnetic displays simultaneously represented music's effect on a model listener—the somnambulist—and produced that effect in every spectator, including the magnetizer himself. Thus when LaFontaine imagines that "if [ecstasy] were prolonged, perhaps we would have nothing left but a corpse; the soul would fly directly to God," the magnetizer's speculation about the impact of his music on a vulnerable adolescent is also a listener's fantasy of submission to music's irresistible authority.[32]

Barbier and Carré's representation of Antonia's death in *Les Contes d'Hoffmann* (1851) stages just such a fantasy of yielding to music's invading power. The scene follows the dramatic plot of LaFontaine's magnetic displays, beginning with a demonstration that Antonia's boundaries—like those of ecstatic somnambulists—have become entirely permeable. The stage directions detail Antonia's attempt to resist Dr. Miracle's invasion of her private thoughts, and Miracle's sudden appearances and disappearances pantomime the irresistible quality of his words, against which Antonia has no defenses:

> ANTONIA, *alone:* I have promised! I will sing no more! *(She buries her head in her hands.)*
> MIRACLE, *rising suddenly behind her and leaning close to her ear:* You will sing no more! Do you know the sacrifice thus imposed. . . ? Art alone will give you peace! It alone consoles, and it alone is faithful! *(He disappears)*
> ANTONIA, *rising:* Tempt me no more! Begone! Demon, I don't want to hear anymore, I have sworn to be [Hoffmann's] . . . Mother! oh, mother! *(She collapses, weeping, on the sofa at right)*
> MIRACLE, *rising behind her:* Your mother! You dare invoke her name?[33]

In the scene that follows, Dr. Miracle compels Antonia to sing until she dies: specifically, he compels her to sing an adaptation of Schubert's

"Gretchen am Spinnrade," with new text by Barbier and Carré. Ther
nothing unusual about the playwrights' providing new words for a
known melody in this context, for boulevard plays typically included
existing "airs" with new texts and newly composed songs; Les (
d'Hoffmann, for example, features two original choruses and a dri
song in addition to Antonia's performance. Yet the selection of "Gre
am Spinnrade" seems significant, and even more significant is the v
which the playwrights and the Théâtre de l'Odéon's music director,
Ancessy, tailored the song's dramatic and musical structure to make
Antonia's death by "magnetic ecstasy."[34]

Schubert's song had dramatized a singer's struggle between self-
pline—the orderly business of spinning a straight, smooth thread-
a nearly overwhelming urge to drop the thread, to yield to the me
of seduction and fantasies of further transgressions—"O könnt ic
küssen, so wie ich wollt / an seiner Küssen vergehen sollt!" The pers
spinning figure in the accompaniment simultaneously mimics the r
tions of Gretchen's wheel and advertises her emotional conflict, a
wheel accelerates and slows with her tumultuous thoughts. The
music may thus be heard to flow from and respond to Gretchen's
sciousness: she herself "spins forth" the music that accompanies her
Thus her exalted "sein Händedrück, und ach!—sein Küss!," in the s
verse, interrupts the musical flow; when the thread of her obse
stretches too taut, it breaks, and accordingly, the piano falls silent.
each return to her quiet refrain she tries again to spin her thread eve
restrain her mind and hands to a steady pace and contain her song
expressive boundaries that it repeatedly exceeds.

Gretchen's oscillations between repressing and succumbing to the
ory of her own seduction become, in Barber and Carré's adaptation, a
ing of a new kind of seduction: this time, the disorderly fantasy is c
yielding to music. Antonia's lover, Hoffmann, represents oppressive
rather than transgression, for Hoffmann has demanded that she aba
music, her deepest desire, for him. Like Gretchen struggling to co
trate on her domestic task, Antonia struggles to discipline her thou
and like Gretchen she is tempted by a forbidden pleasure and the
lution it promises: "Chanter encore, et puis mourir!"[35] Certain ma
lations of the original song, however, were required to make it fi
scenario of magnetic ecstasy on which Antonia's death scene seems
modeled.[36]

First, Barbier and Carré complicated (one doesn't want to say '
tered") Schubert's scenario of a distracted girl singing to herself with
additions of Dr. Miracle, an off-stage voice of temptation, and a mag
olin. Their adaptation abbreviated the song, yet packed it with mel
matic incidents, subdividing it into two episodes: Schubert's first ver

their redaction, became a scene of listening, and the final verse a scene of somnambulist performance, an "ecstasy" taken to that fatal extreme about which LaFontaine had only speculated. A ghostly voice, which Miracle identifies triumphantly as "ta mère!," sings the first verse of Schubert's song as Antonia listens, captivated; at the end of that verse he pushes Antonia to succumb to the music, no longer as a listener, but as a performer. When after the first verse Miracle "seizes a violin and accompanies with a sort of furor," taking up the spinning figure in a melodramatic gesture that identifies him as the music's master, Antonia cannot resist the accompaniment's propulsive power: she sings until finally, "She falls dying. . . . Miracle disappears into the earth, uttering a burst of laughter."[37]

Simply by reorchestrating and redistributing the elements of Schubert's song, Barbier and Carré inverted its dramatic "plot." The spinning music that had once mimed Gretchen's gestures and served as a sonorous index of her interior state now acts on Antonia from *outside*, emanating not from her but from Miracle's violin. The music that had manifested Gretchen's inner conflict has become externalized as Dr. Miracle's playing, which Antonia hears and to which she must submit.[38] The suspicion that the spinning music no longer comes from the singer, but is imposed upon her, is strengthened when we note that Ancessy's adaptation omits the middle verse of Schubert's song, in which the singer had momentarily overridden the propulsive accompaniment. The magnetic scenario cannot tolerate such an interruption of the somnambulist's ecstatic progress: if Antonia could break the music's spell over her, even for the length of the fermata that follows Gretchen's "Ach! sein Küss!," it would undermine the fundamental conceit of her subjection to the external forces of music and magnetism. In eliminating Gretchen's second verse, Barbier and Carré created an uninterrupted dramatic progression in which Antonia yields to music, demonstrating, like LaFontaine's somnambulists, her utter vulnerability to it.

Miracle's seizing of the violin to "accompan[y] her with a sort of fury" is, of course, an overdetermined gesture, one that links the modern "science" of magnetism to ancient notions of the occult, and to earlier theatrical representations of demonic music acting on female bodies. To name only one of several examples contemporary with Barbier and Carré's *Les Contes d'Hoffmann* of 1851, the ballet *Le Violon du Diable* (1849) united ancient superstition with modern scenes of music "magnetizing" the body. The *Revue et Gazette Musicale* remarked that M. St. Léon, the choreographer and star of this *ballet fantastique*, must inevitably have studied "the life of Tartini and the stories of Hoffmann," and indeed the French considered the violin the most "Hoffmannesque" of instruments.[39] *Le Violon du diable* demonstrates how music's imputed supernatural and scientific properties could be mingled indiscriminately in popular theater, where

mesmerism was only one ingredient in a pastiche of supernatural, magnetic, and theatrical clichés derived from such earlier successes as *Robert le Diable* and *La Sonnambula*.[40] Its villain, yet another black-clad Doctor with "cadaverous-looking" features, commands the conventional powers of sorcery and magnetic cliché: his violin summons ghostly women in a scene modeled on Meyerbeer's "infernal" ballet of nuns, and the solo *pas magnétique* that follows makes the heroine, "Hélène," a modern somnambulist:

> [D]ressed in white and holding a candle in her hand, [she] appeared at the top of the stairs . . . and listened, charmed by the rich sound . . . slowly she descended the stairs, then took a step into the room, moving toward the player, then she took two steps, then three, but as if she moved in spite of herself, as if she were pushed by a force more powerful than her own will.[41]

Mesmerist imagery drops out of the mix in the second act, however, when the doctor-villain's demonic aspect becomes explicit and the plot degenerates into romantic-religious kitsch. The violin, then, could signify modern "magic" such as magnetism and somnambulism, but continually slipped back to its folkloric and occult origins. Its demonic associations endured throught the nineteenth century and beyond, while the "medical" science of *le magnétisme animal* receded into the shadows of quackery and charlatanism, and thus later interpretations of Offenbach's villain as a devil or demon is not too surprising. However, reductions of Dr. Miracle to a fiddling bogeyman do not account adequately for his "passes magnétiques" in the opera's purest mesmerist moment, his conjuring up of Antonia's voice from an empty chair in the course of his "medical" examination of his absent patient.

WOMAN AS INSTRUMENT

In addition to using sound to act upon women's bodies, the mesmerist or magnetizer also claimed the ability to conjure up sounds from them, a dramatic process that lent itself irresistibly to the theatrical stage as well as to the clinic and the medical lecture hall. The magnetized body was not only presented as an object that music could manipulate; it was also imagined as a channel through which mysterious and magical sounds could be directed. In 1785 the Italian impresario Pinetti—claiming to be "inspired by the teachings of Mesmer"—presented his magnetized and blindfolded wife, who read minds, guessing the thoughts of members of the audience. By 1805, an American author described a new incarnation of this oracular fantasy on display in Boston, "a certain Philosophical Machine lately arrived from France, which engrosses universal attention."[42] This device, dubbed by its proprietors *The Invisible Lady and Acoustic Temple,* consisted of a small square chest suspended in the middle of an octagonal railing (to convince the visitor that no person was hiding inside the box or under the floor); on top of the chest was a dome with a crystal ball, and a speaking tube extended from each corner of the chest. Visitors could ask the box questions, to which answers emerged "in an effeminate tone of voice."[43] These two spectacles provide the essential ingredients—magnetism producing a voice, and a voice emerging from an unseen source—for Barbier and Carré's scene of magnetic vocal compulsion, in which Dr. Miracle's gestures over an empty chair compel the absent Antonia to sing:

> *(Miracle continues his magnetic passes. He indicates with gestures that he is taking Antonia's hand, leading her to an armchair, and seating her there.)*
>
> MIRACLE *(indicating one of the chairs and seating himself in the other):* Will you sit down there!
>
> CRESPEL: I'm sitting!
>
> MIRACLE *(not answering Crespel):* How old are you, please?
>
> CRESPEL: Who? Me?
>
> MIRACLE: I am speaking to your daughter.
>
> HOFFMANN *(apart):* Antonia!
>
> MIRACLE: How old? *(He listens)* Answer! I must know! Twenty years old? The springtime of life! *(He gestures like a man taking a pulse)* Your hand, please!
>
> CRESPEL: Her hand?
>
> MIRACLE: Shh! Let me count! The pulse is uneven, too fast—a bad symptom! Now sing!
>
> CRESPEL *(rising):* No, no! Stop! Don't make her sing!
>
> MIRACLE: Sing!! *(the voice of Antonia is heard)* See, her face is agitated and her eyes flash! She places one hand over her fluttering heart!
>
> CRESPEL: What does it mean?[44]

Like the scene of Antonia's death discussed above, Miracle's "medical" evocation of Antonia's voice has a long history behind it, a spectrum of ostensibly scientific displays with frankly theatrical elements, and again the testimonies of magnetizers and witnesses resist definitive interpretation. Yet if rational understanding compels us to admit that magnetic "cures" and effects resulted from fakery or at best genuine coincidence, perhaps this only makes them more interesting as philosophical fantasies about uncanny voices, music, and language. In 1837, for example, William Stone described a magnetic cure of mutism: after a head injury, a young woman named Loraina Brackett "sustained a loss of voice, so complete, that for fifteen months she was unable to utter a single guttural sound, and could only whisper almost inaudible tones."[45] Daily magnetic treatments with Dr. George Capron restored her voice. Similarly, in 1847, LaFontaine claimed to have cured 67 of the 88 deaf-mutes he had treated; while admitting that magnetism worked most reliably on "hysterical" speech disorders, he also said it worked on congenital deaf-mutes, those believed to "lack the vocal organ."[46]

Magnetizers made two still more extravagant assertions about magnetism and the human voice, claims that turned the somnambulist's very body into an "Acoustic Temple" and a "Philosophical Machine." Stone reported that while in the trance state, Brackett could "travel" mentally and report on sights and events in places she had never visited, and LaFontaine's somnambulists displayed the same gift. LaFontaine also stated that while in the trance, his somnambulist could answer "any questions, made in it matters not what language."[47] "Scientific" accounts of vocal conjuring seem to have gained with each telling, yet these magnetic tall tales also open the way to an interpretation of their appeal and persistence, the fulfillment of a collective fantasy. LaFontaine insisted that, contrary to popular belief, mediums could not *speak* languages they that did not know, but could only *comprehend* them; this, he explained, "is merely a matter of thought-transmission; the somnambulist does not grasp anything from the word, but from the thought of the person who addresses her."[48] The gift of clairvoyant speech, the ability to listen "behind" words and hear unspoken meaning, was labeled "second sight"—an apparent misnomer, but a clue to the essential synesthetic confusion at work. Ordinary speech, ostensibly used to convey meaning, is inevitably shadowed by untrustworthiness; language, the vehicle of distortion, omission, and evasion, veils thought as readily as it reveals it. In the magnetic trance, the medium seemed to hear behind this veil, enacting a fantasy that language and its inherent unreliability could be transcended. The somnambulist's language is at once less than and more than ordinary speech: less than speech because she appears to "say" nothing, only to channel words through her body; yet more than speech, because her words appear not to be products of fallible human intelligence or of individual interest. Stone, for example, carefully anticipates any suspicions that Brackett's speech was prompted or interfered with by observers: "she can talk only with the person or persons with whom the magnetiser has willed that she shall be in communication. She can hear nothing addressed to her by anyone else, nor can she hear the conversation between any two individuals, nor even the person with whom she is in communication if he directs his speech to any but herself."[49] The magnetizer, controlling and monitoring the somnambulist's speech and hearing, fulfills an impossible human desire to purify discourse, a reassuring fantasy of an idealized speaker who cannot speak impure or untruthful sounds. The magnetized female body becomes, in these displays, an "Acoustic Temple" from which it is not the human medium, but an incorruptible "Invisible Lady" that speaks.

Yet testimonies of witnesses claiming to confirm the truthfulness of these performances also revealed the logical paradox at the heart of this fantasy. William Stone, for example, presents himself as a rational skeptic who was only convinced of Loraina Brackett's second sight when she "traveled" to Saratoga Springs, a place she had never visited; in her trance, Stone reports, Brackett described every detail of his own recently built new house, proving to him that her "second sight" could penetrate the "veil" of physical distance. A second detail convinced him even more firmly: she described a painting that he had purchased previously but had never yet displayed, and which would hang in the new house but was not yet unwrapped. Brackett's "discovery" of this painting thus penetrated veils of secrecy and silence more opaque than mere distance; we might say that she saw through Stone himself. With this elaborate tale, Stone means to convince his readers that no third party could have prompted or prepared Miss Brackett, but he also confirms that the somnambulist's "oracular" language cannot persuade the listener with content of its own: the only test of the somnambulist's authentic insight is for her to tell the witness something he already knows. He listens, fascinated, to her "travels," her speech that appears to emanate from remote or impossible spaces—but the medium's narrative journey, to be compelling, must end at the listener's own house. Her speech, in short, ceases to be speech: the miraculous discourse that emanates from these Acoustic Temples in "an effeminate tone of voice" is no mere human language, but a fantasy discourse akin to music.

Magnetized women and clairvoyant speakers, that is, become musical instruments, producing transcendently truthful sounds of which they are not themselves aware, and which thus can satisfy a listener's impossible desire for a pure language. Nicklausse, in Offenbach's opera, picks up a violin, remarking that it, like Antonia, has an "unself-conscious soul" made audible by a player's touch:

> Entends le céleste accent
> De cette âme qui s'ignore,
> Ecoute passer dans l'air
> Le son pénétrant et clair[50]

[Hear the heavenly tones / of this unself-conscious soul / Listen as the air is filled / with the bright, clear sound]

Nicklausse's analogy between Antonia and the violin was anticipated in the *musique de scène* for Barbier and Carré's original *Les Contes d'Hoffmann*, where the "heavenly tones" produced by Antonia during Dr. Miracle's examination were not sung by the actress, but played by a solo violin offstage. The 1851 Antonia thus belonged to a sisterhood of heroines like Donizetti's mad Lucia (whose final, visionary appearance is announced and accompanied in the autograph by the mesmerist strains of a glass harmonica); Wagner's Senta in her "magnetisch Schlaf," and his Elsa, who responds to men's questions "as if dreaming" with the voice of a solo clarinet. In these operatic trance-maidens' moments of transfiguration, musical instruments seem to "speak" for them, marking their speech as something outside the realm of ordinary human discourse. Similarly, when Dr. Miracle examines Antonia during the trio "Pour conjurer le danger," her song appears as the final term in a series of instrumental answers to his

Example 2.2 Dr. Miracle examines the absent Antonia

Example 2.2, cont.

Example 2.2, cont.

questions: a solo clarinet responds to his "Quel âge avez vous, je prie? Répondez!," followed by a French horn for the "rapid and uneven" beating of Antonia's pulse. At last, in response to Miracle's urgings of "Chantez! Chantez!" her human voice erupts in a wordless cascade from off-stage (see Example 2.2).[51]

What fantastical creature are we to construe off-stage, that has a clarinet to sing with and a French horn for a heartbeat, and, under extreme duress, peals forth the liquid *glissandi* of a human soprano? Once again a proto-type may be found in contemporary magic shows. A late-nineteenth-cen-tury book of parlor tricks instructs amateur musicians to mystify their friends with an "Aeolian harp," a secret arrangement of tubes and res-onating boards inserted in a windowsill to catch the wind and produce "song" without the presence of a singer.[52] The mid-nineteenth-century magician-impresario Jean Eugène Robert-Houdin describes another, more elaborate display entitled "Aeolian Harps made to perform by Spirit Influ-ence" in his *Confidences d'un prestidigitateur:* a tableau in which a quartet of free-standing harps, untouched by human hands, played themselves and "sang" with human voices.[53] Even more than magnetic somnambulists and musical ecstatics, these magnetized harps are the model for Antonia's op-eratic performance—magic instruments that sing with multiple voices, human and inhuman, always unseen, always disembodied. At the magne-tizer's command, the harp sings like a woman and the woman sings like a harp, producing a fantasy of "unself-conscious sound," of pure, unmedi-ated music.

GOING BACKSTAGE

Robert-Houdin, proud of the wonderful theatrical effect he achieved with these singing harps, shared with his readers the acoustical secret behind them: concealed metal rods extending from the frames of the on-stage harps down through holes in the floor, to another room where the rods could be brought into contact with the frames of other harps or with additional instruments, including piano, violin, clarinet, and cello. The sounds of these instruments would thus be "broadcast" through the harps on-stage, and, he continues,

> A still more striking effect was obtained by transmitting (by the aid of a sin-gle harp) a vocal quartette, the performers holding their faces down as close as possible to the sounding board of a piano.[54]

Nor, he admits, could the "unself-conscious sound" of the magnetized in-struments always be sustained:

> The absurdity of their position was occasionally too much for the gravity of the singers, and the quartette would come to an abrupt conclusion amid peals of laughter, which were faithfully transmitted by the harp to the astonished audience.[55]

The laughter emerging from Robert-Houdin's magnetized harps invites us to resist the carefully constructed allure of magnetism, trance, and instru-

mentalized speech. We may always read the ostensibly unconscious magnetized performer as an agent, the hidden intelligence behind the mesmerist illusion, rather than as the passive object of therapeutic manipula-
tion or even coercion. This possibility had haunted the practice of
mesmerism from its inception, and when stage mesmerists disclosed the secrets of their "supernatural arts," it was invariably confirmed:

> There is a second servant, of whose existence the spectators know nothing.
> This is the alter ego of the conjuror, the invisible hand which really effects
> sundry appearances, disappearances, and substitutions, of which magic has the
> credit. This servant remains behind the scenes, eye and ear constantly on the
> alert; and . . . [T]his office demands great dexterity, constant watchfulness,
> and, above all, instant readiness in execution. Women perform this duty to
> perfection.[56]

Behind the trance-maidens, visionaries, and musical clairvoyants worked
discreet, clever, and musically gifted assistants. A number of published "secrets," memoirs, and instructions for aspiring magicians explain how blindfolded or hypnotized pianists and singers might "miraculously" play silent
requests by mastering codes and signals.[57]

Against this background, it seems naive to accept the Antonia act of *Les
Contes d'Hoffmann* at face value, as the tale of a fragile woman preyed upon
by sinister magic: the music and images of Antonia's trance may just as well
signal a deceptive intelligence at work, a subterfuge with which the girl performer gains access to music forbidden by her father and the demands of
bourgeois life. The mutual contamination of medical magnetism and stage
magic invites us to interpret Antonia not only as the instrumentalized victim of Dr. Miracle's magnetic manipulations, but as a willful, desiring subject. Who is the agent behind this mesmerized woman's apparently "unself-conscious" performance?

Barbier and Carré's Crespel, frantic to contain his daughter in the safe
haven of health and domesticity, attributes control of her singing to the in-
trusive figure of Dr. Miracle, construing Miracle as the villain and Antonia
as his helpless victim. Any reader of ghost stories, however, will distrust this
account, for intruders like Dr. Miracle cannot simply muscle their way into
the human realm; they must be invited or summoned by the repressed desire of a member (often female) of the community.[58] The opera-goer will
again think of Senta, whose obsession with the ballad and portrait of the
legendary Dutchman seems to bring him into her very house—she is the
magnet that attracts destabilizing outside energies. When the forbidden desires of a Senta or an Antonia create a gateway through which sinister supernatural forces may enter the human community, mesmeric scenarios
begin to resonate with vampire plots, and indeed both the play and opera
Les Contes d'Hoffmann do present Dr. Miracle as a sort of vampire preying
on musical women: Crespel exclaims, "He wants to kill my daughter, just

as he killed my wife!" But Crespel's fear of Miracle, his insistence on Antonia's passivity before this sinister invader, may equally serve to conceal a deeper dynamic of recognition and identification between the woman and the monstrous outsider.

For might we not read Dr. Miracle as Antonia's own alter ego rather than her opponent? What if Miracle is not the predator of Crespel's imagination (and of conventional stagings of the opera), but rather a fantasy that gives Antonia access to the music that both her father and her lover have forbidden to her? Remember that in the opera, as in the play, Antonia cannot *see* Dr. Miracle in the final scene—that he whispers in her ear, that she does not turn to look at him, that he disappears and then reappears behind her—until at last she cries out, "Ah! Who will save me from this demon, *from myself?*" It is possible, despite Barbier and Carré's elaborate framework of mesmerist tropes and props, to hear Dr. Miracle and his fatal music originating not from outside Antonia, as her father insists, but rather from inside her—to imagine that Antonia is spinning forth her own accompaniment after all. If Dr. Miracle is not a bogeyman, but rather an external projection of Antonia's own subversive desire, then what is the source and object of that desire, her urge for song and glory? Here the operatic version of Antonia's story will converge with narratives of hysteria, medicalized versions of the Romantic ghost story, in which a constrained body becomes legible, able to express through gesture and inarticulate sounds the unspeakable desires, grief, and loss that haunt it. My next chapter proposes that we listen not to the violin-playing "demon," nor the alluringly unselfconscious singer, nor the magnetic quasi-vampire, but to a *Poltergeist:* the "noisy ghost" of Antonia's mother, who appears only in the operatic presentation of the story, the trauma (in proto-psychoanalytic terms) that underlies Antonia's symptomatic song.

CHAPTER THREE

Song as Symptom

ANTONIA, OLYMPIA, AND THE PRIMA DONNA MOTHER

THAT THE hysteric has proved a useful rhetorical figure for feminist discussions of opera and Western art music as a whole is evident in Catherine Clément's references to heroines and singers alike as "girls who jump into space" and "hysteric[s] in [their] midnight hour," and in Susan McClary's invocation of various "madwomen" including Monteverdi's lamenting Nymph, Donizetti's Lucia, and the nameless protagonist of Schoenberg's *Erwartung* to illustrate conflicts between expression and repression in musical discourse.[1] It is easy to label operatic performances, particularly those of female sopranos, as "hysterical," for like the behaviors attributed to hysterics in the nineteenth and early twentieth centuries, opera's high points are marked by excessive emotion, compulsive repetition, and verbal incoherence. The opera performer, like the women put through their paces in Charcot's lecture hall and written up in Freud's published case studies, acts out a loss of bodily and emotional control that simultaneously attracts and alarms her spectators. But there is more to hysteria than shrieks and gestures, and it is, I hope, with more justification and more delicacy that I venture to read the hysteric(s) in *Les Contes d'Hoffmann*.

Numerous scholars have pointed out the ancient and quintessentially feminine associations of hysteria; although men also suffered from the condition, particularly in the nineteenth and twentieth centuries, the hysteric state was seen as both feminine and effeminizing.[2] The condition seems first to have been discussed in ancient medical writings, including those of the ancient Egyptians, who treated it as a disease of the womb; the Greek physician Hippocrates (460–377 B.C.) named it after that organ (*hysteros*), which he claimed could wander about within the female body, causing pain, convulsions, and emotional disorder until it was lured or manipulated back to its proper place. Explanations of hysteria in various eras worked metaphorical variations on this theme of the "wandering womb" as a presence in the body that is at once member and alien; contained within the body's boundaries yet mobile. Hysteria might be compared to demonic possession, the occupation of the body by an evil external presence; in mesmerist therapies, as discussed in Chapter One, hysteric symptoms were interpreted as results of a surplus, deficiency, or congestion of "animal magnetism." The shift to a modern understanding of hysteria occurred in the late nineteenth century, when physical symptoms came to be construed as evidence of mental or emotional blockage rather than physical. Psychoanalysis now conceived of hysteria as a result of alien presences in the psyche: traumatic memories or experiences that were repressed but not resolved, and thus made their presences felt as physical symptoms and dream images.

The key element of this modern understanding of hysteria is the apparent legibility of the hysteric body, whose symptoms seem to tell fragments of a story about the repressed trauma that caused them. Hysteria is a narrative irritant, in that symptoms such as hysterical blindness, lameness, aphasia, and convulsions make the body a metaphorical field. Even Charcot, who declared his patients' speech irrelevant or deceptive, charted their seizures in a progressive narrative and gave his clinical photos narrative titles such as "Crucifixion," "Ecstasy," and "Supplication"; he also noted that most hysterics seemed to rehearse or reenact a recognizable plot during their "crises." I have called hysteria a medicalized ghost story because the patient's body, like a haunted house, seems occupied by an invisible force—"the repressed"—that obliquely and painfully makes its presence feit, demanding recognition and resolution. The hysteric body bears physical traces of tragedy or violence, unquiet ghosts of the past. Hysteria is a kind of haunting, an expression of longing, loss, or trauma that fixes the psyche in the grip of the traumatic experience and compels it to repeat painful or self-destructive symptoms.

The analyst might piece together the traumatic history of *Les Contes d'Hoffmann*'s Antonia from her symptoms, her compulsion to sing which is also an obsession with her dead mother, also a singer. But Antonia's haunted condition, her desire for and endangerment by a prima donna's song, is a condition shared by the nineteenth-century Romantic imagination, as evidenced by the musical tales of E.T.A. Hoffmann, and numerous retellings of those tales in theater, ballet and opera. Each successive adaptation of Hoffmann's "Rat Krespel," "Der Sandmann," and "Don Juan" reflects an ambivalent attitude toward women performers, whose potent voices make them simultaneously desirable and fearsome. Stories about female singers struggled to contain and manage the singing woman's authority, but the prima donna's voice, like that of the hysteric, persisted, eluding and overcoming narrative attempts to shape or contain its turbulent noise.

Let me begin with an excerpt from "Rat Krespel" that might serve as a parable for relationships between female singers and male music lovers in the Romantic imagination. Krespel, a young German musician, traveled in Italy and was fortunate enough to win the heart and hand of a celebrated diva, Angela, whose name seemed only appropriate to her heavenly voice.

Unfortunately, her personality proved less than heavenly, and when she was not actually singing he found her violent whims and arrogant demands for attention very trying. One day as he stood playing his violin, his wife came to him in an affectionate mood:

> [Angela] embraced her husband, overwhelmed him with sweet and languishing glances, and rested her pretty head on his shoulder. But Krespel, carried away into the world of music, continued to play on until the walls echoed again; thus he chanced to touch the Signora somewhat ungently with his arm and the fiddle bow.
>
> She leaped back full of fury, shrieking, *"Bestia tedesca!"*, snatched the violin from his hands, and dashed it on the marble table into a thousand pieces. Krespel stood like a statue before her; but then, as if awakening out of a dream, he seized her with the strength of a giant and threw her out of the window of her own house, and . . . fled . . . back to Germany.[3]

The attractions of the woman's beautiful voice are offset by the repulsion induced by her willfulness and bad temper. Hoffmann's divas lack domestic virtues: when they are not capricious flirts (like Lauretta and Teresina in the story "Die Fermate"), they are rebellious wives. Angela, for example,

> was unwilling to sever her connection with the theater; neither did she wish to part with her professional name, by which she was celebrated, nor to add to it the cacophonous "Krespel" . . . what a strange life of worry and torture Angela led him as soon as she became his wife. Krespel was of the opinion that more capriciousness and waywardness were concentrated in Angela's little person than in all the rest of the prima donnas in the world put together (Hoffmann, "Rat Krespel," 228).

Counselor Krespel was not the only one to fling the willful prima donna out the window; indeed, every author and composer who adapted his story for the stage tried somehow to follow him in exorcising or containing her transgressive presence. Most famously, of course, "Rat Krespel" and "The Sand-Man" evolved from their original versions through various intermediate stages into Offenbach's *Les Contes d'Hoffmann* (1881). More than sixty years separated the opera from its literary sources, but in every version, the problem of the prima donna endured. In fact, authorial efforts to repress or contain the transgressive diva became less successful with each retelling of Hoffmann's story, and in Offenbach's opera she has become so powerful that her presence actually exceeds the boundaries of the tale inspired by "Rat Krespel": she emerges, uncannily, in the Olympia act, and appears once more in the epilogue that follows the hero's three stories. Let us follow her, in her various incarnations, from E.T.A. Hoffmann's tales to those of Offenbach.

THE GIRLS WHO LOVED SINGING TOO MUCH

In "Rat Krespel," Hoffmann resolves the tension between the prima donna's beautiful voice and repellent character in his portrait of Antonia, Angela's daughter. Antonia's voice is even more enchanting than her mother's, her soulful personality the antithesis of Angela's worldliness and pride; she is not so much human as superhuman, the personification of ideal music that would "speak in heavenly language . . . of that far, romantic realm in which we swoon away in inexpressibly yearning . . . penetrate our narrow, paltry lives, and with sublime siren voices tempt forth its willing victims."[4] As David Charlton has written, "In Hoffmann's philosophy, an almost mystical triangle connects composer, singer, and auditor, one that suggests music's acoustic immediacy of impact . . . it was for the singer . . . to embody the very spirit of the composer, and actually become its Romantic essence."[5] The voices of female singers such as Antonia or Donna Anna in the short story "Don Juan" serve as conduits for music from a remote and greatly desired sphere, available to the male listener only through the sound of their singing voices. In both cases, the woman's submission to her role brings about her death; *she,* not the listener, becomes the "willing victim" of her own siren song. Whereas Hoffmann houses the prima donna's voice in a capricious and rebellious body, the bodies of these idealized women singers exist only to be sacrificed for the production of their sublime music.

In Hoffmann's fiction, the most transcendent music enters the world when the singer's body has been eliminated altogether, leaving only her voice ushering from the unseen "far, romantic realms." The narrator of "Johannes Kreisler's Certificate of Apprenticeship," for example, describes a forest spot he used to visit for musical inspiration: "it often happened that as I gazed at the rock, I drifted into a waking dream, and heard a girl's extraordinary singing, which filled my breast with the exquisite pain of ecstasy."[6] This girl, he explains, had loved a mysterious musician who taught her to sing "melodies . . . so strange and ghostly that no one dared to approach."[7] But one day she disappeared, and a search revealed her body buried under the rock where they used to sit and sing. Although the singing girl did not survive her encounter with music, the sound she brought into the world remains available to the Romantic listener. Whereas the prima donna noisily proclaims "I sing," the victim of music *is sung* by a power outside of herself. Standing on the threshold between the mundane world and the transcendent realm, such imaginary singers open themselves to artistic and quasi-demonic possession, Hoffmann's fantasy transforming the woman performer into something performed-upon.

Hoffmann thus represents his idealized singers as musical instruments,

music coming not from but through them. The narrator c
hears Donna Anna's voice in the rustling strings of the pian
nia's voice has "a very remarkable and altogether peculiar
time it was like the sighing of an aeolian harp . . . it seemed
not room for such notes in the human breast."[8] The image c
phasizes the female artist's passivity, for this mythical instru
resonate to the breath of Nature rather than in response t
telligence. In another passage, Hoffmann explicitly equate:
the Cremona violin in her father's workshop:

> Scarcely had [Krespel] drawn the first few notes from [the violi
> nia cried aloud with joy, "Why, that's me!—now I shall sing ag
> truth, there was something remarkably striking about the clea
> like tones of the violin; they seemed to have been engendered
> soul. . . . As [Krespel] ran up and down the scale, playing bold
> consummate power and expression, she clapped her hands toge
> with delight, "I did that well!" (Hoffmann, "Rat Krespel," 23

When Antonia sings herself to death in the tale's musical
Cremona violin cracks and is buried with her. Similarly, t
Kreisleriana is found next to the shattered remains of her lc
instruments breaking from the strain of overuse, these ar
from an excess of music, or passion, or unrequited love.

In the Romantic conflation of female pleasure in perfor
bidden love, music pours through the woman artist and
Hoffmann's "Donna Anna," helpless on stage before Don
magnetism, is helpless in life before the debilitating pow
music. After the intermission of *Don Giovanni,* during whi
materializes in the narrator's private opera box for a discus:
tic aesthetics, her rendition of "Non mi dir" brings on the
vous collapse and death. Antonia's last performance in "Ra
spired by a beloved man, the "young composer B." whom
have nor resist:

> [T]he Counselor fancied one night that he heard somebody pla
> in the adjoining room, and he soon made out distinctly that
> ishing on the instrument in his usual style. . . . Antonia's vc
> singing low and soft; soon, however, it began to rise and rise i
> it became an ear-splitting fortissimo. . . . All at once [Krespel] v
> by a dazzling brightness, in which he beheld B—and Antonia lc
> embrace, and gazing at each other in a rapture of ecstasy. . . .
> ing, Krespel] rushed into Antonia's room. She lay on the sofa
> if asleep and dreaming of the joys and raptures of heaven. *But*
> (ibid., 235).

The notion that excessive passion for performance and for a forbidden lover could combine to kill the woman performer is not unique to E.T.A. Hoffmann's fiction. Heinrich Heine's *De l'Allemagne*, a collection of German folklore published in Paris in 1835, included the legend of the "Wilis," which weaves together Hoffmannesque themes of female performance, romantic disappointment, death, and the supernatural. Adolphe Adam's ballet *Giselle, ou les Wilis* (1841) incorporates the motif of fatal performance into Heine's legend, presenting the heroine as excessively passionate, not only about her secret lover, but about dancing as well. Her mother warns her that "You love dancing too much—you will be turned into a Wili!," and when her lover abandons her at the end of Act I, Giselle dances herself to death and returns in Act II as the newest forest spirit. Offenbach's "romantische Oper" *Die Rhein-Nixen* (1864) features a nearly identical situation involving song rather than dance. According to a ballad sung by Armgard, who will shortly sing herself into a fatal frenzy provoked by disappointed love:

> Dort, wo hundertjähr'ge Eichen,
> Dunkele Tannen steh'n,
> Luft'ge Schatten sich zeigen,
> Singen seltsam und schön.
> *Das sind jene jungen Schönen,*
> *Die gesungen allzuviel,*
> *Krank von hinschmelzenden Tönen,*
> *Früh erreicht ihres Lebens Ziel.*
> Jetzt ziehen sie vorbei
> Mit ihrer süßen Melodei.[9]

[There, where centurion oaks, / dark tree-trunks stand, / airy shadows show themselves, / singing strange and beautifully. / They are all the fair maidens / who loved singing too much, / sick from their own melting tones, / their life-spans cut unfairly short. / Now they reveal themselves, / with their sweet melodies.]

Uncontainable passion, for singing or dancing or for a forbidden lover, pushes these female performers to collapse and death.

Hoffmann rigorously segregates his two female-performer archetypes, denying any common ground or connection between the human prima donna and the transcendent artiste. "Don Juan" allows us to measure Donna Anna against both standards, and her failure to succeed on mundane terms simply confirms her sublimity. Anna's absolute submission to the music and to her role, so admired by the Romantic narrator, is criticized later by a Philistine in the audience:

> Donna Anna had been too passionate. One must, he opined, be moderately pretty and avoid too much violence in a theatrical performance. Her account

of the catastrophe ["Or sai chi l'onore"] had truly upset him. Here he took a pinch of tobacco and said some entirely, unprintably stupid things to his companion, who maintained that the Italian actress had been a right pretty woman, but insufficiently careful of her costume and toilette; in each of her scenes, a lock of hair had come undone and obscured her profile![10]

Anna abandons the elegance and detachment required of a prima donna; her inability to posture for the bourgeois audience confirms the narrator's conclusions at their mystical encounter in the intermission, when he recognizes her as an incarnation of Music itself. One whose whole life is music cannot also be concerned with such worldly questions as coiffure, costume, and personal ambition. "Rat Krespel" goes to more elaborate lengths to segregate the earthly diva from the sublime artiste, for in this case one archetype is mother to the other, and her influence must be carefully contained to prevent contamination. Counselor Krespel's physical casting-out of his wife's transgressive presence governs the story's structure, and no one—neither the "Traveling Enthusiast" who tells the tale, nor any speaker within it—mentions Angela as long as her vulnerable daughter is alive. The story of Antonia's cloistered life, her beautiful voice, her illness and her mysterious death unfolds with no mention of her prima donna heritage, and Hoffmann confines the "back-story" of Antonia's estranged parents, and of the diva-mother in whose care she grew up, within a long, embedded narrative that Krespel recounts at Antonia's funeral at the end of the story. There at last Hoffmann raises the possibility that Angela might have bequeathed her undesirable character to Antonia, along with her soprano voice, only to disavow it: "Antonia inherited all her mother's amiability and all her mother's charms, but not the *repellent reverse-side* of the medal. There was no *chronic moral ulcer,* which might break out from time to time" (Hoffmann, "Rat Krespel," 232). Unlike her mother, Antonia gives up singing at her father's request, submitting to a life of silent health and domesticity. The narrative thus exorcizes the troublesome mother, leaving father and daughter pottering over their violins; but like all repressed powers, the exiled prima donna continues to haunt the margins of the tale. Hoffmann's adaptors would not be so skilled at keeping her at bay.

CHÈRE ENFANT, JE T'APPELLE . . . C'EST TA MÈRE!

Barbier and Carré, in adapting "Rat Krespel" for the third of their three dramatized *Contes d'Hoffmann,* worked substantial changes on E.T.A. Hoffmann's original. The playwrights replaced the "Composer B." with "Hoffmann," and made him a helpless witness to Antonia's song and death, rather than an agent in it; while a wholly new character, Dr. Miracle took up the narrative function of containing the subversive mother and mediating her influence over her child. Barbier and Carré erased Angela's original difficult personality, presenting Crespel's dead wife only as a victim of Dr. Miracle's evil. Crespel tells us that Miracle is no doctor, but "un assassin, un fossoyeur, un vieux croquemort . . . les malades qu'il a touchés du doigt sont condamnés d'avance . . . Il était venu chez ma femme le jour même qu'elle mourût" [an assassin, a grave-digger, an undertaker . . . those invalids he touches are doomed from that moment . . . he was with my wife on the day she died.][11] Barbier also disposes of Angela's Italian name and her prima donna status. The "distant voice" in the play admits the mother's influence and implicates it in Antonia's death, but the maternal presence remains ambiguous: only Dr. Miracle's assertion, "C'est ta mère!" guarantees that the unseen singer truly is Antonia's dead mother. The text of the play suggests that this Voice is only diabolical ventriloquizing, for the putative, unseen mother sings of herself in the third person: "C'est ta mère, Entends *sa* voix" [It is your mother, hear *her* voice].[12] Antonia's fatal outburst involves only herself and Dr. Miracle, who invokes maternal authority in order to manipulate her. The daughter, in Barbier and Carré's version of the tale, has inherited her mother's vulnerability to the mesmerist, rather than her genius or her irresistible and subversive desire to sing. Bonds between female generations must be severed so that each cohort of daughters may be fully assimilated into patriarchal order; however, this repression has not been completed in Antonia's case. The prima donna mother remains alive both "outside" the family and "inside" her daughter, encouraging her to rebel against silence and domesticity, to sing. Operatic Antonia, less tractable and less silent than her previous incarnations, displays will and ambition. Reunited with her lover, she initiates their song in defiance of her father's injunction: "mon père à présent m'impose la vertu du silence. Veux-tu m'entendre? . . . Tiens, ce doux chant d'amour que nous chantions ensemble." [My father imposes silence upon me. Would you like to hear me? . . . Let us take up the sweet love-song which we once sang together].[13] Antonia's nascent prima donna passion for worldly success makes her lover jealous: "Pour m'y suivre, chasse de ta mémoire ce rêves d'avenir, de succès et de gloire" [Follow me, and banish from your mind these dreams of the future, of fame and glory], he begs her.[14] She agrees, but when Dr. Miracle appears, she is already regretting her acceptance of the prohibition. In despair she cries out, "Ma mère! O ma mère!" opening the door to that long-repressed presence, and to the fatal trio.

Dr. Miracle is credited with provoking Antonia's frenzy in all plot synopses since the opera's 1881 premiere in Vienna, when Hanslick described the scene in his review: "Miracle . . . reveals himself as a hugely evil phantom and seems to flutter about madly, inducing Antonia to sing again. He plays wildly on his violin, and finally brings the life-sized portrait of Antonia's dead mother to life."[15] But while Dr. Miracle does indeed manipulate the heady waltz tune of the trio, and the tempestuous swirl of the violin, he did not bring this subversive music into Crespel's house: both the theme that he plays on his violin and the "Chère enfant" melody had haunted Antonia from the act's beginning, musical traces of the mother whose portrait hangs on the wall. The music that Dr. Miracle "plays wildly" on his violin was first heard in the minor mode, played by a solo flute in the recitative that introduces Antonia's opening Romance, "Elle a fui, la tourterelle." This theme, marked by a wide upward leap and a winding descent, is a characteristic "lament" figure that recurs, in a more subdued form, at the end of the song's first verse and again as a brief coda after the second verse (see Example 3.1). It also punctuates the recitative after the song, in which Antonia and Krespel discuss the lost mother and her vocal reincarnation in her daughter. The wistful woodwind melody is the still-inarticulate mother's voice that Antonia hears in her heart as she sings. Solo woodwinds often speak for silent women, as elsewhere in *Les Contes,* when a solo clarinet voices the absent Antonia's responses to Dr. Miracle's interrogation; this trope in French opera dates back at least to 1828 and Auber's use of the clarinet to speak for the mute Fenella in *La Muette de Portici.* Evoked by the woodwind lament themes and the clarinet's fragment of the "Chère enfant" melody, a muted woman calls to Antonia subliminally, and these fleeting strains sing the mother's presence long before the trio grounds them in her visible body and Miracle's violin.

Example 3.1 "Elle a fui, la tourterelle," measures 13–15

Antonia's "Elle a fui" also implies an inaudible presence, always hovering just out of reach. Her voice climbs higher and louder in the course of the verse, and the harmonic and vocal tension increases until she reaches her highest note, accompanied by a loud and emphatic diminished seventh chord. But the tension is never resolved; voice and accompaniment cease abruptly and instead of resolution we hear only a beat of silence. Antonia repeats the final line of each verse on one low, quiet note as the tense harmony of the diminished seventh chord evaporates, falling by means of half-step movement and enharmonic respelling back to the B-flat tonic and the refrain, "Elle a fui, la tourterelle." These elusive musical gestures underscore the song's themes of unfulfilled longing and nostalgic sadness, emotions ostensibly addressed to Antonia's absent lover, Hoffmann; but the daughter who sings this wistful song is also missing her mother: she tells her father, "My heart, in singing, hears her voice," and the clarinet whispers a fragmentary wordless melody, which in the trio will become the mother's embodied song, "Chère enfant, je t'appelle, comme l'autrefois—c'est ta mère! Entends ma voix!" The trio makes the mother's call audible, not only to Antonia's heart, but also to her ears, while Dr. Miracle's violin takes up the old lamenting melody and transforms it into an exhilarating major-mode swirl.

In the final trio, the mother recovers both her identity as a diva and her long-denied authority over Antonia. Where Barbier had quoted Schubert, Offenbach invokes Gounod's *Faust,* modeling his trio on "Anges pures, anges radieux." Both pieces are in an expansive $\frac{12}{8}$ meter, with three repetitions of a simple theme that modulate upward by step from G major. The deployment of the voices is also similar: a theme presented by solo soprano, then repeated with counter-melodies and interjections from the other two voices, then presented one final time by the two high voices together, with comments from the bass. The allusion to *Faust* emphasizes (perhaps heavy-handedly) Dr. Miracle's demonic energy and the imperiled soprano's hysteria, but achieves a subtler end as well. Antonia's mother, taking Marguerite's place in the trio as bearer of the main theme, escapes the domestic musical environment in which the spoken play had confined her and reclaims her prima donna status. The portrait that comes to life and begins to sing is an operatic innovation and restores Angela's presence and authority: thrown out of Hoffmann's story, and kept on the margins of Barbier and Carré's play, she at last sings to her daughter in a voice no longer distant, but emanating from an on-stage body.

As the trio progresses, Antonia falls increasingly under her mother's sway, listening to the first statement of "Chère enfant," then punctuating the second statement with exclamation of joy and fear. Before the third verse, she begs for rest and release, and at this point, the mother suddenly begins to sing "entends *ma* voix," replacing Barbier's ambiguous "entends *sa* voix." Antonia, who cannot resist this first-person entreaty, merges her voice with her mother's in the final unison statement of the theme, and in the frenetic concluding section the two sopranos echo each other's phrases so rapidly that we can no longer differentiate them.[16]

Antonia's desire has preserved the prima donna mother, whom, following Lacan and Kristeva, we might call a pre-Oedipal or Imaginary mother, an incoherent and infinitely pleasurable voice that surrounds the infant before it recognizes itself as an individual (solitary) being. Antonia, hearing the lost voice of her mother, occupies the rapturous listening position that Michel Poizat posits as the essential component of operatic experience.[17] This mother is a *supplément* of undomesticated female power that survives in each generation, an echo of mythic sorceresses and sirens; a subversive voice that disturbs the daughter, beckoning her off the right path. Romantic opera had begun with the repression of the prototypical renegade mother in Mozart's *Die Zauberflöte,* when the Queen of the Night's treacherous and beautiful maternal voice had ordered the daughter to resist her own assimilation: stab the father, ditch the prince, and escape back into darkness and the maternal embrace. (Pamina of course was not allowed to respond hysterically, but cured by Sarastro's intervention.) The dark mother's appeals and threats were in vain; she was cast out of the temple of reason and enlightenment, and her daughter rescued. But perhaps she could not be killed, only exiled, and was always waiting in the night. Does not Wagner's *Lohengrin,* for example, rework the *Magic Flute*'s plot in a new setting? Ortrud, the wicked stepmother and pagan queen, feigns domestication in order to plot against the Christian order, while Elsa, unluckier than Pamina, succumbs to maternal temptation and dies for it. Antonia also encounters this exiled mother, a figure repressed—and thus kept alive—within a dutiful daughter. And because this is opera, the mother's repressed energy takes the form of seductive and fatal song.

Thus despite elaborate narrative efforts to repress and exclude her, the mother claims her daughter in the end, and the Krespel of the opera can no longer sigh with relief that Antonia inherited nothing of her mother's "repellent reverse-side." In rewriting "Rat Krespel," its French adaptors ultimately reversed its original premise, for where Hoffmann's tale had silenced "Angela" and made Antonia a sublime martyr to Music and the "Composer B—," the opera's climax confirms the irresistible and subversive authority of the woman singer. This authority, which is unique to the opera, derives from Offenbach's musical setting rather than from Barbier's text; the mother's words in the libretto do not hint at the potency of her music and its ability to sweep her daughter away from patriarchal control. The apparently inescapable link between talent and organic defect in the singing woman's offspring inspired one last fiction, the fantasy of a musical child with no mother at all.

"ASSEZ, ASSEZ, MA FILLE!"

This fantasy was initially realized in Hoffmann's "The Sand-Man," where the beautiful Olympia bows to her audience, smiling demurely, and begins to sing "an *aria di bravura* in a voice which was, if anything, almost too brilliant, but clear as glass bells."[18] Here a perfected singer had obediently warbled forth her song unmarred by "organic defects," bad temper, or unmanageable ambition—until Hoffmann revealed the secret of Olympia's perfection: she is a musical robot, the final, fantastical solution to the problem of the prima donna mother and her influence. Olympia has no mother;

rather she had two fathers, the inventor Spalanzani and his demonic col-
league Coppélius, for in this Pygmalion fantasy Hoffmann throws the
transgressive mother out the window for good, eliminating her entirely
from the conception of her singing daughter. Olympia, the all-male creation, sings and behaves flawlessly; no one detects that she is a machine, although she makes some people uneasy:

> We think—you won't take it ill, brother?—that she is singularly statuesque
> and soulless. Her figure is regular, and so are her features, that can't be gain-
> said; and if her eyes were not so utterly devoid of life, I may say, of the power
> of vision, she might pass for a beauty. She is strangely measured in her move-
> ments, they all seem as if they were dependent upon some wound-up clock-
> work. Her playing and singing have the disagreeably perfect but insensitive
> timing of a singing machine, and her dancing is the same. We felt quite afraid
> of this Olympia, . . . she seemed to us to be only acting like a living creature,
> and as if there was some secret at the bottom of it all (Hoffmann, "The Sand-
> man," 207).

Despite her strange awkwardness, Olympia fools everyone. She fools bourgeois society because her fixed smile and limited conversation (she can say
only "Ah! Ah!") conform so perfectly to their idea of how a young girl
should behave. She fools Nathanael, the poet who has fallen in love with
her, because he always views her through Coppélius's magic spectacles. But
her apparent humanity always resides in the eyes of those watching her: although Hoffmann conceals the truth about her mechanical nature until
the climactic moment when she is broken, his narrative never claims that
she is anything but "dependent upon some wound-up clockwork." At no
point does he depict her coming to life, beginning to move or sing of her
own volition. French theatrical versions of Hoffmann's fantasy, however,
repeatedly stage the erosion of its carefully maintained boundary between
the robot and the humans observing her.

Two comic adaptations turned Hoffmann's tale into simple farce:
Adolphe Adam's one-act opéra-comique *La Poupée de Nuremberg* (1852);
and Léo Délibes's ballet *Coppélia,* after a scenario by Charles Nuitter
(1870). Hoffmann's Romantic psychodrama is here transformed into comedy, as the demonic Coppélius becomes a buffo villain, a cranky old man
posing obstacles to true love, and a sentimental young lover replaces the
deluded poet Nathanael. Most importantly, both versions add a new event
and a newly created character: a scene in which a plucky servant or peasant
girl impersonates the doll and "runs amok" before the astonished inventor
who has been interfering with her romance. Both the "Nuremberg doll"
and the puppet "Coppélia" seem, at their comic and dramatic high points,
to be transformed from mechanism to organic life, but the plot provides a
rational explanation: the "ghost in the machine" is a real girl. The inven-

tor, like the legendary sorcerer's apprentice, is initially delighted by the success of his experiment and then made frantic by his creation's misbehavior, while the audience remains comfortably aware that the actual doll is still slumped in the cabinet, and that the thing dancing wildly is a real person, logically accounted for. The boundary between machine and woman remains secure.

Act I of *Les Contes d'Hoffmann* destabilizes Adam's and Délibes's comical representations of Olympia's liveliness. The opera retains the climactic "running amok" moment in the Act I finale, but refuses to explain Olympia's misbehavior as the obedient singing and dancing machine goes out of control, heedless of her inventor/father's cries of protest. Once again there is a girl in the machine, but neither the characters on stage nor the audience know who she is. If Olympia is "only acting like a living creature," who programmed her to act so lively? Olympia thus possessed resembles the haunted Antonia, subject to a disorderly feminine principle that resists containment and refuses to be exorcized, her voice singing in defiance of paternal authority. But whereas Offenbach presents Antonia's disobedience as the resurgence of her mother's influence, urging her to transgress the boundaries, Olympia's story does not allow such a logical explanation: with no mother to influence her, how did the performing machine learn to behave like a diva? We must look outside the plot to find the mother of Offenbach's Olympia: a prima donna mother whose presence at the role's conception is reflected in the mechanical daughter's music. She was the Opéra-Comique star Adèle Isaac:

> When [the impresario] Carvalho accepted the work for the Opéra-Comique changes had to be made to accommodate the singers available in the new company . . .the lyric coloratura Adèle Isaac had recently made successes in the title role of Gounod's *Roméo et Juliette.* . . . Isaac, who visited the composer at Saint-Germain, persuaded him to exploit her coloratura with a new "doll song" for Olympia. . . . Offenbach re-set the words to the melody that became famous, including passages that gave Mlle Isaac full scope for her skill.[19]

Prompted by Isaac, Offenbach's revised music for Olympia traces the robot's transformation from mechanical perfection to human—specifically, feminine—disorder. In her first appearance, Olympia performs the Doll Song, "Les oiseaux dans la charmille," which has many features in common with earlier representations of her mechanical voice. These features are designed to hide the human performer in the role by creating the illusion that a machine or musical instrument is making the sound: like Adam's "Nuremberg Doll," Offenbach's and Isaac's Olympia sings *vocalise* and piercing high notes, rapidly repeated, and her staccato coloratura purges the voice of its human affect, depriving it of grain and texture.

The singer playing Olympia sounds like a woodwind instrument, and the corollary is also true: when Olympia is an actress or ballerina, woodwinds sing for her. Délibes indicates the silent puppet Coppélia with a stilted little theme for flute and English horn, while in Barbier's spoken play, Olympia "sings" a wordless obbligato, actually played by an off-stage English horn (see Example 3.2).[20] Here the poet's friend remarks that "elle chante avec l'accent sonore et vibrant d'un harmonica" [she sings with the sonorous accents and vibrations of a harmonica].[21] The soprano, to succeed in the role, must impersonate a machine—she must sound as if she were *not singing,* denying both her effort and her physical presence.

Example 3.2 Olympia's song, played by an off-stage English horn (Ancessy, 1851)

Although Olympia's song fits generically with the coloratura waltz songs of the period, including Juliet's "Ah je veux vivre," with which Mlle Isaac had had such a success, it differs from them in the crucial respect that its brilliant language, the prima donna's native tongue, has been deliberately drained of expressive meaning. The singer must efface herself and the fact of her performance if she is to be effective. The song, which has two identical verses, leaves no room for the diva to indulge in the vocal inventiveness that she might have regarded as her right, either in improvised cadenzas or with new and more elaborate ornaments for the second verse. A brief survey of recordings of the opera in this century reveals that most performers have nobly resisted the urge to vary the ornamentation in the second stanza. The regular phrase structures, unvaried repetition of the verse, and generic waltz accompaniment all contribute to the "programmed" effect of the piece, which conceals the laboring human performer. The notion of genre pieces hiding the woman performer inside was made explicit in *Coppélia,* where Swanhilda veiled herself, first with a tartan and then with a mantilla, and danced appropriate character pieces—a jig and a bolero—to conceal the fact of her presence animating the supposed doll. Similarly, the prima donna inside Olympia hides behind a mask of stiff gestures and deliberately hollow, inexpressive vocal quality.

But the Finale unmasks the singer's charade, the limits of her mechanical impersonation, for as the puppet's programmed melody breaks down in her extravagant final *vocalise,* a genuine prima donna replaces the doll-instrument. This moment of revelation undoes the paradox of a virtuoso performance that had vainly tried to efface its own production: the more successfully the singer produces that "inhuman" coloratura, the more astonished the audience becomes at her technical mastery. This finale acknowledges the way that the performer always "breaks character" in a coloratura showpiece, because her singing is so breathtaking and strenuous that we cannot escape our knowledge of the particular live woman doing it. In such moments, the prima donna plays only herself.

Olympia's manic final performance, which is unique to the opera, begins with a solo flute theme to which her father's guests are waltzing. She and Hoffmann begin to dance, but the girl suddenly refuses to follow, she lurches around, throwing the bemused poet back and forth and finally flinging him to the ground, where his magic spectacles shatter. The breaking of the spectacles destroys the illusion—for Hoffmann, and for the audience, who now see the live soprano dropping her mask of wooden programmability. In response to the paternal command, "Assez, assez, ma fille!" she warbles her obedient word, "Oui!," but goes nowhere; she has *not* had enough. Her syllable "Oui!" melts into the nonsignifying noise of "Ah!" that it was all along, and she takes up the waltz theme, replacing the solo flute with her voice. But almost immediately she exceeds that theme's formal constraints, and the orderly expectations set up by her Doll Song, as she runs away with the tune: her *roulades* get out of control; she gets stuck in the cadential trills; she rewrites the piece to the surprise and alarm of everyone around her. Like her crazy dance with Hoffmann, this disorderly music comes from outside the logic of plot, contrary to paternal programming. Bereft of his magic spectacles, the disillusioned Hoffmann, like the audience on-stage and off, can only gape at the *new* spectacle of a cooperative girl-machine transformed into a disorderly diva.

Not surprisingly, the prima donna's song, pouring out of the child from whom her influence was supposed to have been expunged, provokes a violent retaliation: Olympia exits and is immediately dragged back on-stage in pieces. The plot rationalizes Olympia's destruction as Coppélius's revenge against Spalanzani, but the music tells another story, the story of Angela being thrown out the window, and of Antonia dying for her joyful indulgence in her mother's voice. Ultimately, the opera implies, the construction of Olympia was only another futile attempt at the repression of the prima donna's spirit.

We may read the Olympia and Antonia acts, then, as two versions of one story, the old story of a repressed Mother's voice returning with fatal results. *Les Contes d'Hoffmann,* however, moves beyond this familiar tale and makes the *telling* of it part of the action, inviting speculation about the one

who tells and about what purpose the tale might serve for the teller. Re-
calling that the stories of Olympia and Antonia are carefully framed in the
opera as Hoffmann's narrative performance, we may suspect that they are
less about the women than they are about Hoffmann himself. Antonia
functions as Hoffmann's stand-in at the encounter with magic and the
primitive mother, represented as both sublime and fatal: for the duration
of the Antonia act, the beloved woman becomes the archetypal Romantic
artist, while Hoffmann, encouraging her to abandon art and music, takes
the side of bourgeois normalcy.[22] The Hoffmann of *Les Contes d'Hoffmann* needs Antonia as a surrogate in his encounter with the sublime: she
is his defense against the perceived effeminizing effect of art on the male
artist.

Recall that French authors since 1840 had represented Hoffmann and
his admirers as both effeminate and hysterical. The state of poetic inspiration as represented by *Hoffmannistes* frequently involved such hysteric
symptoms as fainting, hallucination, self-alienation and the fragmentation
of personality, and compulsive, repetitious, and fabulous speech.[23] Théo-
dore, the sensitive narrator of Gautier's "La Cafetière," has a somnambulist episode at the end of which he faints; in the morning his friends find
him sprawled on the floor in a white nightgown and tease him about how
pretty he looks, to which he responds, "Ce ne'st qu'une faiblesse qui m'a
pris; je suis sujet à cela"[24] [It's only a little weakness that overtook me; I
suffer from them]. Gautier's Onuphrius has hallucinations, as a result of
which "les liens qui le rattachaient au monde s'étaient brisés un à un" [the
chains that bound him to the real world were broken one by one], while
the narrator of "La Morte Amoureuse" spends half the story in a state of
somnambulism and cannot tell which of his two identities is real and which
a dream.[25] As for the opera's Hoffmann, Antonia's death is the first event
he tells without having witnessed, and for the first time his narrating authority is separated from his first-hand experience as protagonist. As I noted
in my first chapter, it is at the moment when Antonia is left alone with her
hysterical visions that the narrative reveals itself most clearly as Hoffmann's
invention, and his account of the events leading to Antonia's death can only
be a product of his imagination. We must distrust this unreliable narrator,
his three tales, and their Romantic visions of women, for there are no
women here—Woman, to vary Lacan's oft-invoked phrase, is a symptom
of the poet. Hoffmann, not Antonia, is the "real hysteric" of the piece, and
the entire opera is his hysteric performance: an unreliable narrative, a symptom of past trauma, and a compulsive reenactment of that trauma.

More generally, this might suggest that opera is not a place for securing
male subjectivity, and that we need not take its narratives—especially those
about singing women who die—at face value. Rather we may see them as
fantasies about "going under" to music, and about installing temporary

boundaries around the sublime experience. The singing woman is not, after all, the "hysteric" in the singer-listener dyad; rather opera is an hysterical pleasure for *listeners* in that it allows, indeed *demands,* vicarious identification with another's suffering and emotional extravagance.[26] Finally, opera adds one last ironic twist to this not-quite-clinical scenario in that both the performer's loss of control and the listener's identification with that loss are staged constructions.

LA STELLA

> It irritated my intense individualism to be pointed
> out as a musical spirit possessed by a voice from
> the ether, or a magnetized automaton controlled
> from other spheres.
> (*Geraldine Farrar,* Such Sweet Compulsion)

With this remark, real-life diva Geraldine Farrar derided the poetic fantasies about singers that would defuse her authority or wish away her presence. Similarly, the epilogue of *Les Contes d'Hoffmann* takes us back-stage to show the diva in her "intense individualism." Stella's appearance in Luther's tavern writes large the moment when the human singer peered around from behind Olympia, dropping her robot-mask. The diva, her performance over, walks out from behind the three dead heroines, having survived them all.

With Stella's appearance back-stage in the tavern, the epilogue invokes the prima donna one last time. This episode, like the poet's three narratives, retells one of E.T.A. Hoffmann's tales, but transforms it even more drastically. Stella is further from "Don Juan," than Olympia is from "The Sand-Man," or Antonia from "Rat Krespel." "Don Juan," like the opera's epilogue, tells of an off-stage encounter; since Hoffmann's Donna Anna speaks only Italian and the narrator only German, their conversation takes place in some transcendent musical language, Donna Anna's native tongue: "She said her whole life is music, and she often believes that her innermost being is a secret that words cannot express, but that she understands only in singing" (Hoffmann, "Don Juan," 60). This performer can never be out of character, for she does not exist independently of her role, having no language other than music and no name other than "Donna Anna." Barbier and Offenbach's Stella has also been performing in *Don Giovanni* before her appearance off-stage, but she is otherwise quite unlike her sublime counterpart, and the epilogue provides a cynical final variation on the prima donna theme of *Les Contes d'Hoffmann.* The epilogue of Barbier and Carré's play had continued the theme from the three internal tales of having the demonic antagonist control the scene; Stella comes for Hoffmann, but Lindorf persuades Hoffmann to reject her and leads her away himself, making worldly conversation. (Is it an accident that Stella's last two lines consist solely of "Ah!" and "Oui!" like Olympia's?) In Barbier's libretto, approved by the Parisian censors in 1881 but never set by Offenbach, Hoffmann is simply drunk, sending Stella and Lindorf away with a satirical verse about the dwarf Klein-zach and his futile love for an expensive courtesan.[27]

The tradition of Stella's silence seems to begin with this libretto, for in the play she spoke the same mixture of verse and prose as all the other characters. In the libretto, and in most subsequent realizations of the Epilogue, she says nothing. In the 1907 version she makes a brief, silent appearance: "Stella, accompanied by Lindorf, appears at the side door. Seeing Hoffmann's condition, she turns and leaves, escorted by Lindorf" (39). In Michael Powell and Emeric Pressberger's 1951 film of the opera, Moira Shearer, as Stella, wears an expression of regret and nonchalance perfectly calibrated to reflect the prima donna's ultimate indifference to the poet whose obsession she is. In an "alternate ending" attached to the 1907 version she speaks only two words: "Hoffmann! Endormi?" In Oeser's 1977 reconstruction of the scene, based on the 1851 play, Stella is also silent.[28]

Why, in Catherine Clément's words, does this opera "put on the stage a real prima donna—who does not sing"?[29] Like the story "Don Juan," the epilogue problematizes the prima donna's discourse, but makes the opposite point, for Stella does not have her whole existence in music; it is neither her only language nor the outpouring of her soul. Rather it is her work, and she leaves it behind when she leaves the stage. Paradoxically, this prima donna character is the only one who does not "go around singing songs all the time," to borrow Edward T. Cone's phrase about the people in the fantasy world of opera.[30] The characters may go around thus, but the performers do not, and the nonsinging Stella reminds us, even more cogently than Olympia's "breakdown" did, that we are watching a performer. Thus the Stella episode overturns the analogous episode in E.T.A. Hoffmann's tale, for where Donna Anna represents a fantastical poetic spirit at large in the mundane world, Stella is a mundane intruder on the opera's fantasy. Off-stage and off-duty, Stella should not sing, for it is precisely her *not* bursting into song that differentiates her final appearance from the preceding episodes, and the role she had played in them.[31] And when she strolls away from Hoffmann, we remember that her three prior appearances all happened on the stage of the poet's imagination; her three "deaths" were only his stories. In each tale, the poet imagined her broken or smashed for having overstepped the bounds, but in the end the compulsive repetition of the smashing and breaking gestures only emphasizes their ineffectiveness.

The opera's conclusion defies the dull final sonority of E.T.A. Hoffmann's "Rat Krespel": "*But she was—dead.*" A sentence of death, and the story is over. But Offenbach's version admits that the soprano's story is never over, for the curtain rises and there she is again. The prima donna can be silenced in the poetic imagination and its fictions, but the practical reality of opera performance rewrites the endings of Hoffmann's musical fantasies by allowing the soprano to survive her "most dread moment" night after night. Elaborate narratives may attempt to cast out the prima donna, to confine her within a wooden shell or a dutiful daughter's fragile body—but she always breaks free, makes herself heard, and transcends the narrative's seemingly inevitable punishment. Stella, the diva off-stage, is the suppressed truth of opera: the girl inside Olympia, Antonia's secret self. Selfish, splendid, disdainful, willful and difficult, she survives the collapse of musical martyrs and the "undoing" of performing dolls. The prima donna's song has not been extinguished, but the poet can neither command it nor confine it, for in the last analysis the singer does not exist to serve the Romantic artist. She may "have sung [him] and have been [his] melodies"—but only on stage, and only for a price.

CHAPTER FOUR

Offenbach, for Posterity

Les Contes d'Hoffmann is Offenbach's
testament for posterity. Before such creative
power, particularly that manifested in the
Antonia act, even his most prejudiced critics
must fall silent.
(*Anton Henseler*, Jakob Offenbach)

"They will do me justice after I am dead,"
Offenbach said to us one day.
(*Andre Martinet*, Offenbach)

EVERY CRITIC who reported on *Les Contes d'Hoffmann's* 1881 premiere
agreed that it represented not only a departure from Offenbach's characteristic style, but a conscious bid for artistic success and lasting esteem. Auguste Vitu of *Le Figaro* described it as "the dear, treasured work, Offenbach's supreme hope; he wished that the score of *Les Contes,* avenging at
last all the misfortune that had dogged his previous efforts at the Opéra-
Comique, should at last assure his renown, above and beyond operetta, in
the ranks composed of musical dramas. . . . After *Les Contes,* the name of
Jacques Offenbach, already so well-known, is found singularly enhanced."[1]
The opera's status as a testament was enhanced by such biographical
ephemera as André Martinet's description of Offenbach dropping dead at
the moment of finishing the score "to the last chord." Posthumous inter-
ventions such as the reordering of the acts, the rearrangement of numbers,
and the recomposition of the Venetian act all contributed to the opera's traditional form, a form that perfectly serves narratives about Offenbach's
artistic progress beyond operetta and opéra-comique, toward serious opera.

According to most accounts, it was *Les Contes'* much-vaunted *sincerity*
that established its difference and distance from the operettas, and that
quality has been essential for its privileged reception among his works. But
the piece's kaleidoscopic character is difficult to interpret: if *Les Contes* is a
testament, to what does it testify? What message did Offenbach leave "for
posterity"? As the musical language switches among the registers of farcical operetta, sentimental opéra-comique, tragic opéra-lyrique, and fantastical Romantic opera, the composer's refusal to create a consistent tone

makes the piece slippery, resistant to interpretation or *reading*. Confronted with so many odd characters, so many ironic twists, so many abrupt shifts of tone, who is supposed to deserve our sympathy? Certainly not the comic-book villain, nor the wind-up doll, nor the heartless courtesan whose too-easy seduction of Hoffmann doesn't even earn our admiration. Are we to identify with Hoffmann, the dupe? with Antonia, the martyr? or with the sardonically patient Muse, whose music never quite measures up to her dramatic importance? Later in this chapter I will use the phrase "fun-house mirror" to describe Offenbach's parodic operetta style, and *Les Contes*, too, has some of the disorienting effect of a hall of mirrors: Where, if anywhere, can the composer's true voice be heard? Which, if any, of the opera's discursive modes shall we take as the real Offenbach?

Different interpreters have answered this question differently. Eduard Hanslick, perhaps reacting to the nostalgia for early Romanticism most evident in the prologue, saw Offenbach as the last of Hoffmann's "Serapion-Brethren," arriving in Luther's tavern just before closing time to spin tales within tales about crazy artists, seductive women, and mysterious strangers: "That Offenbach took up this subject so passionately seems not so inexplicable to his friends. Hoffmann's world of phantoms exercised a strong charm over Offenbach; in his last years the poor man appeared a transparent pale thing, a fading, laughing spirit out of the *Serapion Brotherhood*."[2] A watercolor portrait of the composer in his study in 1879 represents him as already half a ghost, a small pale face peering out of the shadows. No biographer has failed to note his melancholy wit in the face of his impending death, nor his prediction of that death the night before it occurred. Like Antonia, Offenbach seemed to sing himself into the grave with *Les Contes d'Hoffmann*.

Indeed, since the time of the opera's composition, sympathetic biographers and commentators have associated Offenbach with Antonia, and the biographical romance surrounding *Les Contes*'s composition has a pathos and a tragic inevitability that matches and surpasses the somewhat incoherent drama of the opera's plot. The anecdotal pull is almost irresistible: the classic scenario of a clown longing to play Hamlet, to be taken seriously by a society that regarded him only as a *farceur*. The composer—old, ill, and in pain—struggled to finish the work that would lift him into the immortal company of true artists. Because Offenbach was not given to writing long or detailed confessions of his inner state, a few phrases have attained almost talismanic status in accounts of his last days: the remark in a letter to his wife Herminie that "I have been working all day on my *Contes*," and his oft-cited request to the impresario Carvalho to hurry the production along so that he might see it before he died. The unprecedented time and care that he lavished on this last work, and the illness that worsened during the final year of its composition, have given rise to the mythology of a "Pact with Death," Offenbach's concession that if Death would only permit him to finish *Les Contes d'Hoffmann,* he would gladly die at its conclusion.[3] André Martinet's elaborate and influential account of the composer's last days begins with a fainting spell during the first rehearsal he attended—as if the sound of his opera had been too much for him to bear—and ends with the scene of his death over the just-completed score. The fatal work became a Requiem when Andre Talazac, the tenor who would create the role of Hoffmann, sang two excerpts with the texts of the *Dies irae* and *Agnus dei* at the composer's funeral. At its premiere, many critics received the opera as Offenbach's legacy in music, the fulfillment of his desire to transcend the operetta-style of the bygone Second Empire and to create a work for all time.

The intersection of music, silence, death, and testament seem to have mandated the acceptance of *Les Contes d'Hoffmann* as a sincere work, one in which Offenbach at last dropped the masks of irony and grotesquerie that had marked his early style. The seriousness of *Les Contes* might be judged overdetermined, the product of biographical romance, vigorous promotion by the composer and his supporters, and the historical and aesthetic prejudices that have elevated tragedy above comedy, the work "for posterity" above the quotidian, and sincerity above facetiousness. Indeed this interpretation began to be promulgated two years before the opera's public premiere, as the *Revue et Gazette Musicale*'s comments after a private concert of excerpts in May 1879 makes clear: "The composer has completely changed his manner. . . . No more leaping rhythms, no more showy couplets, no more light and brilliant choruses; the coquettish muse who inspired *La Belle Hélène* has taken a graver and more measured step, and even become for this occasion dreamy and tender."[4] This new gravity and tenderness, most strongly manifested in the Antonia act, would prove the key to the work's acceptance, and to Offenbach's place in music history.

Yet although opera's most serious, or most sincere, part has been allowed to determine its reception, the Antonia act is not the whole opera. It is gratifying to believe that here, at the end of his last work, we have finally heard Offenbach's true voice, purified of irony and facetiousness; that the "gifted musician who hated music," as Debussy described him, is letting himself sing at last. But the composer's voice is not so easily located within his work, his sincerity not so unimpeachable. He pours sympathetic music over Antonia but makes that very music the cause of her death; he makes Hoffmann's disastrous loves as risible as they are tragic. He engages our emotions, only to push them away with an abrupt reversal or a violent eruption. He juxtaposes musical styles, not only between acts but also within them—sandwiching the deaf servant's absurd couplets about "la méthode," for example, between a delicate love duet and the ominous trio "Pour conjurer le danger," and lurching from the sensual tranquillity of the Barcarole into Hoffmann's rowdy drinking song. The end of one act sets up no expectation about the act that will follow, and each descent of the curtain serves as a black-out, a stroke of almost perfect discontinuity.

How, with its episodic construction and its melange of musical styles, does the opera nonetheless impress us as more than just a patchwork of individual numbers? The question of how those numbers are stitched together into a whole that manages to be *coherent* without being *consistent* proves somewhat elusive, but perhaps the sense of musical continuity results from recurrences of a markedly lyric idiom. Waves of lyricism course through the score, cresting at unpredictable but always effective moments: Hoffmann may be jolly, facetious, convivial, but when he sings rapturously about his lost love, or apostrophizes Olympia's sleeping beauty, his yearning draws us to him, temporarily removing us from the environment of joking patter. When Antonia sings sweetly about the turtledove, or the young rose smiling at the spring, we feel her sincerity as strongly as we felt the hollowness of Olympia's brittle little waltz. Nicklausse teases Hoffmann in staccato $\frac{3}{8}$ time about his susceptibility to Olympia's mechanical charms, but later hymns Antonia's soulfulness, and the poet's sensibility, in a magnificent aria. Overall, the opera may be divided into two parts, for the appearance of Antonia's mother in Act III marks an abrupt inversion of the positive value assigned to lyricism. If we trace the lyric idiom and the changing values attached to it through the score, *Les Contes* suggests itself as a testament to the composer's complex and contradictory relationship to the lyric tradition epitomized by Weber and Gounod, to his own Second-Empire past, and to the Parisian musical culture of the 1870s.

FOR POSTERITY

Two years before its premiere performance in 1881, *Les Contes* was already advertising its own sincerity. On May 18, 1879, Offenbach staged a concert at his house with the goal of attracting a producer for the nearly finished opera. Critics and impresarios saw evidence of a change in the formerly frivolous Offenbach: the *Revue et Gazette Musicale* reported that "the death trio has an elevated and severe style that we are not accustomed to hearing from the author of *La Grande Duchesse*," and continued, "In the Rêverie d'Antonia ['Elle a fui'], M. Offenbach has absolutely departed from his style and manner; this reverie vaguely recalls some passages of Gounod, and is harmonized with great elegance."[5] Harmonic elegance and reminiscence of Gounod's style will do for a definition of the "lyric idiom" in *Les Contes*: following Frits Noske, we may point to the coloristic use of dissonant notes against repeated pedal tones and the reliance on triplet and compound triplet accompaniments as hallmarks of the Gounod

Example 4.1.a The lyric idiom: Antonia's Romance

style, and to these we might add syllabic text-setting, "heartbeat" accompaniments, smooth melodic contours, and moderate *tessiture* with high notes reserved for expressive climaxes.[6] The following examples show these elements not only in "Elle a fui" but also in the rhapsody that interrupts Hoffmann's *Légende du Klein-zach;* the love duet "C'est une chanson d'amour"; Nicklausse's aria, "Voici l'archet frémissant"; and the "Reflection Duet" for Hoffmann and Giulietta.

The program suggests that Offenbach designed his preview concert to promote the opera's Gounod-style lyricism, and that creating a consistently sincere tone in the concert mattered more to him than airing his *newest* music, for four of the eleven pieces he presented were made over from previous works.[7] In addition to the two numbers borrowed from *Die Rhein-Nixen,* he made over a *mélodie* that he had written in 1845—before the beginning of his career as a parodist—for the Epilogue's quartet with chorus, and took a tune from the overture of *Fantasio,* the least farcical of his opéra-comiques, as the main theme of the Antonia trio. Reviews of this preview concert celebrated Offenbach as the heir of Weber and Gounod, and Carvalho was persuaded to accept *Les Contes d'Hoffmann* for the Opéra-comique. Praise for the finished opera would continue in this same vein; at the premiere, for example, the men's trio "Pour conjurer le dan-

Example 4.1.b The lyric idiom: Hoffmann's visionary rhapsody

ger," was repeatedly singled out as "a true masterpiece . . . [in which] a *new Offenbach* really reveals himself. The andante is of a somber and penetrating effect, and the stretta in e-minor is truly terrible. One would say that the spirit of Weber passed here."[8]

Offenbach, as he worked on *Les Contes* in this final stage of his life, very much wanted to be accepted as the heir of Weber and Gounod. Up to the point of the fatal confrontation between Dr. Miracle and Antonia, *Les Contes* argues in favor of the conservative musical values that Offenbach, not ordinarily given to aesthetic polemics or manifestos, had articulated in an essay of 1879. This tract avows his loyalty to French tradition, and includes several themes that will be useful for my reading of *Les Contes d'Hoffmann*

Example 4.1.c The lyric idiom: Antonia and Hoffmann's love duet

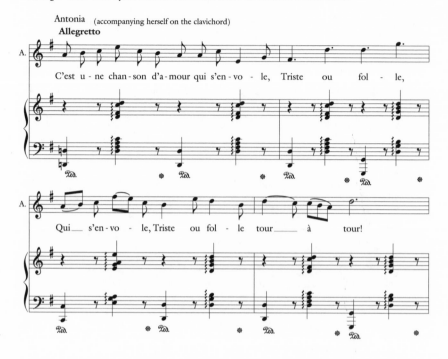

and its ultimately ambivalent relation to national, generic, and affective categories. Reminding his readers of his seniority in the musical community, he censures the "younger school" who currently "affect a great disdain for French composers."[9]. Yet his nationalist rhetoric screens a conservative aesthetic more properly defined by time and tunefulness, with 1840 as an unstated *terminus ante quem*. The sphere of his approval extends beyond the national tradition, for he counts such French masters as Auber, Hérold, and Halévy among "the melodists of every land . . . all the master-singers" (245). His canon includes not only *Le Pré-aux-Clercs, La Juive, La Dame blanche, La Muette de Portici, Les Huguenots,* and *Guillaume Tell,* but also Mozart's *Don Juan,* Weber's *Le Freyschütz* [sic], the "adorable symphonies" of Haydn and Mendelssohn, and "Beethoven's sublime fantasies, in which melody reigns" (247). His argument subsumes Italian, Austro-German, and French composers of the past under one utopian lyric tradition.

The prologue and first act of *Les Contes* testify on behalf of this lyric tradition. The prologue establishes Hoffmann as the poet, the sincere man of feeling, in contrast to the sardonic villain and boisterous male chorus

Example 4.1.d The lyric idiom: Nicklausse's aria, "Voici l'archet frémissant"

around him. When he tries to confine himself to their jolly idiom in the ballad of "Klein-zach," he cannot repress his true musical personality and pours out the first extended lyric passage, his rhapsodic account of obsessive love. The chorus's failure to understand him only emphasizes his difference and superiority, and his sincerity also makes him the outsider in the workshop of Spalanzani, the facile inventor and bamboozler who "n'aime pas la musique." The plot and music of the first act chart Hoffmann's progressive disillusionment with the ticking waltz rhythms, charming *couplets,* and marvelous spectacles—both Olympia's *brillante* singing and Coppélius's deluding *Brille*—of Spalanzani's Paris salon.

OLYMPIA AND THE "MOST PREJUDICED CRITICS"

Olympia embodies French operetta with her wind-up *couplets,* her comical moments of "winding down," and her gratifying yet meaningless responses of "Oui, oui!" to any remark addressed to her. There could be no more perfect figure for the genre which, as Fabrizio Della Seta has written, staged "one of the universal principles of humor, the apparently objective representation of human reality, but threatened by tiny worms able to lay bare

the characteristics of inauthenticity, interior aridity, and mechanical repet-
itiveness."[10] These were the very terms on which Offenbach had been
harshly criticized in the 1870s, and even reviewers who enjoyed the gaiety
and charm of the Olympia act agreed that it perpetuated Offenbach's operetta style rather than departing from it: Jacques Herman, for example,
remarked in *Le Constitutionnel* that, "Nicklausse's air, 'Une poupée aux
yeux d'émail,' and the doll's *couplets,* are in reality only operetta airs, such
as Offenbach has written a hundred times before, and the merit of this act
is only in the libretto, the performance, and marvellous mise-en-scène."[11]
Auguste Vitu reported in *Le Figaro* that, "[Nicklausse's] *couplets* about the
doll with enamel eyes would, I think, have been better written for the
Bouffes or the Renaissance,"[12] and Philbert Joslé, in *L'Événement,* added
that, "the most Parisian of Offenbach's operettas are full of such numbers."[13]

They were not wrong to hear the musical language of operetta in the
Olympia act; indeed Nicklausse's *couplets* about a wind-up rooster's infatuation with a music-box doll is a perfect example of that comic-mechanical
style, with its jerky arpeggiated melody, staccato chordal accompaniment,
very short repeated phrases, and hiccuping little flourish at the end of each
line. Léon Kerst, in *La Presse,* grumbled that "The music is always Offenbach, that Offenbach with whom so many works have acquainted us. . . The
result, for a judicious and disinterested observer, is a disappointment that
promptly changes into indifference. . . . He has written a chimerical opera
in which he never distances himself from that which makes the basis of his
personality, the refrains of operetta."[14] But such a reading of the Olympia
act as a mere backsliding into operetta, as proof that Offenbach could only
"mechanically repeat" his habitual style, seems wilfully obtuse. It may be
that Kerst gets it exactly wrong, and that Offenbach does in the course of
the Olympia act distance himself from those "refrains." The doll and the
doll-songs in *Les Contes* are not merely remnants of operetta, but rather figures that *stand for* operetta in an allegory about musical style.

At the time of *Les Contes d'Hoffmann's* genesis, operetta was enmeshed
in a web of nationalist aesthetics and musical insincerity. In a pairing that
would have disgusted them both, Offenbach and Wagner had become
linked in the French critical imagination of the 1870s as twin threats to the
purity of the musical homeland—Wagner from without, and Offenbach
(more destructively) from within. Gustave Chouquet's essay, "Wagner et
Offenbach," for example, presented the "false" and "intellectual" music of
Wagner and the ironic cosmopolitanism of Offenbach as a Teutonic Scylla
and Charybdis between which "true French musicians" had to navigate.
Chouquet praised composers and audiences for thus far resisting Wagnerian temptations, but the problem of Offenbach appeared to him more

grave, for here France had already sustained damage: operetta, he declared, was "a moral sickness that recently threatened the entire social body with gangrene . . . effronteries which seem[ed] to take a malign pleasure in corrupting the spirit of our nation, without its being noticed that they were helping to throw our unhappy country to the edge of the abyss."[15] Chouquet described operetta explicitly as a political and social infiltration perpetuated by "the caricaturist Jacques Offenbach (born in Cologne, 1819), the lyrical Lancer [*Uhlan*], pillaging here, pillaging there . . . a dangerous scoffer, who won his glory by transforming our Parisian stages into lunatic asylums."[16] Chouquet's emphasis on Offenbach's German birthplace, together with the military imagery to underscore his assertion that operetta had "declared war on opera," makes it clear that the composer's ironic, insincere discourse was now to be understood as a form of aggression, at once producing and preying upon French weakness and decadence.[17]

Chouquet did not misrepresent Offenbach's parodistic technique, which might indeed be described as a kind of "pillaging" of serious music for distortion in a fun-house mirror. (Recall that Offenbach first made his name as an instrumental ventriloquist, of whom it was said that he could make the cello sound like anything but itself.) His early successes as a composer of operettas derived in part from his outright misappropriations and skillful parodies of other composers' melodies: the unexpected eruption of the celebrated love theme from Meyerbeer's *Les Huguenots* in the farcical *Ba-ta-clan;* the hastily improvised recitatives, duet and trio in pidgin Italian of *Monsieur Choufleuri restera chez lui;* the grand trio from Rossini's *Guillaume Tell,* outrageously spoofed in *La Belle Hélène.* In a revue entitled *Le Salon de Parodie* in 1860, Offenbach presented a *Symphonie de l'avenir,* a heavy-handed burlesque of the operatic excerpts that Wagner had just presented in three scandalous concerts at the Théâtre Italien. In addition to inspiring Wagner's undying enmity, the *Symphonie* epitomized the relationship of Offenbach's musical slapstick to self-proclaimed serious music, and its reception testifies to how much the Second Empire public enjoyed the malicious fun. *La France Musicale*'s description of the *Symphonie de l'avenir* reveals the obvious pleasure that audiences took in Offenbach's blurring of the authentic and the false: "There are those who pretend that [the *Symphonie*] is a witty parody of the music of the future; they are completely in error; this is simply a page from one of M. Wagner's scores that Parisians have not yet encountered, furtively detached by M. Offenbach. It is a finished scene, and M. Offenbach has done nothing but transport it onto his stage."[18] The journalist's description of the *Symphonie* as a leaf from Wagner's own portfolio foreshadowed the growing dissolution of boundaries between the parodistic and the real in the 1860s, as residents of Parody's Salon spilled out into the "real world" outside the Bouffes-

Parisiens. Characters from the operettas stepped off the stage and traveled about in daylight, as when Hortense Schneider spent much of the Universal Exposition of 1867 in the guise of the "Grand Duchess of Gerolstein," while other operettas, most notably and most successfully *La Vie Parisienne,* put Paris itself on-stage. "Parody's salon" had become a hall of mirrors, in which *le tout Paris* beheld itself intoxicated by its own delights.

The Franco-Prussian War, however, upset the balance of pleasure and danger in parody's intoxicating ambiguity. After the war and the siege of Paris, the French public began to express disapproval of Offenbach's jesting style (and of his removal to Germany during the war), and some went so far as to condemn his operettas as the epitome of a bad art that had pushed the nation toward moral ruin. Thus Chouquet retrospectively represented parody as perversion and madness and claimed that sincere French music had been degraded by Offenbach's burlesque "pillaging" of its melodies and situations. Critic Jacques Herman, more sympathetic to Offenbach, accepted *Les Contes* as posthumous proof that "this man was marked with the sign of the artist, and, if he had not been caught up by the dizzying currents that swept away France's last vestiges of good sense and dignity, he would have composed opera-comiques, more amusing and more novel than many others."[19] Herman numbers Offenbach among operetta's victims, rather than blaming him for its harmful effects, yet in either case, Offenbach was stigmatized by his association with the genre and its milieu. An anonymous contributor to *Le Figaro* reminded his readers of this post-war condemnation, noting that at the premiere of *Les Contes,* "Numerous representatives from the official world were in the hall. Evidently, for the Republicans in power, Offenbach has ceased to be the 'great corrupter.'"[20]

Such vilifications of Offenbach's comic style during the 1870s betray the ideological foundations of the emerging French aesthetic, and suggest what difficulties the composer confronted as he worked on his serious opera, *Les Contes d'Hoffmann.* Oscar Comettant declared, in *Le Siècle,* that Offenbach could never be absolved of his former bad associations, and that it was presumptuous of him even to try: "[With *Les Contes,*] he believed he could take his place, whenever it pleased him, on our second official lyric stage, side by side with Grétry, Méhul, Boïeldieu, Hérold, Auber, Halévy, Adam, etc."[21] Comettant banned Offenbach from this august company, calling him a "spirited, yet vulgar musician, who thanks to his slapdash operettas won such fame in the world of coquettes and dandies that nourished him," and declared that Offenbach's attempt to come clean was hopeless, for "while it's true that one may become rich in a day, through an inheritance or a stock-market coup, *respect*—of the artistic or moral variety—is a peculiar kind of fortune that one must amass oneself, over time, discreetly, through patient economies every day." Most tellingly, this writer compared Offenbach, attempting to compose a respectable opera-comique, to a "woman of easy virtue" seeking acceptance in good society:

> Fortunately for the dignity of art and its austere servants, it is not easy for a musician grown fat on polkas and refrains to inscribe his own name on the list of serious composers, and to make serious works like theirs, works of true style—any more than it is easy for a woman of light morals to give up her past,—when she sees that the present threatens to make her pay for it—to adopt the manners and speech of a woman of the world, and to receive with her the respect and consideration that we accord only to virtue.[22]

We have already seen how Chouquet blamed Offenbach and operetta explicitly for France's "decadence," and now Comettant's rhetoric equates Offenbach and his music with two long-standing enemies of decent bourgeois society: the speculator and the prostitute.

The accusation that Offenbach, even on the respectable stage of the Opéra-Comique, could offer only a cynical and calculated imitation of true art, echoes Richard Wagner's characterization of "French opera music" circa 1850 as a "coquette" whose "mainspring is an icy coldness."[23] (Contemporary audiences may most readily interpret Olympia's coloratura as an Italianate effect, thanks to the modern habit of programming the "Doll Song" alongside Lucia's mad scene and other *bel canto* warhorses, but Olympia's *couplets* fits securely within the tradition of French opera; her excessively decorative "bird-song" coloratura recalls Queen Marguerite's "O beau pays de Touraine" or Ophélie's mad scene.) In a diatribe against Meyerbeer, Wagner had called French opera "a masterpiece of mechanism"[24] without authentic content or inspiration, no more than a mechanistic interior and a polished surface: "the cold smile she gives us. . . seems like a distorted reflection of ourselves."[25] Like Wagner's coquette, Olympia is literally a mirror and a mimic whose "seductive power and exercised individuality were first derived from the love-approaches of the man."[26] She embodies hostile contemporary perceptions, originating both within and outside of France, of a bankrupt French music that could create only the *appearance* of authentic feeling.

A similar rhetoric, and the same urge to embody operetta in a "woman of light morals," propels Emile Zola's almost hysterical condemnation of the genre in his novel *Nana* (1875). Allusions to Offenbach in *Nana* are easily enumerated: the operetta in which Nana debuts at the Variétés fuses elements from Offenbach's two most enduring successes, featuring the Olympian characters of *Orphée aux Enfers,* and a climactic scene (Vulcan's discovery of Venus *in flagrante* with Mars) identical to the Act II finale of *La Belle Hélène.* Nana, with her sturdy build, promiscuous sexuality, and long red-gold hair, physically resembles Offenbach's diva Hortense Schneider. But Nana does not merely star in operetta, she incarnates Zola's particularly hostile vision of it. She is completely unmusical, and "[The audience] had never heard a worse-trained voice, nor one singing more out of tune. Her manager had summed her up exactly: she sang like a corn-crake . . . as she was reaching the end of the song her voice gave out completely."[27] But no one cares; she's an overnight sensation. When Zola compares Nana to "a plant flourishing on a dung-heap" or a "golden fly. . .escaping from its dung-heap and . . . slip[ping] through the window of palaces," one is reminded of Wagner's judgment that "Offenbach has the warmth lacking in Auber, but it is the warmth of a dunghill; all Europe is wallowing in it."[28] For Zola, operetta epitomizes a fatal cynicism and vacuity in Second Empire art and culture.

Can one claim any commonalities, then, between the raucous, fleshly Nana and the prim Olympia? Zola's penultimate description of Nana apotheosizes the operetta's cold and mechanical aspects, for as Nana lies dead upstairs in the Grand Hotel, her friends downstairs reminisce about her final appearance on stage:

> at the Gaietés. . . in *Mélusine*. . . in that crystal grotto! . . . . Wasn't it queer to think she was dead? . . . The grotto round her, made up entirely of mirrors, was glittering with cascades of diamonds, streams of white pearl necklaces . . . and in this sparkling mountain spring, gleaming in a broad beam of electric light, with her skin and fiery hair . . . blazing with light in the middle of all that crystal.[29]

Although Nana "seemed like the sun" in this scene, she was a frozen, artificial sun, reflecting external light like the cold white stones. Nana, in her dazzling radiance, is silent: "she didn't say a word, the authors had even cut out her only speech because it spoilt the effect."[30] With this vision of illusory, cold, and electrical radiance, Zola created a composite portrait of operetta as a frigid, inorganic, and manufactured feminine mask over socially destructive energy.

Offenbach's Olympia also embodies operetta as a woman who only *seems* to possess the warmth of organic life. Hoffmann is first captivated by the still, gleaming beauty of Olympia asleep, and even when awake, she remains strangely stiff and chilly, inspiring his ardent plea, "Let my warmth fill you with the sun!" Spalanzani's admission that Olympia does not eat, accompanied by a whir of mechanical sounds, further signals that her apparent liveliness is a dupe and a swindle, and Nicklausse, never deceived, teases Hoffmann with the cryptic remark that "she is dead . . . or she's never been alive!" Even Hoffmann is forced to recognize this when the object of his deluded infatuation turns on him, shattering his spectacles and his illusions. Thus the first act of *Les Contes d'Hoffmann*, in the gaiest and most tuneful way imaginable, manages to endorse the general contemporary verdict on operetta as destructive and false.

Leon De Froidmont, in *Le Voltaire,* observed that, "There are two distinct parts in this work: that which is of the realm of pure operetta, and that which strives toward the tender measures of opéra-comique," and the caesura between these two parts is the smashing of Olympia.[31] We may read this gesture as a symbolic destruction and silencing of operetta, a composer's attempt to disavow the genre he had created and in which he had once been "the god."[32] Anticipating this disavowal, Offenbach's 1879 preview concert had already suppressed all traces of his coquettish former muse from early publicity for *Les Contes d'Hoffmann,* for although he had completed the entirely new music of the Olympia act in 1877, he previewed only the "Trio des yeux."[33] The showy *couplets* and *flon-flons* of the rest of the act would have undermined his effort to have *Les Contes d'Hoffmann* heard as a departure from his old ways. Within the opera's narrative, the end of the Olympia act stages the end of operetta, as Hoffmann's final outburst, "Un automate!" concludes the first act's narrative of disillusionment with the past and its fraudulent gaiety and glitter. And in case we've missed the point, Hoffmann's first exchange with Nicklausse spells it out: Antonia, his new love, is nothing like Olympia, that "cold and heartless *poupée.*"

AFTER OLYMPIA

Durranc, reviewer for *La Justice,* spoke for the majority of critics when he called the Antonia act "the best act of the score, if not the libretto. Offenbach seems to have worked as if to raise the coefficient of his whole musical work. One feels in it a belated intention to repent. Truly, it would be unfair not to recognize that the maestro has surpassed himself this time."[34] Antonia's "Elle a fui, la tourterelle," with its melancholy melody, sentimental strophic poem, and pianistic orchestral accompaniment, opens up a new sound-world in which the superficial frivolity of operetta has been left behind. Gounod-style lyricism, the musical hallmark of sincerity, has apparently triumphed, and the love story between singer and poet progresses in a series of touching musical performances. Antonia, alone at the piano, pines for Hoffmann, and Hoffmann in his turn summons her with a fragment of song. Reunited, they naturally sing "that sweet love song that we used to sing together." The thought of Antonia inspires even the cynical Nicklausse to poetry and song, in the lovely aria "Vois sous l'archet frémissant"—or perhaps the disguised Muse of Poetry simply finds it harder to maintain her mask of disaffection in this overwhelmingly lyrical environment.

In a radical shift from the values of the previous act, the act of singing and the sound of singers' voices now signal the presence of authentic feeling. We are far from Spalanzani's workshop, where brilliant song and performance were exposed as a deceptive mask over emptiness or absence. There are no more delusions, no more ambiguities about the truth or humanity of a beloved woman's songs. Furthermore, because there is no chorus to provide an on-stage surrogate for the theater audience as in the other acts, these are all private performances: the characters sing only to themselves and to each other. Their chansons do not break the "fourth wall" as operetta numbers do, and their sincerity is never compromised by the suggestion that the characters are playing, operetta-style, to an audience. Unlike the crowd-pleasing performers heard previously in the opera—Hoffmann in the tavern, or Olympia in Spalanzani's workshop—Antonia and Hoffmann sing for no audience but each other. Modest and domestic, removed both in style and context from the world of the stage, the songs in the Antonia act constitute a denial of theatrical performance. The only exception is the unaccountable—and, it seems, quite innocent—incursion of the old-fashioned operetta idiom in Frantz's comic *couplets*. Yet even as this little song-and-dance number reminds us of operetta, it consigns it to a subordinate position, for unlike Hoffmann's or Antonia's songs, Frantz's goes unheard by other characters (even by Frantz himself, who is deaf). Of no concern to anyone but the poor singer himself, deprived of intoxicating powers and of listeners, the number is merely a charming grotesquerie.

But perhaps this harmless snippet of operetta, sung in the parlor while all the lyric characters are out of the room, warns us that lyricism's triumph is not yet complete. Like everyone else in the Antonia act, Frantz sings about singing, but he parodies them with a song about *not* being able to sing. He explains to the audience that he obeys Krespel's whims as dutifully as a singer follows a conductor:

> Jour et nuit, je me mets en quatre,
> Au moindre signe je me tais,
> C'est tout comme si je chantais[35]

[Night and day, I put myself out / I hush up at his least sign / It's just as if I were singing!]

But Frantz immediately reconsiders this analogy, noting that singers get respect, and he gets none: "Encore non, si je chantais, / De ses mépris il lui faudrait rabattre!" [Not quite: if I sang / he would have to be less scornful!] An outsider in this lyrical household, he confesses, "Je chante seul quelquefois, / Mais chanter n'est pas commode!" [I sing when I'm alone, sometimes / But singing isn't easy!], and the refrain demonstrating his incompetence, with its nonsense syllables and a parodistic cadenza that culminates in an antimusical "couac" on the high note, conforms to the farcical style that Offenbach disavows in the rest of the act (Example 4.2).

Even in the lyric utopia of Krespel's house, then, we are reminded of

Example 4.2 Franz's voice breaks in the refrain of his couplets

contemporary accusations that Offenbach "mock[ed] both proper spelling and musical syntax," an assertion that would become central to French analyses of his corrupting artistic influence.[36] Shortly after Offenbach's death, for example, Saint-Saëns would cite a famous grotesquerie from *La Belle Hélène*'s Act I finale to prove that the operettas, with their patter songs, misplaced accents, and verbal grotesqueries, had ruptured the relationship between French verse and music.[37] From Offenbach's ability to make words jingle, pop, and sputter as well as sing, French academic composers manufactured a paranoid fantasy about foreign musical elements that needed to be purged from contemporary practice. Frantz—with his lack of "méthode," comically stilted delivery, nonsense refrain, and squawk on the high note—reminds us again of postwar hostility toward Offenbach and operetta. This little ditty, unheard by anyone, at first seems to represent operetta's newly "defanged" place in the lyric environment as subordinate, a figure of fun. But only a few moments later, it is Frantz who opens the door to Dr. Miracle. Perhaps his charming, apparently harmless *couplets* foreshadow the more powerful direct attack on lyricism that shortly follows—the *scena* "Tu ne chanteras plus?" in which the lyric idiom's own resources will ultimately be turned against it.

"Tu ne chanteras plus," the climactic confrontation between Miracle and Antonia, puts lyricism to the test, confronting it with a new challenge in the extended "development" of the villain-motive. This recurring music is by now familiar, having accompanied Lindorf's entrance in the prologue and Coppélius's appearance in the Olympia act; later it will announce Dapertutto as well. The presence of recurring themes in *Les Contes* may tempt us to introduce the Wagnerian notion of the *Leitmotif* into the discussions, and divested of its Wagnerian associations the word has some relevance; the villain-music does lead us through the opera's larger argument, confirming and reminding us that the four villains represent a single nemesis figure whose true face we never see. Perhaps he has no true face except for this musical icon of the sinister. But musically, the motive participates in the opera's conservative discourse insofar as it functions as an "old-fashioned" musical label, familiar from grand opera, Romantic opera, and mélodrame; indeed, the four villains of Barbier and Carré's boulevard play in 1851 had been accompanied by a similar name-tag, eight measures labeled *allegro diavolo* (Example 4.3).

Example 4.3 The *allegro diavolo* that accompanies the villain in each of his incarnations (Ancessy, 1851)

Offenbach's villain-motive adheres closely to the character it introduces: we hear it only when he appears on-stage, and its component parts describe his gestures and persona in music. Like Hoffmann's antagonist(s), the villain-theme sounds deliberate, malicious, and old; its trill foreshadows and echoes his sardonic laughter, and its closing figure has an ironic suavity (Example 4.4).

The motive does more than announce each villain's arrival, for its unchanging presence in the frame-narrative and the three embedded tales signals the identity of the four "nemesis" characters. The villain-motive, only

Example 4.4 The villain-motif that introduces Lindorf, Coppélius, Dr. Miracle, and Dapertutto

four measures long and tonally closed, is static, iconic, "inanimate." In all its appearances *except* "Tu ne chanteras plus?," the recurring theme stays closed, never permeating the surrounding musical texture.

Yet when Dr. Miracle and his attendant motive appear in Antonia's chamber, they initiate a struggle between two musical discourses, between Antonia's lyric sincerity and a more modernist operatic process. As Dr. Miracle begins to tempt Antonia with visions of future artistic glory if she will sing as he urges, his formerly static, iconic label comes to life for the first time, actively serving his sinister purpose. The motive announces Miracle's entrance (as it had announced Lindorf and Coppélius), but it at once exceeds its customary function, ending on a deceptive cadence to ♭VI rather than the expected C-minor closure. With this harmonic swerve, the closed four-measure theme "breaks open" and its fragments dissolve and suffuse the musical texture: the first measure, in E, is repeated twice in measures 10 to 11, while the accompanying melody of measures 20 to 24 develops the half-step rocking motion (see Example 4.5).

The presence of this "Wagnerist" moment in *Les Contes,* however, should not be taken as a testament to the composer's embrace of that new model of musical seriousness. Rather the *scena* stages the assault of an alien musical process on native French lyricism, in which Offenbach uses Dr. Miracle to demonize modernist musical procedures.

The motivically developing music that accompanies Dr. Miracle opposes itself to the natural or authentic lyricism embodied in Antonia, as the iconic motive breaks out of its traditional frame and moves around causing trouble. The villain-motive can no longer be confined within its four-measure form: as Miracle paints a dark picture of Antonia squandering her beauty and individuality for "les plaisirs bourgeois," the theme (now in G minor) expands to three times its original length. The musical label detaches itself from the villain and like his insistent words, it is heard everywhere; like him, it dodges around the orchestra, disappearing in one place and popping up in another. The theme surrounds Antonia and the audience with Miracle's sinister presence as it loses its status as an isolated label or cliché and permeates the musical atmosphere, whispering its own wordless answer to An-

Example 4.5.a The villain-motif in Dr. Miracle's final confrontation with Antonia: Dr. Miracle appears in Antonia's room: "Tu ne chanteras plus?"

Example 4.5.b The villain-motif: Dr. Miracle and his music menace Antonia

tonia's terrified question: "Quelle est cette voix qui me trouble l'esprit?" [What is this voice that troubles my spirit?] (Example 4.6).

When the recurring music momentarily crosses over from the melodramatic realm of musical icon into the realm of musical action, simultaneously reflecting and performing Miracle's persistence, the elaboration of the motif becomes a form of entrapment.

The scena thus composes out ideas that Offenbach set forth in his 1879 essay lamenting the decline of the French lyric/melodic tradition. Ostensibly, he writes out of concern for the current generation of French composers, whose genuine talent would win them so much success if they would only trust in their proper powers and "fly with their own wings." What distracts and demoratizes them? They pursue a "Medusa's head" that has paralyzed them all: the example of Richard Wagner. (For an index of what Paris regarded as Wagnerist modernism, remember that a mere four years earlier, Bizet's *Carmen* had been accused of "Wagnerism" and of unmelodiousness.) Nearly twenty years before he wrote this essay, Offenbach had made raucous and careless fun of Wagner's "music of the future" in his parodistic *Symphonie de l'avenir*, but now he speaks as an exasperated elder, wondering, "when exactly is this future scheduled to arrive?" and expressing concern over Wagner's influence: "I see the composers whom he

Example 4.6 Antonia: "What is this voice that troubles my spirit?"

has troubled, but I see none whom he has inspired."[38] It becomes apparent that the category of "troubled" young composers, like that of master-melodists, exceeds national boundaries, because Wagner is bad for everyone: "For many years now they have played these so-called 'operas à la Wagner' on the major German stages. Ask the public for the titles of these works, or the names of their composers. . . . Each attempt is made with great fanfare. Triumph precedes each work, but never follows it."[39]

Who are the composers who have lost confidence in their individual vocation, whose new works are forgotten, who are paralyzed by the "Medusa's head" of Wagner and his music of the future? Offenbach never names one, but we might at least note that at this moment the French composer most troubled by the demands of a new aesthetic, and struggling hardest to compose in a voice in which he felt less than fluent, was Offenbach himself. Almost every review of the 1881 premiere noted how, in the words of *Le Figaro*, "This great improviser, who generally wrote his scores with such astonishing speed, continually re-began and reworked this one, never entirely satisfied, always wanting to attain perfection. . ."[40] In 1879 he had already devoted three years to *Les Contes d'Hoffmann*, longer than any of his previous works, and he would not have finished it to his own satisfaction when he died a year later. Beneath the facetious tone of his essay, we may detect a clinging to traditional ideals in the face of a potent new influence. If the past dangers of operetta were feminized in the post-war imagination of the 1870s, Offenbach personifies Wagner in a series of sinister or repressive masculine figures, equally dangerous for the future of true art, artistic productivity or inspiration. As if to echo Wagner's own model of artistic creation as fructification, Offenbach calls him an impotent father whose work "engenders" nothing. A false Apollo, inspirer of a collective delusion in his followers, "he is an aurora borealis they have mistaken for the sun" (ibid., 247). Finally he is a school master "with a ferrule in his hand"—a measuring stick that has become a means of intimidation and punishment. By associating motivic-developmental procedures only with the villain and his diabolical intrusion, *Les Contes* tacitly argues against the alien-modern threat to French musical culture, and so Offenbach's brief invocation of Wagnerist *Leitmotif* in *Les Contes*—the animation of a traditional iconic motive into an active principle, an "assailant"—serves the conservative agenda set forth in this 1879 essay.

Antonia, like Offenbach, calls upon traditional lyric resources to defend her against the developmental energy of Miracle's motive, in a short passage that recalls the style of her "Elle a fui, la tourterelle." She successfully resists his modern blandishments, and refuses to hear or trust him until he tempts her with more traditional music: the sonorous specter of her mother, who sings a melody imported from Offenbach's *Fantasio* (1872). Antonia can resist Miracle's argument and the echoes of his motive that surround her, but she has no defense against this lilting, pure-hearted opéra-comique melody—the French composer's "mother tongue." The charming melody, firmly in the Gounod tradition, becomes the tool of her worst enemy. Something has gone very wrong with our parable, for while the effectiveness of the mother's song may seem to pay tribute to the enduring power of lyricism, it is precisely this music that proves fatal to Antonia. If the opera's first "chapter," the Olympia act, staged the artist's disillusionment with operetta's deceptive, glittering charms, the second seems to confirm lyric melody as the language in which love and art would flourish. But the scene of Antonia's death makes Gounod-style sincerity into another kind of deception. When Dr. Miracle turns lyricism against itself, appropriating its moral and emotional power for his nefarious ends, *Les*

Contes d'Hoffmann becomes at best an ambivalent expression of fealty to any tradition.

On this apocalyptic note—the death of much more than just Antonia— the opera has traditionally ended, with the pathetic spectacle of the inno- cent, dying girl to distract us from any lurking music-historical allegory or critique. The opera works as a Romantic tragedy culminating in the death of a beautiful woman: how sad, how affecting, how satisfying. This is what operas are supposed to be about, and how they are supposed to end. Leav- ing the theater with that trio still pulsing in our ears, we can declare that Offenbach has written a real opera at last, one before which, as Henseler wrote, "all his previous critics must fall silent." This is the Offenbach whom posterity would remember, the one who with his last breath transcended his early "low" associations and left a powerful, genuinely operatic testa- ment for all time.

It seems ironic, then, that the Antonia act was never meant to be Offen- bach's last word. This death should have been the middle of the story, not the end, for Antonia was to be the second of the three tales. The traditional dis-order of the acts resulted from Carvalho's suppression of the Venetian act at the Opéra-Comique premiere, and from Ernest Guiraud's subse- quent placement of that act in the middle of the opera rather than at its conclusion. These two pragmatic decisions shaped the opera in its tradi- tional form, with the *scena* and final trio as the musical climax, and the death of Antonia as the culmination of the drama. Both the opera and Of- fenbach's career thus ended up in the right place, a *serious* state of dramatic intensity and pathos. The final curtain that shrouds Antonia also covers over the questions raised by her mother's fatal song, and the implications of the final trio's unexpected demonizing of old-fashioned lyricism need not be explored. But if, for the purpose of *reading*, we do not end the opera with Antonia's death—if we proceed to the disorderly Venetian act and try to reconstruct the conception behind its layers, its juxtaposition of styles— we will perceive a kind of musical grasping at straws. The death of Anto- nia, brought about by the unholy alliance of the devil and opéra-comique, was also the death of sincerity. Having shattered operetta and handed the lyric mode over to the villain, Offenbach seems to have painted himself into an expressive corner, and all that remained for the Venetian act was a kind of post-sincere discourse that either rejects lyricism outright, or under- mines it by tainting it with absurdity and delusion.

Offenbach's numbers for the Venetian act comprise a catalogue of cyn- ical music, beginning with Hoffmann's clumsy drinking song. This is the opera's most explicit encoding of lyricism as human feeling and true emotion: the text derides those things, and the music rejects lyric melody together with love. With its *couplets* form and choral refrains, its boisterous rhythmic motion, and its "shouted" conclusion to each line, this number represents a backsliding back into the old, rejected realm of operetta. The same could be said of the prologue's "Klein-zach" ballad, but unlike that earlier number, the drinking song has no rhapsodic digression to reveal Hoffmann's lyrical inner being: nothing breaks its jaunty, cynical mask. The opera's fragmentary narrative has almost come full circle: the Hoffmann we meet in Venice is the same disillusioned Hoffmann we first encountered in the prologue. In Venice, however, his character is rougher and his disillusionment more recent; here he derides love in his own voice rather than channeling his bitter humor into mockery of a legendary dwarf. The orchestra echoes his sneers at the lost virtues of chastity and purity, and his refrain jeers at the fascination of "deux beaux yeux" with a sarcastic, misplaced C-major harmony. Offenbach had initially assigned this Mephistophelean drinking song to Dappertutto, and only in the post-Antonia, post-lyrical world could musical numbers be traded freely between the hero and his nemesis.

Even when Hoffmann resumes his characteristic lyric urgency in response to Giulietta's manipulative rhetoric, that urgency appears no more than a reflex, a quasi-automatic response to external stimulus. There is something comical about the way Hoffmann's cynical detachment gives way to abject devotion, his sudden and all-too predictable capitulation when Giulietta's urgent sextuplet accompaniment broadens out into the *Largo-Andante*. His ecstatic "O Dieu! de quelle ivresse," with its characteristic triplets and melodic sequences that create waves of escalating excitement and blissful sinking, is a textbook example of lyricism—yet this glorious melody nonetheless partakes of the absurd and banal. Assembled from gasping one-measure phrases, it leaps upward a bit *too* headily; it has too many swoony triplets, over-heated turns staggering up and down the scale a half-step at a time. Lyric sincerity and authentic feeling are nearly caricatured in this intoxicated wallowing, this boozy indulgence in emotion for its own sake (Example 4.7).

If "O Dieu de quelle ivresse" gives us the full-fledged rhapsodic experience that we were denied in the Olympia act, it also reveals for the first time how these lyric markers teeter on the edge of cliché. The Romance addressed to Olympia also had short phrases repeated in sequence, and concluded with one of those long slow climbs up the scale, but it was undermined by the comedy of Olympia's participation, the chirpy "Oui! oui!" that answers Hoffmann's ardent statements and the abrupt final cadence that pulls the rug out from his ecstatic conclusion. Within the context of the Olympia act, this comedy supported an overall representation of operetta as the enemy of lyric sincerity. But in retrospect—having heard the

Example 4.7 Hoffmann: "Oh God! how you intoxicate my soul!"

Example 4.7, cont.

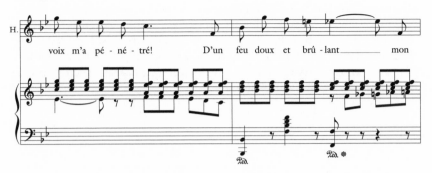

voix m'a pé - né - tré!   D'un feu doux et brû - lant_____ mon

uninterrupted exultation of "O Dieu de quelle ivresse"—one realizes that
Olympia's interjections had also supplied an ironic defense against the potential banalities of such effusions. In the prologue's "Klein-zach" ballad
and in the Olympia act, Offenbach had always framed Hoffmann's lyricism
with ironic commentaries or interruptions, and when in the Venetian act
we experience it without that frame, it sounds clichéd and overwrought.
With Lindorf we may be tempted to mutter, "Un poète? Un ivrogne!"

As for Giulietta, the most recent research on the Venetian act reveals her
as a musical chameleon. Where Olympia could sing only "mechanical"
songs, and Antonia could sing only sincerely, Giulietta adopts various idioms to suit her needs and situation. To entertain her guests she sings a lilting *couplets,* "L'amour lui dit: la belle," whose coloratura refrain will be discussed in my next chapter. Her most important number, the "Reflection
Duet" with Hoffmann, sounds carnal rather than lyrical. The "Reflection
Duet" abjures melody in favor of declamation on single pitches with ap-
poggiaturas, and, in keeping with Hoffmann's intoxicated outburst, which
immediately precedes it, its effect derives from throbbing rhythms. And although the crucial "theft of the reflection" episode defaults to the $\frac{12}{8}$ accompaniment that is customary for lyric melodies, the context undoes the
sincere values attached to lyricism, again making those Gounod-style elements into marks of insincerity. The audience undergoes a process of disillusionment similar to that which we had experienced along with Hoffmann in the Olympia act, as feeling and passion are revealed as a calculated
effect.

Carvalho omitted the Venetian act from the premiere because it could
not be finished to anyone's satisfaction, and this failure seems inevitable if
we consider how the composer had, in the course of the Olympia and Antonia acts, rejected or ironized all the musical discourses available to him.
Once lyricism had been tainted with *insincerity,* once the allure of the

mother's opéra-comique chanson had proved as dangerous as operetta's glitter, we reach a musical impasse beyond which no authentic/human musical discourse remains. This act had to be rescued, completed, and restored to the score by other, freer hands than Offenbach's. His "testament for posterity" testifies not only to his genius but also to a contemporary politics of musical style, to the elusive nature of musical sincerity, and to one composer's ambivalence about it.

CHAPTER FIVE

Reflections on the Venetian Act

This fourth act was omitted in Vienna and will remain
so in Paris. Odd, like the whole piece, is the fact that
the omission of an entire act in no way alters the
dramatic coherence; it may be just as well to add two
acts as to take one away.
(*Eduard Hanslick, "Hoffmanns Erzählungen" [1881]*)

Music is a Woman.
(*Richard Wagner, Oper und Drama [1851]*)

As LONG AS human beings have represented abstractions as allegorical figures, Music has been a woman. The conceit is as old as the muses, Calliope and Polyhymnia; as old as Monteverdi's La Musica descending from Parnassus to tell the story of Orfeo and his lyre. Prior to poets, prior to song, there is music, and music is a woman. Bizet, for example, "love[d] Italian music as a mistress," and Auber wryly remarked that his early infatuation with music had long ago faded into a marriage. Music—as lofty Muse, enchanting mistress, infuriating coquette, dutiful wife—was a woman to all these. But it was Wagner who took the ancient, universal equations of music with femininity and made them particular, attributing to national musics the features of French, Italian, and German women. Furthermore, he reversed the values implicit in the equation so that music's womanly character became a sign not of its beauty, seduction, grace, or sublimity, but rather of its degradations and limitations. The Universal woman-music had in his judgment fragmented into several decadent and "horrifying" feminine types: *Oper und Drama* takes the reader on a brief and futile tour of operatic Europe in search of that universal woman, true Music, but finds her everywhere fallen into some error or perversion characteristic of her nation: coquetry, harlotry, and prudishness.

Wagner's assertion that "Music is a Woman," and his catalogue of existing national feminine and operatic "types," seem to have been woven into a dramatic plot in the traditional version of *Les Contes d'Hoffmann*: as in the passage from *Oper und Drama,* we follow an ardent young German artist's quest for perfect love, embodied in women of three nations, each a musician of a different type and character. Wagner's rejection of French

opera as a coquette—insincere, cold, and inhuman—is echoed in Hoffmann's reaction to Olympia; if she embodies French operetta, then the
poet-protagonist's despairing recognition of her as "un automate!" disavows that musical style. In contrast to the coquette, who withholds herself from would-be lovers, Italian opera trades her commodified passions
"for purposes of pleasure or profit," and in similar fashion, Giulietta seduces Hoffmann to win a diamond from Dapertutto (*Opera and Drama,*
187).[1] The final revelation of Nicklausse as the disguised Muse of poetry
seems to complete the allegory, and the opera's conclusion stages the fulfillment of Wagner's promise that the artist who escapes from old forms
and styles will find his art regenerated by a "true Woman" who surpasses
human women. The Muse who appears to Hoffmann in the epilogue de-
clares, "L'homme n'est plus, renais poète! Je t'aime, Hoffmann! Appar-
tiens-moi!" [The man is no more, be reborn as a poet! I love you, Hoffmann! Be mine!][2] Hoffmann sublimates human desire to poetic devotion,
answering the Muse with a reprise of "O Dieu, de quelle ivresse," the Romance with which he had once greeted Giulietta's meretricious declaration
of love. The traditional score provides a catalogue of national music to ac-
company these feminine types: French waltzes for Olympia, the Italianate
Barcarole of the Venetian act, and Antonia's sentimental songs, descended
(via Gounod) from German *Lieder.*

Yet appealing though it may be to imagine that Offenbach's final, sincere achievement is itself a parable about the progression toward true
art, the now-familiar plot of *Les Contes d'Hoffmann* actually took shape
through a series of historical and theatrical contingencies involving the
Venetian act. Carvalho's decision to cut the Venetian act shortly before the
work's premiere in 1881 set in motion a history of efforts at compensation
and reconstruction. We might wonder, given its textual instability and proliferation, whether the Venetian act itself contains some irritant provoking
reconstruction and recomposition, for since the moment when Carvalho
suppressed this act, it has had an ambivalent existence: there is no authentic form in which it has had the unquestioned right to exist, and yet it
persists, continually appearing in new forms. As a textual puzzle and an
artistic challenge, this act has inspired multiple solutions in the form of recompositions and reconstructions. The discussion that follows is not designed primarily to endorse any one of these solutions (though my preference will become clear); nor will it produce a new authentic or integral text.
Rather it will interrogate the notion of such an integrity—the motivations
behind it, and the possibility of its achievement.

In this, the last of his three tales, the poet Hoffmann meets the courtesan Giulietta, who is in thrall to the sinister Dapertutto. On Dapertutto's
instructions, she has already acquired the shadow of her lover, Schlemil,

and now she seduces Hoffmann into giving up his reflection in her magic mirror, an event whose symbolic meaning may be interpreted in a variety of ways.[3] Hoffmann's yielding up of "mon reflet, mon âme, et ma vie," is at once a loss and a multiplication: the detachment of his reflection from his physical body means that there are now two of him, and he no longer knows which is real—is he the body, or is he the image that Giulietta has captured? None of the versions restores Hoffmann's psychic integrity; rather the curtain simply falls as if to black out the dead end reached by the plot.

The textual condition of the Venetian act is thus curiously akin to the condition of its protagonist: like Hoffmann after the theft of his reflection, the act seems to have lost its integrity and coherence—and yet, like Hoffmann, it lives on, compulsively retelling its own story. Yet both the dramatic action and the literary origins of the Venetian act foreshadow this unfinished state; indeed we might even suspect that they guarantee it, for the story of Hoffmann's encounter with Giulietta and the loss of his reflection descends from a series of similar stories in which the protagonist sustains a loss or damage that leaves him alienated, deficient, and unable to be at home anywhere. The immediate source of the opera's Venetian act is "Le Reflet Perdu," the fourth act of Barbier and Carré's *Les Contes d'Hoffmann*. In the play, it is the third of Hoffmann's three tales: after the disastrous endings of his infatuation with Olympia and his love affair with Antonia, the narrator-protagonist travels to Florence to forget his sorrows in loveless revelry. There the sinister Dapertutto instructs Giulietta to make Hoffmann love her: "I order you to do for [Hoffmann] what you have done for our friend Peter Schlemil, and all the others whom I needn't name. . . . Make him give you his reflection! . . . I will take such joy in watching him turn from mirror to mirror without ever finding his own face."[4] Having scoffed at the idea that anyone could fall in love with a courtesan, Hoffmann succumbs to Giulietta immediately, even committing murder in the hope of acquiring her key. Barbier and Carré's "Le Reflet Perdu" was in turn based on "Das verlorene Spiegelbild," an embedded narrative that forms the penultimate episode of E.T.A. Hoffmann's tripartite story "Die Abenteuer der Sylvester-Nacht."[5] This tale-within-a-tale is communicated to the protagonist, the Traveling Enthusiast, by one of Hoffmann's grotesques, a neurotic and belligerent little man named Erasmus Spikher. Spikher's account of his Italian journey and the loss of his reflection to Giulietta and Dapertutto provided the basic plot of the adventure that Hoffmann, in the play, enacts (and we might recall that Hoffmann's enactment is also framed as a narration, both to his friends and to the audience), but Spikher's original story had continued past the point where it ends in Barbier and Carré's play. In "A New Year's Eve Adventure," Spikher goes on to tell how he escaped from Florence, leaving his reflection behind, and subsequently found that without a reflection he was not welcome in human society. Rejected by his wife and family, he "went into the wide world" to wander forever (Hoffmann, "New Year's," 128). As for the shadowless Peter Schlemiel, he was not a resident of Giulietta's Italian palazzo in Spikher's story, but he does appear in an earlier episode of the Traveling Enthusiast's "New Year's Eve Adventure," in the *Rathskeller* where the Enthusiast first encounters both him and Spikher.

The presence of Peter Schlemiel in "A New Year's Eve Adventure" and *Les Contes d'Hoffmann* signals the common inspiration for both Hoffmann's tale and Barbier and Carré's play. Hoffmann's invention of Erasmus Spikher, the wanderer without a reflection, pays tribute to his contemporary and friend Adelbert von Chamisso, author of *Peter Schlemiels wundersame Geschichte,* the "wonderful history" of a man who sold his shadow and was henceforth condemned to wander the earth alone.[6] Barbier's and Offenbach's versions of the Venetian tale, of course, include Schlemil as Giulietta's most recent lover and victim. The genealogy of *Les Contes d'Hoffmann's* Venetian act does not, however, end—that is, begin—with *Peter Schlemiel,* for von Chamisso himself had borrowed the name of his luckless antihero from an earlier source. Von Chamisso explained to a prospective translator that the name of his antihero must never be altered, because it had a particular meaning: "Schlemiel is a Hebrew name and means Gottlieb, Theophil, or Beloved of God. This, in the everyday parlance of the Jews, is their designation for clumsy or unlucky souls who succeed at nothing in this world. A Schlemiel breaks his finger in his vest pocket or falls on his back and breaks his nose."[7] Thus the name Schlemiel descends from the oral tradition of a people whose cultural identity was linked to diaspora and displacement. Tracing the opera's Venetian act back to Hoffmann's tale of the lost reflection, and farther back through and beyond its origin in von Chamisso's novel, we find that the story always already comes from somewhere else; more importantly, we may note that each generation of the story turns around a central event of loss and the subsequent fragmentation of the protagonist's Self, whether in the comic form of "reaching into his pocket and breaking a finger," or selling his shadow for gold, or giving his reflection away to a demonic seductress. These tales, each new one a response to and a varied repetition of those that have gone before, all lie behind and are embedded within *Les Contes d'Hoffmann's* repeatedly reconstructed Venetian act.

It is not difficult to recognize at least one meaning of the loss at the heart of Hoffmann's, Barbier's, and Offenbach's tales of the Lost Reflection. Post-Freudian eyes can easily identify the textual traces of castration in both plot and rhetorical details: Spikher's wife, for example, sends him away when she discovers his loss, explaining, "if you do not have a reflection, you will be laughed at, and you cannot be the proper father for a family" (Hoffmann, "New Year's," 128). Schlemil's loss also renders him ineligible for marriage, for his sweetheart's father rejects him on the grounds that, "'every low-down dog has a shadow, and to think that my beloved only child should wed a man who—no, you must put him out of your mind at once'" (von Chamisso, *Peter Schlemiel*, 55). Evasions, like this refusal to characterize what exactly is wrong with Schlemiel ("a man who—no"), are another textual mark of castration, as Barthes notes in *S/Z*—perhaps the most influential reading of the most famous account of a European artist's debilitating encounter with an Italian singer.[8] The evasions continue in E.T.A. Hoffmann's text, where Schlemiel explains to the Traveling Enthusiast, "'there's no getting it back—I've lost . . . I've lost . . . my . . . oh, I can't go on . . .' and he leapt up and dashed out into the street" (Hoffmann, "New Year's," 112). Erasmus Spikher discovers that the loss of his reflection has made him unnameable when people in a tavern chase him away: "'He's not in the mirror?' everyone cried in confusion. 'He's a *mauvais sujet,* a *homo nefas*'" (ibid., 124). Hoffmann's French and Latin phrases simultaneously point to and resist naming Spikher's condition, a classic verbal fetish that may be compared to Freud's famous and self-contradictory insistence that there is no danger in speaking frankly of taboo matters: "I call bodily organs and processes by their technical names, and I tell these to the patient if they—the names, I mean—happen to be unknown to her. *J'appelle un chat un chat.*"[9]

Barthes further suggests that "the contagious force of castration explodes. Its metonymic power is irreversible: touched by its void, not only is sex eradicated, but art too is broken . . . language dies" (Barthes, *S/Z*, 200). Perhaps it is to guard against this catastrophe that Spikher does not *tell* his story to the Traveling Enthusiast directly, but rather writes it down—an act that fills the room with "the chill of the supernatural"—and leaves it to be read after he is gone. Barthes also notes that Balzac's narrator tells the story of Sarrasine and his encounter with the castrato to a woman who has "a burning desire to know the secret"; their unspoken agreement is that if he tells, she will take him as her lover. But to trade castration for love, even through the medium of narrative, is an impossible bargain, for the woman is so repulsed that she rejects the narrator and thus the story rebounds on its teller (Barthes, *S/Z*, 200). Perhaps Erasmus Spikher fears that his own narrative carries a similar danger of contagion, and he hopes to protect his audience, the Traveling Enthusiast, by writing his story down rather than telling it directly. Spikher's comes much too late, however, for by the time the Enthusiast reads the "Tale of the Lost Reflection" he has already sustained losses of his own. Indeed, the Enthusiast's losses have propelled the story from its beginning, bringing him at last to Spikher and his revelation. The Enthusiast's New Year's Eve adventure began at a party, where he encountered his lost beloved, Julia:

> "I will never let you go," I was saying. "Your love is the spark that glows in me . . . without you, without your love, everything is dead and lifeless . . ."
> At this very moment there tottered into the room a spindle-shanked cretin, eyes a-pop like a frog's, who said . . . "Where the Devil is my wife?"
> . . .
> The spindle-legged monkey reached for her hand and she followed him into the living room with a laugh. "Lost forever," I screamed aloud (Hoffmann, "New Year's," 108).

The humiliating loss of Julia, which by his own admission renders the narrator "dead and lifeless," had driven him from the party and human society, "bareheaded and without a coat" (108). His mundane lack of outerwear, in turn, forced him to take refuge in the tavern where he first encountered the shadowless Peter Schlemiel and Spikher without his reflection, and although he did not know them by name, he felt them to be kindred spirits, remarking, "It seems to me, gentlemen, that all of us lose something, just as right now I have no hat or coat" (111).

Hoffmann's original story, then, is a chain of narratives that recedes infinitely back in time: tales of alienation and severance from the social order, and specifically of lost masculinity and generative power. The (anti)hero, cut off from his origins and his former happiness by the loss of some essential part of himself, is never at home and never able to *return* home. Nor is Hoffmann's "Adventure" ever properly finished: Erasmus Spikher has already departed when the Traveling Enthusiast discovers his manuscript, and Peter Schlemiel simply "disappear[s] into the night" (112). The Traveler's own postscript ends with the elliptical fragment, "Forgive me . . ." (129). Although a narrator might hope to repair his condition, restore himself to wholeness, by recounting the story of his own or another's loss, his every effort simply propagates the central lack in the text. Each successive narration attempts to recuperate the text's integrity, yet ends by replicating its unfinished state. The "Tale of the Lost Reflection" has never been satisfactorily concluded, either in literary or musico-dramatic form; rather, it seems only to multiply through compulsive retelling. The loss of Spikher's/Hoffmann's reflection, like the echoes of that event in other episodes of "A New Year's Eve Adventure" and the dissolution of the Traveling Enthusiast's narrative in an unfinished sentence, has been repeated in the original "cutting" of the Venetian act and reproduced in its fragmented source situation and multiple versions.

To dwell exclusively on the familiar tragic and fatal aspects of castration, however, may cause us to overlook another way in which the metaphor

connects the unfinished text of the Venetian act to its plot and its protagonists. We may bring the grotesque and comic aspects of the castration
trope into focus by turning away from the pathetic Schlemil and consider-
ing another imported character, Giulietta's jester Pitichinaccio. Barbier and
Carré found this small but significant figure in Hoffmann's novella *Salvator Rosa*, where he had been described as an "ill-bred eunuch dwarf."[10]
This "hideous little monster" worked as a ladies' maid, was forced to wear
women's clothing by his bizarre master, and—most importantly—never
spoke, but rather squealed, groaned, bleated, and wailed (Hoffmann,
"Signor Formica," 330). Thus his voice, appearance, and persona, like those
of Erasmus Spikher in "A New Year's Eve Adventure," were those of a castrated grotesque. Barbier and Carré's play (1851) perpetuated the representations of these creatures as risible and possessed of broken voices, for
Giulietta's jester Pitichinaccion [*sic*] barely speaks, but punctuates the conversations of others with a sarcastic laughter described as "barking"; Giulietta calls him "une curiosité, une façon d'homme, ou de singe, qu'on m'a
rapportée de je ne sais où" [a curiosity, a type of man—or perhaps a mon-
key—that someone sent to me from I don't know where].[11] By adding
Pitichinaccio to Giulietta's retinue, Barbier and Carré situated her within
the orientalist tradition of exotic, fatal queens with a retinue of subhuman
slaves and eunuchs, a trope that would gain importance in Barbier's 1881
libretto and would influence Offenbach's music for the prima donna. Perhaps this trope culminates, in serious theater, with Friedrich Dürrenmatt's
"tragi-comedy" *Der Besuch der Alten Dame* (*The Visit of the Old Lady*), in
which Claire Zachanassian—the wealthiest woman in the world, and a
femme fatale in every sense—is accompanied by "Koby and Loby," a pair
of men who once wronged her and whom, for revenge, she has caused to
be castrated and blinded.[12] (In Gottfried von Einem's opera of the same
title, the blind pair are—not surprisingly—played by two grotesque-comic
tenors.) Such eunuchs, literal or figurative, share one additional feature
with Giulietta's lovers: they cling to the *femme fatale* in the face of infi-
delity, insults, and humiliations, displaying a masochistic devotion that—
like their missing parts—resonates with Western European imaginings of
the Jewish male rendered both perverse and castrated by the ritual of cir-
cumcision. Again, these fantasies did not inspire sympathy for the Jewish
"other," but rather revulsion and mockery.[13] The jester's voice remains
bestial and effeminate in the opera, for Pitichinaccio is played by the same
comic tenor who plays the monosyllabic Andres in Act I, the stammering
Cochenille in Act II, and Franz, whose Act III *couplets* had demonstrated
his inability to sing: each successive incarnation of the grotesque character
is marked by a worse vocal defect. The recently recovered 1881 libretto
contains more spoken and sung lines for Pitichinaccio than any previous
version, but still the *comprimario* mainly cackles and shrieks. He is also sub-

ject to insults from everyone around him as Giulietta mocks him for his devotion, and Hoffmann repeatedly threatens and taunts him.

The cruelly comic representation of the eunuch Pitichinaccio reminds us that the Venetian act's sources date from an era when the "unmanning of men" could still be taken lightly. In *Salvator Rosa*, in Spiker's narrative, and in von Chamisso's *Peter Schlemiel*, such grotesques inspire mockery rather than pity or existential terror, descending perhaps from early modern *charivari* traditions of taunting and mocking impotent, weak, or cuckolded men.[14] In an early scene of von Chamisso's novel, Schlemiel is spotted by a crowd of schoolboys, who "proceeded on the spot to hurl lumps of dirt and deride me: 'Honest people don a shadow when they step out into the sun'" (von Chamisso, *Peter Schlemiel*, 14). We might also recall that the real-life eunuchs of Western Europe, the castrati, were still alive and singing in Hoffmann and Chamisso's time, and were as much the objects of ribald humor and derision as of veneration, not yet having acquired the phantasmatic charge that Balzac's generation would project onto them. Thus although Spikher's wife is frightened by the sight of the empty mirror gazing back at her husband, she is also pragmatic enough to realize that he will be laughed at by outsiders; and although women express pity for Peter Schlemiel in his "shadowless state," he is also greeted by "the disdainful scorn of the men, particularly those well-dressed burgers who themselves cast such a broad and imposing shadow" (14). Castration and emasculation may represent social death in these tales, but they do not confer sublime or fatal status on the one who suffers them.[15]

It seems appropriate, then, that in each successive version of the Venetian act Hoffmann's recognition that he has lost his reflection is followed not only by a violent death but by an outburst of mocking laughter. Furthermore, precisely *who* laughs and *who* dies in each version is an index of the seriousness with which the castration trope is presented. Gunsbourg, like his predecessors Guiraud and Carvalho, treated the Venetian plot rather lightly. Not only is this act the briefest of the three tales, but it occurs in the middle of the opera, and thus the metaphorical force of Hoffmann's symbolic castration does not "explode," bringing about the death of subjectivity, plot, or narrative. The ending in this version is essentially a practical joke on Hoffmann, whom Giulietta dupes into killing Schlemil and then abandons. Leaving him with nothing but the *femme fatale's* laughter (and Pitichinaccio's), floating from off-stage over the strains of her Barcarole, this version retains not only the nightmarish quality but also the maliciously comic tone of the sources.

Both of the recent critical editions, by contrast, place the Venetian act at the end of the opera, as if to fulfill Barthes's claim that castration brings about the end of narrative, and they emphasize the serious and fatal aspects of the plot in other ways as well. Oeser's version, based on Barbier's 1851 play, ends with Giulietta's death, tacitly punishing the *femme fatale* for her treachery. With a certain poetic justice, she receives the poisoned cup from her most devoted victim, the grotesque Pitichinaccio. Yet this conclusion also sentimentalizes Giulietta by representing her as the last victim of Dapertutto's machinations, for she is ultimately as much a dupe as Schlemil and Hoffmann, and Dapertutto laughs at her death, remarking, "Ah, Giulietta! Maladroite!" Perhaps in "softening" their portrayal of Giulietta, Barbier and Carré's first priority was to emphasize the structural parallels among their play's three episodes rather than to follow the *femme fatale* trope to its conclusion, for the ending of their 1851 Venetian act (and therefore of Oeser's) replicates the conclusions of the two previous tales, in which Hoffmann had rushed to the broken/dead body of Olympia/Antonia while Coppélius/Dr. Miracle stood by, laughing.

Castration, laughter, and death are most strongly linked in Barbier's 1881 libretto, set by Offenbach and restored in Kaye's critical edition: not only does Hoffmann kill the unfortunate Schlemil, but he attempts to stab Giulietta and accidentally kills Pitichinaccio, who is elevated from "barking" clown to victim as the curtain falls on the mocking laughter of the entire chorus at Hoffmann's stupefaction and Giulietta's grief.[16] Yet it seems to me a flaw in this libretto that no dramatic irony mediates between the intense, tragic emotions experienced by the principals and the mockery demonstrated by the laughing chorus. Additionally, the chorus's collective cruelty introduces an element of sadism beyond that displayed by the evil *individual*, Dapertutto, in earlier editions. The spectacle of a community knowingly laughing at the murder of one of its members has a bizarre and unpleasant effect that exceeds prior operatic representations even of the most decadent and cynical courtiers—we might contrast Barbier's Venetians, for example, with the *corteggiani* in *Rigoletto*, whose ribald laughter at the suffering jester falls silent when they realize that they have delivered his virgin daughter, not his mistress, into the Duke's hands; or with the laughing chorus in Act II of *Un Ballo in Maschera*, who laugh to see Amelia unveiled because they do not realize that they have just exposed her to her husband as an adulteress. The contrast between the joking ending of Gunsbourg's version and the more evil spectacle that concludes Barbier's libretto highlights the way in which a discrepancy between form and content, always problematic in the Venetian act, has gradually been exacerbated. In the versions of this act that appeared during the twentieth century, increasingly "comique" forms, such as spoken dialogue, pantomime-melodrama, and *couplets*, have been made to bear ever more serious and even tragic content.

———

Giulietta's menagerie is properly a literary pastiche, and a musical one as well, for like the residents of her palace, musical numbers came to the

Venetian act from diverse places. The version restored by Guiraud in 1881 included only two numbers that might be considered "native": Daper-tutto's "Tournez, miroir" and the Reflection Duet for Hoffmann and Giulietta, which Offenbach composed expressly for *Les Contes d'Hoff-mann*.[17] Apart from these two numbers, the Venetian act was home to a variety of foreign visitors, guests, and interlopers, beginning with Offen-bach's own importation of the Barcarole and Hoffmann's *chanson à boire,* "Amis l'amour tendre et rêveur, Erreur!" from his earlier *Die Rhein-Nixen* (1864). The inclusion of these two "recycled" numbers in the May 1879 concert suggests that they were part of his initial conception of the Venet-ian act, as if Offenbach himself wanted to retell a story that he had not com-pleted satisfactorily the first time.

As we have seen, the same compulsive retelling that produced the chain of source tales seems to have been at work in the opera; however, both the motivations for such retelling, and the form and content of the end-prod-ucts have changed dramatically over time. During the first quarter-century of performing editions, restoring and repairing the work was essentially a pragmatic task, as the Monte Carlo director Raoul Gunsbourg explained: "I wrote almost all of the [Venetian] act of *Les Contes d'Hoffmann,* that which is today performed on every stage; I received five hundred francs for my work from Paul Choudens, and for this amount I renounced all claim to the piece."[18]

Gunsbourg's statement that he was paid for his work and "renounced all claim" on the product distinguishes his version from those that succeeded it, for even as Gunsbourg's version took hold in the standard repertoire, the notion persisted that there had once been a different Venetian act, dra-matically and musically superior to the available one, and furthermore re-flecting Offenbach's authentic and completed vision. When scholars took it upon themselves to reconstruct Offenbach's original Venetian act— rather than pragmatically assembling a new and better version, as Guns-bourg and numerous impresarios after him had done—the opera's history acquired what we might call a psychoanalytic dimension, for both the plot and the performance history of this act crystallize the opera's Romantic theme of identity as fragile and mutable. Thus although the textual and musical incoherence of the Venetian act has been taken as a problem to be solved, it may also hold a key to *Les Contes d'Hoffmann's* meaning, for by a kind of contagion, scholars and performers of the opera have become (like Hoffmann) desiring Subjects and compulsive retellers of tales, with the "complete" opera as their elusive Object of desire.

Several new German productions in the 1950s and 1960s attempted not only to repair the opera's theatrical weaknesses, but also to remove inau-thentic elements and restore it to a presumed original and integral state, and more was at stake in such efforts than simply improving the Venetian act. These versions were part of a larger scholarly project of recuperating the German-born Offenbach as a serious composer and of revealing a German Romantic spirit under *Les Contes d'Hoffmann*'s French surface. This work culminated with Fritz Oeser's critical edition of 1976, based on a cache of new sources discovered in the home of one of Offenbach's descendants. The new sources on which Oeser relied, unfortunately, provided scant information about the Venetian act, and therefore his edition of that act, like Gunsbourg's of 1907, is a recomposition rather than a reconstruction.[19] Rationalizing that he could bring the work closer to Offenbach's imputed intentions by purging the inauthentic "Scintille, diamant," the septet, and Guiraud's recitatives, Oeser followed Offenbach's own process of raiding *Die Rhein-Nixen* for much of his new version. To illustrate both the impact of Oeser's recuperative project and the rhetoric surrounding it, let me turn to the crucial moment in the Venetian act when Dapertutto invokes the magic diamond with which he will draw Giulietta to him and compel her to steal Hoffmann's reflection.

The aria "Scintille, diamant," introduced into the opera by Gunsbourg in 1907, is plainly inauthentic: while revising *Les Contes d'Hoffmann*, Gunsbourg and his collaborators had access to Offenbach's drafts, and they were also familiar with his earlier operas. When they constructed a new solo for Dapertutto, they had imported a tune from the overture to Offenbach's opéra-comique, *Le Voyage dans la lune* (1875), a tune that resembled Offenbach's penultimate draft of the diamond aria. The result captures the *fin-de-siècle* French aesthetic that informed Gunsbourg's work; both an autograph manuscript and the early printed sources, however, confirm that Offenbach's final version of Dapertutto's solo had been very different, emphasizing his demonic and aggressive side.[20] Oeser's replacement of the clearly inauthentic "Scintille, diamant" with the just as clearly authentic "Tournez, miroir" is most interesting for the paranoid tone of the praise it received. Oeser had done more than simply emend the score, for as critic Egon Voss explained, the luxurious lyricism and undeniable beauty of "Scintille, diamant" had exercised a malevolent power over the piece: it "degrade[d] this text to empty superficiality," until the meaning of both the poem and the Venetian act were "sucked away by the lovely music."[21] Voss's rhetoric attributes sinister, even *vampiric* qualities to the aria, as if this musical representation of Dapertutto's diamond had somehow stolen the opera's authentic self. The opera's *authentic* music is seen as a besieged textual body whose boundaries must be defined and policed, and whose integrity must be secured by the laying to rest of the intruder in an appendix of Oeser's edition.

But the line between authentic and alien elements—between Offenbach's Venetian act and the parasitic elements that had attached to it over time—cannot be so clearly drawn. Oeser claimed proudly that his edition contained only music by Offenbach—but he also reintroduced music that the composer had rejected, wrote a new libretto for the Venetian act, and freely imported both recitatives and set pieces from *Die Rhein-Nixen* (1864). He added a duetto for Dapertutto and Pitichinaccio, and a scene and quartet with chorus, both based on Offenbach's discarded early drafts.[22] He also introduced an aria for Giulietta and new, longer recitatives, all borrowed from *Die Rhein-Nixen*. Ironically, his edition perpetuated the strictly inauthentic condition that he had set out to solve.[23]

Oeser's efforts at rebuilding the Venetian act had been hindered by the absence of a complete libretto, and he had solved this problem by writing one himself, following the 1851 play as Jules Barbier had done. In 1987, however, Josef Heinzelmann located the censor's libretto of *Les Contes d'Hoffmann*, authorized on January 6, 1881 for performance at the Opéra-Comique, and this discovery allowed work on the Venetian act to move to more solid textual ground.[24] This discovery solved the single biggest problem for editors—the lack of a definitive text or even plot synopsis for the Venetian act—and became the basis of a new source-critical edition by Michael Kaye. Kaye had access to a second trove of manuscript musical sources from the Opéra-Comique preparation period, up to and including the February 1, 1881 dress rehearsal when the Venetian act was cut. These include a gambling scene for full chorus, Giulietta's aria, "L'amour lui dit: la belle," and her ensuing seduction duet with Hoffmann; a shadow-play melodrama for Dapertutto and Schlemil; and a *parlando* duel scene to replace the pantomime introduced by Guiraud.[25] Kaye's edition seems to realize a long-sought ideal, the reassembly of a fragmentary and apparently irreparable text, and the restoration of the Venetian act as it was immediately before the premiere; in short, an end to the story.

Yet paradoxically, and perhaps inevitably, the satisfaction of this desire for textual wholeness has not repaired the opera. On the contrary, the reconstructed *Les Contes d'Hoffmann* demonstrates how a once-idealized object, in the moment of its becoming material, loses its ideal qualities and becomes simply itself. Any lingering nostalgia for Offenbach's lost score as the solution to the opera's flaws may now be put to rest, for Kaye's version is substantially "as Offenbach left it," and still something is lacking: ironically, the piece has been restored to the unsatisfactory condition in which it originally had to be cut. The musical numbers are inconsistent in tone, and separated by long stretches of spoken dialogue. Each number is also reprised at least once as incidental music for a pantomime or dialogue, and a spoken scene in which Dapertutto taunts Schlemil with the loss of his shadow, which might have been a marvelous bit of stagecraft in 1881, now simply slows the musical action. Perhaps the very lack in the old Venetian act had accounted for the allure of this unfinished work, its magnetic power and the fantasies it inspired: as long as the Ideal remains in the realm of fantasy, it is compelling, irresistible. But on becoming material, it risks becoming no more than the sum of its parts. With the reconstruction of the suppressed 1881 version we must give up blaming the deficiencies of the Venetian act on posthumous interference, and begin to look elsewhere for understanding.

What might account for the unconvincing condition of the Venetian act? Consider again the challenges of representing this story on the stage. Its only dramatic event is Hoffmann's succumbing to Giulietta and the consequent loss of his psychic integrity, and this is more an archetypal situation than a plot, a dream of encountering the Other personified in a seductive exotic woman. The music of this act should therefore work on the listener as Giulietta works on Hoffmann, seducing us into her soundworld, but the foreign woman's language cannot be translated into vernacular forms and phrases without losing its effect. As Hoffmann's Traveling Enthusiast explains, describing a mystical encounter with another foreign soprano, "Her sweet words resounded like a song. . . . How can I represent to you, my dear Theodor, every word of the marvelous conversation that began between the Lady and myself? Only that although I will transcribe her utterances in [our own language], every word seems flat and stiff, every phrase ungainly."[26]

This is the very task of transcription that Offenbach faced in the Venetian act, as he attempted to shape Giulietta's utterances and the exotic atmosphere of Venice into conventional modes of expression. Kaye's reconstruction reveals that Offenbach had not solved this problem at the time of his death, for the hallucinatory events of the Venetian plot had been forced into the vernacular form of an *opéra-comique,* an ungainly sequence of songs, melodrama, and spoken dialogues. The gap between the vernacular music and the magical effects attributed to it creates a frustrating sense of incompleteness, as if the truly enchanting music of Venice were hovering just out of reach behind the din of the music on stage. Giulietta's aria, "L'amour lui dit: la belle," restored in Kaye's edition of the score, will illustrate some of the limitations of the recovered Venetian act.

THE SIREN'S SONG

Unlike the other two heroines, Giulietta has traditionally had no solo showpiece, although operatic conventions, the literary sources, and the dramatic situation all demand that she should. Hoffmann's original tale includes a description of Giulietta singing for her guests, emphasizing the sensuous impact of her voice: "Giulietta sang, and it was as if the tones of her beautiful voice aroused in everyone sensations of pleasure never felt before but only suspected to exist. Her full but clear voice conveyed a secret ardor which inflamed them all" (Hoffmann, "New Year's," 118). An aria for Giulietta became even more necessary when Barbier and Offenbach "orientalized" Hoffmann's Italian tale by moving the scene from Florence to Venice. The tale of the lost reflection fit neatly into an orientalist paradigm, for its Venetian setting was well-established in French and German imaginations as an ambiguous, even uncanny space, simultaneously "home"— because European—and "foreign," a place where rational rules do not apply. Dapertutto, with his machinations against visiting Westerners, became a cruel potentate, and his suave hypocrisies are consistent with literary and operatic clichés of Venetian treachery. But perhaps the most indispensable element in an exotic scene is the *femme fatale* with a siren song.[27] Orientalist formulae contributed perhaps the strongest impetus for Giulietta to perform a seduction song, in the course of which she would captivate the listening Hoffmann. Yet Barbier and Carré's drama, which provided the outlines of the libretto, included no basis for such an aria: their Giulietta had not sung at all, and indeed the play had denied any lyrical qualities to Giulietta's seduction of Hoffmann. The scene was written entirely in prose rather than the free verse used for the emotional and expressive high points of the other tales.

Thus Barbier, in fashioning his libretto, was compelled to devise not only an aria for Giulietta, but also a scene in which that aria could occur.[28] Hoffmann, having sworn off love and specifically vowed never to fall for Giulietta, gambles with her other guests while the courtesan sits alone, fanning herself and singing a song addressed to no one in particular. Her *couplets* is a dialogue between "L'Amour" and "the Beauty": Cupid invites her to "drown your soul in joy" in verse one and "to be a queen" in verse two, but the Beauty refuses, claiming that she prefers "a bitter love, drunk on tears" and that she wants only to "hide myself under the shadow of the dark night, so I may hear and see him!"[29] The poem is thus a seduction in the ambiguous "talking to myself" mode of Carmen's *Seguidilla,* as Giulietta—easily identified as "the Beauty"—conveys slyly that there is someone for whom she wants to renounce all other pleasures, and Cupid's "Aimez! aimez!" can equally be understood as Giulietta's invitation. Hoffmann—like a Don José—interprets and accepts this performance, which is also a proposition. He succumbs in music when, after a brief exchange of recitative, he picks up the verse, taking on Cupid's persona to address Giulietta: "L'amour lui dit: la belle / Vos yeux étaient fermés! / Puis, la touchant de l'aile: / Voyez le jour, aimez!" [Cupid said to her: Oh Beauty, your eyes were closed! Then, touching her with his wing: Behold the day, and love!] The seduction is complete.

Hoffmann succumbs to the insinuating charms of Giulietta's song, yet nowhere in this act is the discrepancy between music and its imputed effect more pronounced. The melody and its operetta-style accompaniment sound more jaunty than seductive, and the coloratura passages seem arbitrarily tacked on to the simple tune; furthermore, it is inconsistent with the narcotic opening Barcarole, music that has already defined Giulietta's seductive vocal character so strongly that this virtuosic aria seems almost to belong to some other voice entirely. Nor is the bright effect of this aria, out of keeping as it is with the sinister and sensuous Venetian atmosphere, the only quality that makes it jarring at this particular moment in the opera as a whole. Giulietta, fanning herself and singing, might be the very doll against whom Nicklausse's *couplets* had cautioned Hoffmann during his infatuation with Olympia: "Une poupée aux yeux d'émail / Jouait au mieux de l'éventail" [a doll with enamel eyes, playing with her fan] who "Soupirait et disait: Je t'aime!" [sighs and cries, 'I love you!'].[30] Her coloratura conclusion, absolutely identical to the final cadence of Olympia's Doll Song, gives the game away: in succumbing to this song, Hoffmann falls for the very same trick that snared him in Spalanzani's workshop.[31] And although Hoffmann fails to recognize the hollowness of Giulietta's coloratura flourishes, they are more likely to inspire in the audience a sense of ironic detachment. For the audience, there is no unlearning the lesson taught in the Olympia act: we saw this doll shattered at the end of Act II, and the alluring songbird has already been categorically undone, revealed as an instrument of the villain. Having heard Olympia, we remain undeluded by Giulietta's song even as it enraptures Hoffmann, recognizing it as a parody of a siren song rather than the real thing.

One might argue that this ironic effect, and the way that it undermines the Venetian plot, does not matter; Hanslick, for example, had compared the opera's whole dramaturgy to a dream-logic that juxtaposes events in an arbitrary and striking, rather than logically coherent, fashion.[32] But if we accept this rationale, there is no need to restore "L'amour lui dit: la belle" at all, for Hoffmann's submission to Giulietta in Guiraud's and later Gunsbourg's versions of the Venetian act already made triumphant *non*-sense as an arbitrary and apparently spontaneous response to the atmosphere and his own susceptibility. Giulietta need not make verbal promises or dazzle with coloratura like Olympia, because her real siren song was always present in the Venetian act: the music that overcame Hoffmann was the Barcarole, hovering over the scene of night and sensuality. Although sung by Giulietta, the Barcarole is not addressed to Hoffmann nor to anyone in particular, and this adds to its power. Beginning as a phenomenal performance by Giulietta and Nicklausse, it comes to saturate the musical texture, exceeding its initial realistic presentation. Where "L'amour lui dit: la belle" depends on words for its effect, the Barcarole's text is virtually meaningless; adding little or nothing to the plot, its words are purely atmospheric, dissolving repeatedly into wordless melisma and hummed accompaniment. This is music of the body—in Dahlhaus's words, "as physically present to the listener as music is capable of being"—and makes its presence felt as sonorous materiality rather than verbal sense.[33] Recall again the untranscribable language spoken to the Traveling Enthusiast in the short story *Don Juan* by "Donna Anna," whose "sweet words resounded like a song."[34] The words of the foreign woman are music in the ear and cannot be shaped into verbally signifying phrases without loss of effect. In the same way, Giulietta's siren song inevitably suffers from translation into the vernacular idiom of opéra-comique *couplets*. The Barcarole renders other, more conventional solos for Giulietta redundant, even counterproductive, for they detract from her power rather than enhancing it.

The condition of the reconstructed Venetian act resembles that of Giulietta's song in that its once-alluring gaps are now filled with words and ungainly phrases, and its musico-dramatic weaknesses no longer represent a tantalizing absence in the opera—rather, they *are* the opera. No longer an alluring mystery, *Les Contes d'Hoffmann* once reconstructed is simply an opéra-comique. The lost music, now recovered, reveals the idealized "authentic version" as a fantasmatic space, the product of a collective nostalgia for something that never existed. The differences between the reconstructed score from 1880 and Gunsbourg's inauthentic through-composed version of 1907 also invite a brief consideration of genre and reception. The opéra-comique version on which Offenbach was working when he died had been haunted from the start by the opéra-lyrique—in five acts, sung throughout—that he had initially wanted to write, and which he had begun composing in 1876.[35] But as I have discussed in previous chapters, circumstances had compelled Offenbach to revise the opera to conform to the generic and institutional requirements of the Opéra-Comique and its company. The Venetian act, as preserved in the censor's libretto and in materials from the last stages of rehearsal, regresses back to opéra-comique and melodrama (for example, the shadow-duel between Dapertutto and Schlemil). It contains much more spoken dialogue than the previous acts, and these pose their own challenges of plausibility, interest, and delivery.[36] But the more basic problem is the shifting of mental gears required for the audience to switch our attention back and forth between speech and song. Turning the music off and on during an opera is disruptive, for singing, in a work with spoken dialogue, will be tinged with self-consciousness, and the more speech there is, the less natural the music must seem. Used successfully, dialogue can emphasize the contrast between the mundane world and the magical or sublime, elevating music to a "super-natural" status. But the supernatural is always in danger of collapsing into subnatural or farcical expression, from the sublime to the ridiculous. This is one reason for the effectiveness of alternations between speech and song in comic genres, for by singing where they "could" speak, characters enter a topsy-turvy world of absurd juxtapositions. Yet the numbers restored to the reconstructed Venetian act are neither sublime nor comic. (Dapertutto's demonic "Tournez, miroir," for example, erupts out of nowhere, musically, and vanishes after only fifty measures.) The musical thinness of the Venetian act is only exacerbated by contrast with Hoffmann's other two tales, which are "about music" and are played out in music that carries, amplifies, and performs the action.[37] It seems entirely possible that *Les Contes d'Hoffmann* would not have entered the international repertory in the opéra-comique form that Offenbach created for Carvalho between 1879 and 1880. The theatrical effectiveness of the 1907 version, on the other hand—an effectiveness that cannot be disputed, given the opera's long record of success, although deploring it has become *de rigueur*—resides in the ability of its interpolated materials, inauthentic or not, to create and sustain a musical sound-world.

Can a "corrupt" version be superior to the real one? So long as the fantasy of an authentic Venetian act persisted (that is, a version composed by Offenbach and uncorrupted by editorial interference), Guiraud and the 1907 editors have appeared as villains blocking our view of the opera. The Offenbach scholar Robert Pourvoyeur, for example, praises *Les Contes's* ability to survive "a hundred years of the most unexpected mutilations and distortions."[38] Now, however, I would argue that these editors did what Offenbach himself had not done; that is, they created an *operatic* Venetian act with musical interest and dramatic momentum, unimpeded by spoken dialogue and instrumental reprises. Yet despite my affection for the "bad" old version, and my sense that Gunsbourg's version, despite its manifold inauthenticities, conveyed the spirit of the tale more effectively than either of the more recent recompositions or restorations, I have not made this argument in order to reject any of the numerous efforts to rescue the Venetian act between 1881 and 1992. It seems more interesting to meditate on the fact that there is no "Venetian act"—or rather, that there are innumerable ones. To borrow Jean-Jacques Nattiez's terms, the *poietic* process—by which the "producer" of a musical work addresses performers/listeners in a trace, in this case, a written score—and the *esthesic* process—by which these "receivers" make sense of that trace—are hopelessly entangled.[39] The Venetian act can hardly be said to preexist its performance, nor can it be separated from its performance, and thus it undermines any comfortable notions we may be harboring about the musical work as a secure or stable entity; thus this problem piece will provide, in the final section of this chapter, an opportunity for meditation on the performative aspects of opera.

IDENTITY AND PERFORMANCE

La femme n'existe pas.
(*Jacques Lacan*)

If we regard the Opéra-Comique version of the Venetian act as the cobbled-together product of Offenbach's compromises with Carvalho, we might turn to the numbers written before 1879 in search of the act's authentic core. But it is here, at the least adulterated stage of composition, that the fantasy of a return to origins eludes us most definitively, for these numbers reveal that the Venetian act *began* as a patchwork of citations from other operas. Three of the four numbers with which Offenbach began were self-quotations from earlier works: not only Giulietta's song from 1852, but also the Barcarole and Hoffmann's drinking song, which he imported from his *Die Rhein-Nixen* of 1864. The only original music for this act is, appropriately enough, the duet during which Giulietta steals Hoffmann's reflection. All of the music surrounding that event originates outside *Les Contes d'Hoffmann,* and thus the search for an authentic Venetian act, like the search for an origin to the tale of the lost reflection, recedes endlessly back in time: the text was always already assembled from fragments.

Returning now to my opening conceit that "Music is a Woman," I would like briefly to consider the problem of the Venetian act's origins and authenticity in light of anti-essentialist theories of identity as performance and citation, or what philosopher Judith Butler has called "the stylized repetition of acts."[40] Butler, adapting the speech-act theory of J. L. Austin to questions of human self-knowledge and self-presentation, theorizes gender as a performative utterance rather than an innate or immutable quality, a set of norms, signals, and masks that the individual subject occupies. What implications might this quietly radical notion—that an aspect of the self without which one can barely conceive the self does not inhere in the self, but must be constructed through the repetition of stylized acts that simultaneously express and constitute an indispensable component of the self and its intelligibility—have for musical, rather than human, objects? What happens if we replace "the self" with "the work," and "gender" with "authenticity"?

Butler refuses to see gender as *natural,* construing it rather as an *artifice* and *fiction* whose apparent naturalness must repeatedly be re-inscribed. Most recently, she has used the example of male cross-dressers to illustrate her theories, for these are subjects for whom gender is undeniably "constructed" through reference and citation to an ever-receding horizon of the natural or authentic.[41] Such transgressions against the fiction of authenticity or naturalness—Butler's "gender trouble"—menace and destabilize culture in a way all out of proportion to the apparent size of the of-fense, for "drag enacts the very structure of impersonation by which *any gender* is assumed" (Butler, "Imitation," 21). Essential to Butler's theo-rization of gender as performative rather than inherent (or constative) is the premise that a sex/gender performance acquires its authority through its relation to a model—to be comprehensible, an identity must cite, imi-tate, or refer to a known model. Yet "*gender is a kind of imitation for which there is no original* . . . a kind of imitation that produces the very notion of the original as an *effect* and consequence of the imitation itself" (Butler, "Imitation," 21). Might one substitute the "identity" of a musical work for the identity of a human subject in Butler's performative model? What if the naturalness of Music is equally a necessary fiction, an elaborate arti-fice, and what if such an aberrant, marginal work as *Les Contes d'Hoff-mann's* Venetian act is no exception to but rather a limit-case for the rule? The Venetian act, whose ongoing construction and reconstruction in imi-tation of a fantasied "natural" ideal cannot be disputed, is a sort of textual drag queen, a subject whose identity exists in the repetition of stylized acts. To invoke Butler once again, what are the multiple reconstructions of the Venetian act if not "performance[s] that *produce* . . . the illusion of an inner depth"? (Butler, "Imitation," 28). If, as I argued above, the opera acquired a psychoanalytic dimension at the very moment when a recuperation of its authentic state seemed to became possible, giving rise to a nostalgic long-ing for that wholeness, then we need not reach too much farther to see that opera-psyche as "a compulsive repetition, as that which conditions and dis-ables the repetitive performance of identity. If every performance repeats itself to institute the effect of identity, then every repetition requires an in-terval between the acts . . . in which risk and excess threaten to disrupt the identity being constituted" (ibid.). This musical subject, too, is an imita-tion of a fantasy-original, a series of invocations of an Itself that does not exist in any authentic form.

Perhaps the Venetian act, permanently under construction, could be cel-ebrated on post-modern terms as a work that continually undoes itself. Certainly it has facilitated, even demanded, "resistance" on the part of per-formers; the ideology of faithful or obedient performance that Suzanne Cusick has critiqued in "Gender and the Cultural Work of a Classical Music Performance," for example, is quite untenable in the case of *Les Contes d'Hoffmann*. Cusick, bringing Butler's ideas to bear on cultural practice, proposes that modern traditions of interpreting, analyzing, and perform-ing "classical music" can and should be subverted, starting from the premise that "the music's Self [i]s not essential, but contingent on choices and performative acts governed as much by 'audience' and 'performer' as by 'the music itself.'"[42] Note, however, that musical texts in Cusick's model remain the "givens" with or against which the performer works: in order to valorize the performer's ability to overcome or to resist the work, paradoxically, we must leave "the work itself" intact as a thing-to-be-resisted.[43] This is precisely what the Venetian act will not allow, and following Butler, we might rather suggest that musical works and their performer have contingent identities—that the work is not an independent entity to be obeyed or "sung against," but rather a subject like the performer, constituted through the repetition of stylized acts. If the Venetian act seems aberrant in that it exists in so many versions, each the result of such extreme intervention on the part of editors and performers and leading to so few firm conclusions, it nevertheless may highlight the dynamics behind all performance: perhaps its true aberration is simply that it presents no seamless surface, no score or original text behind which performers may hide.

Les Contes d'Hoffmann ultimately undoes the apparent dichotomy of "obedient" and resistant, leaving only performance, which it reveals as always a creative act—always, that is, an *act*, even when it masquerades as a naturalized submission to authenticity or to composerly intentions. The multiple versions of the Venetian act expose our nostalgia for, and submission to, a composer's voice as a strategy for broadcasting the voices and tastes of the present.[44] It is for this reason that the Venetian act, like Hoffmann as he narrates the opera's three tales, seems destined to compulsive, imperfect retelling, for the musical numbers can only be patched together in a semblance of organic design and made to cohere by the assembler's will—first that of Offenbach, and then of the generations who have tried to finish the work for him.

But if the Venetian act's restless and permanently incomplete condition resembles that of Giulietta's hapless victims, the work also resembles her magic mirror in its ability to capture the reflections of those who have looked into it, and to record the image of their desire. The versions of the Venetian act preserve snapshots of Offenbach and his "serious opera" as different eras have wanted to see them: *fin-de-siècle* editors, for example, suppressed the operetta-style numbers and built an entire act on variations of the Barcarolle, while Oeser's edition captures the mid-twentieth-century rejection of that salon aesthetic as kitsch. Oeser's edition reflects the elevation of Offenbach's German Romantic aspirations in its thickened orchestral textures, materials borrowed from *Die Rhein-Nixen,* and expansion of through-composed scenes beyond any Offenbach precedent. Kaye's opéra-comique version might be seen as a reaction to and compensation for Oeser's too-German version, and in restoring the opera's parodistic aspects, it also speaks to a modernist embarrassment at Romanticism's perceived excesses. The Venetian act has always lacked an essential or authentic identity; like the "Woman" posited by Lacanian and post-Lacanian theorists, this Music "does not exist" save as the repetition of stylized acts. If this is disconcerting, it may also be useful for the way it undoes our nostalgia for fugitive and impossible originals. The Barcarole—seductive, irrational, mildly embarrassing, and always already from "elsewhere"—is this opera's siren song. Sounding outside of time and plot, it envoices not only Giulietta and a *fin-de-siècle* fantasy of Venetian decadence, but also opera as a genre, drawing each generation of editors, performers, and listeners into the labyrinth.

Notes

Introduction

1. Antonia de Almeida, letter to Michael Kaye (May 12, 1990). Quoted in Kaye, "'Hoffmann' after Offenbach," liner note for Jacques Offenbach, *Les Contes d'Hoffmann*, Staatskapelle Dresden, cond. Jeffrey Tate (Philips 422-374-2, 1992) 31.

2. Jean-Christophe Keck, "La Genèse et les légendes," 15–17.

3. J.J.A. Ancessy, incidental music for *Les Contes d'Hoffmann* (1851), F-PBn Vms 803.

4. Jacques Offenbach, *Revue et Gazette musicale de Paris* (July 20, 1856), repr. in *Le Ménestrel* (July 27, 1856). Translated in Alexander Faris, *Jacques Offenbach* (London: Faber and Faber, 1980).

5. *Les Contes d'Hoffmann*, piano-vocal score (Paris: Choudens, 1881), Act II, no. 8.

6. Petrus (pseud.), "Première représentations/Opéra-Comique. *Les Contes d'Hoffmann*," *La Petite république* (February 13, 1881): 3.

7. Hervé Lacombe, *Les Voies de l'opéra française* (Paris: Librairie Arthème Fayard, 1997).

8. Jacques Offenbach, "Duo du 3e Acte des *Contes d'Hoffmann*," MS draft piano-vocal score (May 29, 1877). F-Pn ms. 20649.

9. André Martinet, *Offenbach*, 284.

10. *I racconti di Hoffmann/Hoffmanns Erzählungen* (Paris: Choudens, 1881) includes Guiraud's recitatives and his reconstruction of the Venetian act, and follows his order of the four acts and epilogue. A vocal part-book based on the Opéra-Comique production in the 1882 season follows this same configuration, with spoken dialogue replacing Guiraud's recitatives; see Offenbach, *Les Contes d'Hoffmann: Partition Chants et Paroles* (Paris: Choudens, 1882).

11. Martinet, *Offenbach*, 284.

12. Jacques Offenbach, *Hoffmanns Erzählungen/Les Contes d'Hoffmann, phantastische Oper in fünf Akten*, new source-critical edition by Fritz Oeser (Alkor: Edition-Kassel, 1977).

13. Offenbach, *Les Contes d'Hoffmann*, ed. Michael Kaye (Mainz: B. Schott's Sons, 1988).

14. Eduard Hanslick, "*Hoffmanns Erzählungen:* Phantastische Oper von Offenbach: Erste Aufführung in Wien 1881," in *Hoffmanns Erzählungen: Texte, Materialien, Kommentare*, ed. Attila Csampai and Dietmar Holland, 245.

15. The most useful source-book is *Jacques Offenbachs Hoffmanns Erzählungen: Konzeption, Rezeption, Dokumentation*, ed. Gabriele Brandstetter. Robert Didion's discussion of the sources remains the most exhaustive and useful account of the opera's textual history: see Didion, "A la recherche des *Contes* perdus: Zur Quellenproblematik von Offenbachs Oper," in Brandstetter, *Jacques Offenbachs*

Hoffmanns Erzählungen, 131–292. Didion did not have access to the manuscripts edited by Michael Kaye (Friedrich R. Koch Collection, No. 345, NY-Pm.), now published in Kaye's critical edition (Mainz: B. Schott's Sons, 1988). Jean-Christophe Keck provides the most up-to-date summary of the published editions, and his variorum edition of the libretto compiles variant texts and musical settings most lucidly: see J.-C. Keck, "Le Genèse et les légendes," in *L'Avant-Scène Opéra* 25, 2nd ed. (October 1993): 8–17; and Keck, "Commentaire littéraire et musical," in ibid., 27–124.

The first critical edition was *Hoffmanns Erzählungen/Les Contes d'Hoffmann: Quellenkritische Neuausgabe,* ed. Fritz Oeser (Alkor: Edition Kassel, 1976). The condition of the opera before Oeser's intervention is documented by Anna Eisenberg in *Jacques Offenbachs Hoffmanns Erzählungen* (Ph.D. diss., Cologne, 1973); and by Jean-Louis Dutronc in *"Les Contes d'Hoffmann:* une genèse laborieuse, une partition contestée," *L'Avant-Scène Opéra* 25, 1st ed., 13–17.

16. Judith Butler, *Gender Trouble: Feminism and the Subversion of Identity,* and "Imitation and Gender Insubordination," in *Inside/Out: Lesbian Theories, Gay Theories,* ed. Diana Fuss; Eve Kosofsky Sedgwick, "Queer and Now," in *Tendencies* (Durham, NC: Duke University Press: 1993), 1–20.

Chapter One
Telling the *Tales*

1. Théophile Gautier, *Histoire de l'art dramatique en France depuis vingt-cinq ans,* Vol. 6, 232–35.

2. Eduard Hanslick, *"Hoffmanns Erzählungen,* Phantastische Oper von Offenbach: Erste Aufführung in Wien 1881," in *Hoffmanns Erzählungen: Texte, Materialien, Kommentare,* ed. Attila Csampai and Dietmar Holland (Hamburg: Rowohlt Taschenbuch, 1984), 242.

3. E.T.A. Hoffmann, "Don Giovanni, A Strange Episode in the Life of a Music Fanatic," in Heinrich Von Kleist, Ludwig Tieck, and E.T.A. Hoffmann, *Six German Romantic Tales,* trans. Ronald Taylor, 108. [Hereafter cited in text as "Don Giovanni."]

4. Théophile Gautier, "Étude sur les Contes Fantastiques d'Hoffmann," in *Hoffmann: Contes Fantastiques,* trans. X. Marmier (Paris, 1843).

5. Jules Barbier and Michel Carré, *Les Contes d'Hoffmann,* Act V (Paris, 1851), 80.

6. Ulrich Schönherr provides a fascinating reading of another tripled soprano character, Bettina/Zulema/Julia in "The Sanctus," as a vehicle for working out aesthetic problems, in "Social Differentiation and Romantic Art: E.T.A. Hoffmann's 'The Sanctus' and the Problem of Aesthetic Positioning in Modernity," *New German Critique* 66 (fall 1995): 3–16.

7. Deborah Harter, *Bodies in Pieces: Fantastic Narrative and the Poetics of the Fragment* (Stanford, CA: Stanford University Press, 1996).

8. Of the Muse and her ultimate claiming of Hoffmann's soul, David Rissin remarks that the maternal consoler is in reality a "possessive and castrating character." See Rissin, *Offenbach, ou le Rire en Musique* (Paris: Fayard, 1980), 331.

9. E. F. Bleiler, Introduction to *The Best Tales of Hoffmann,* ed. Bleiler, xxii. See also Todd Kontje, "Biography in Triplicate: E.T.A. Hoffmann's 'Die Abenteuer der

Sylvester-nacht,'" *The German Quarterly* 58, no. 3 (summer 1985): 348-60.

10. E.T.A. Hoffmann, "Opuscules rélatifs a la musique: *Kreisleriana,* Sur la musique instrumentale de Beethoven," in *Revue Musicale de Paris* 9 (December 4, 1830): 97.

11. See Sir Walter Scott, "Sur Hoffmann et les compositions fantastiques," Introduction to Hoffmann, *Œuvres complètes,* 18 vols., trans. Loève-Weimars (Paris: Renduel, 1830-32), and F. J. Fétis, "Hoffmann," *Revue et Gazette Musicale de Paris* 6, no. 41 (1839): 324-27.

12. Jules Janin, "Hoffmann, conte fantastique" (part 1), *Gazette Musicale de Paris* 4, no. 13 (March 30, 1834): 100.

13. Jules Janin, "Hoffmann, conte fantastique" (part 2), *Gazette Musicale de Paris* 4, no. 14 (April 6, 1834): 110.

14. In the Ballad's final strophe, heard in the epilogue, the distance between these two voices collapses altogether, for it becomes clear that Hoffmann himself is a "Kleinzach" pining after Stella, his "fair Phyrne."

15. Peter Brooks, *Reading for the Plot: Design and Intention in Narrative* (Cambridge, MA: Harvard University Press, 1984), 114.

16. F. J. Fétis, "Hoffmann," 327.

17. H. L., "Audition des *Contes d'Hoffmann* d'Offenbach," *Revue et Gazette Musicale de Paris* 46, no. 21 (May 25, 1879): 173.

18. Jules Barbier, *Les Contes d'Hoffmann* (Livret de la censure, 1881). Reproduced in Brandstetter, ed., *Jacques Offenbachs Hoffmanns Erzählungen,* 464.

19. Each of the opera's source tales uses the sinister double differently. In "The Sand-Man," Coppélius represents the dark side of Nathanael's father, whose secretiveness, cabalistic experiments, irresponsibility, and neglect are attributed to the outsider, allowing Nathanael to preserve the memory of a good dead father: kind, loving, and gentle. Another alternative is to mingle good/bad, protective/destructive, and kind/cruel traits in one grotesque figure, as in "Rat Krespel."

20. Offenbach, *Les Contes d'Hoffmann,* act 1, no. 2 (Lindorf's *couplets,* "Dans les rôles d'amoureux langoureux.")

21. Slavoj Žižek theorizes perverted paternal authority in *Looking Awry: An Introduction to Jacques Lacan Through Popular Culture* (Cambridge, MA: MIT Press, 1992), 23-26, 146-51. He discussed Alberich and Titurel as operatic examples of the "obscene" and "undead" father in "The Wound Is Healed Only by the Spear That Smote You," in *Tarrying with the Negative* (Durham, NC: Duke University Press, 1993), 165-99.

22. Barbier, *Les Contes d'Hoffmann* (Livret de la censure, 1881), act 3, no. 29. Reproduced in Brandstetter, ed., *Jacques Offenbachs Hoffmanns Erzählungen,* 464.

23. Offenbach's ineffectual and impotent "Hoffmann" anticipates twentieth-century revisions of Don Giovanni's character: few if any critics and directors today would accept E.T.A. Hoffmann's interpretation of the character as an omnipotent "fallen angel," and some read him instead as an unsuccessful sexual compulsive, a victim of his unresolved Oedipus complex. See *Don Giovanni: Myths of Seduction and Betrayal,* ed. Jonathan Miller (New York: W. W. Norton, 1990).

24. Gautier, "Étude d'Hoffmann," 8.

25. Edward T. Cone, "The World of Opera and Its Inhabitants," in *Music: A View from Delft,* 125-38.

26. On narrative ballads as conveyors of omens and coded messages, see Carolyn Abbate, "Erik's Dream and Tannhäuser's Journey," in *Reading Opera,* ed. Roger Parker and Arthur Groos (Princeton: Princeton University Press, 1991), 129–67.

27. See David Charlton, "Hoffmann as a Writer on Music," in *E.T.A. Hoffmann's Musical Writings,* ed. Charlton, 1–20. See also Klaus-Dieter Dobat, *Musik als romantische Illusion: Eine Untersuchung zur Bedeutung der Musikvorstellung E.T.A. Hoffmanns für seine literarisches Werk;* and Helmut Gobel, James McGlathery, and Ellen Gerdeman-Klein, "E.T.A. Hoffmann's Language about Music," in *Music and German Culture: Their Relationship Since the Middle Ages,* ed. James McGlathery (Columbia, SC: Camden House, 1992), 143–53.

28. Hoffmann, "Rat Krespel," in *The Best Tales of Hoffmann,* ed. E. F. Bleiler, 224, 232, 235; Dumas, *La Femme au collier de velours* (Paris, 1850), 32.

29. Hoffmann, "Rat Krespel," 220.

30. Hoffmann, "A New Year's Eve Adventure," in *The Best Tales of Hoffmann,* ed. Bleiler, 115.

31. J.J.A. Ancessy, Musique de scène for *Les Contes d'Hoffmann* (1851), no. 14, F-PBn Vmd MS 803.

32. Hoffmann, "The Sand-Man," in *The Best Tales of Hoffmann,* ed. Bleiler, 183–14.

33. Sigmund Freud, "The 'Uncanny,'" in *The Standard Edition of the Complete Psychological Works of Sigmund Freud,* ed. and trans. James Strachey (London: Hogarth Press, 1955), Vol. 17. See also Tobin Siebers, "'Whose Hideous Voice Is This?': The Reading Unconscious in Freud and Hoffmann," *New Orleans Review* 15, no. 3 (fall 1988): 80–87.

34. Hoffmann, "Rat Krespel," 235.

Chapter Two
Mesmerizing Voices: Music, Medicine, and the Invention of Dr. Miracle

1. Gautier, *Histoire de l'art dramatique en France depuis vingt-cinq ans,* Vol. 6, 232–35.

2. E.T.A. Hoffmann, "Rat Krespel," trans. J. T. Bealby, in *Best Tales of Hoffmann,* ed. Bleiler. In-text citations will refer to this edition.

3. Gabriele Brandstetter discusses Krespel's obsession with Antonia and violins in "Die Stimme und das Instrument, Mesmerismus als Poetik in E.T.A. Hoffmanns 'Rat Krespel,'" in *Jacques Offenbachs Hoffmanns Erzählungen,* 15–38; see also Brigitte Prutti, "Kunstgeheimnis und Interpretation in E.T.A. Hoffmanns Erzählung 'Rat Krespel,'" *Seminar: A Journal of Germanic Studies* 28, no. 1 (February 1992): 33–45.

4. Hoffmann, "Rat Krespel," 222.

5. Ibid., 234.

6. E.T.A. Hoffmann, "Les Aventures de la Nuit de la Saint-Sylvestre," in *Hoffmann: Contes fantastiques,* trans. Henri Egmont (Paris, 1836).

7. Jules Barbier and Michel Carré, *Le Docteur Miracle* (Paris, 1857).

8. Hoffmann, "A New Year's Eve Adventure," in *Best Tales of Hoffmann,* ed. Bleiler, 119.

9. Hoffmann, "Rat Krespel," 222. Loève-Weimars's French translation of 1832 renders this image as "il me sembla que je n'étais que le magnétiser qui excite le somnambule" (repr. Paris: GF-Flammarion, 1980), 225.

10. See Maria Tatar, *Spellbound: Studies on Mesmerism and Literature*, and Götz Müller, "Modelle der Literarisierung des Mesmerismus," in *Franz Anton Mesmer und der Mesmerismus: Wissenschaft, Scharlatanerie, Poesie*, ed. Gereon Wolters, Konstanzer Bibliotek, vol. 12. (Konstanz, 1988), 73-76.

11. Jules Barbier and Michel Carré, *Les Contes d'Hoffmann*, Act IV, scene 4 (Paris, 1851), 64.

12. J.F.P. Deleuze, *Instruction pratique sur le magnétisme*, trans. and ed. Thomas C. Hartshorn as *Practical Instruction in Animal Magnetism; Le petit physicien* also recommends the use of jewels.

13. Dumas, *La Femme*, 169.

14. Ibid., 145.

15. On the demonic image of the "Black Hunter," see Egon Voss, " 'L'alouette ou la femme . . . l'une y laisse la vie, et l'autre y perd son âme'.: Zur Bedeutung von Dapertuttos es-Moll-Chanson," in Brandstetter, *Jacques Offenbachs Hoffmanns Erzählungen*, 317-27.

16. *L'Auxiliaire Breton*, January 1841, cited in Charles LaFontaine, *L'Art de magnétiser* (Paris, 1847), 96.

17. Elaine Showalter, "Feminism and Hysteria: The Daughter's Disease" in *The Female Malady*, 145-66. I should emphasize that the majority of feminist theory on hysteria appears in critiques of Freud; the "pre-history" of psychoanalysis has attracted relatively little attention, although Janet Beizer's *Ventriloquized Bodies*, and Elisabeth Bronfen's *The Knotted Subject: Hysteria and Its Discontents*, on hysteria in the Salpêtrière (as documented in Georges Didi-Huberman, *L'Invention de l'hystérie*) suggest the rich potential of this area of inquiry. Peter Brooks's *The Melodramatic Imagination* (Cambridge, MA: Harvard University Press, 1976, rev. 1990) also proposes intersections between melodrama and hysteric "theater." I will return to Charcot, Freud, and the legibility of the hysteric body in Chapter 3.

18. Her blindness was also most likely a hysterical effect, since doctors could not find an organic cause for it and it did respond to Mesmer's treatment. The story of the von Paradis case is central to every biography or discussion of Mesmer, beginning with the doctor's own *Collected Writings*. Sympathetic modern biographical accounts all tell basically the same story; see for example R. B. Ince, *Franz Anton Mesmer, His Life and Teaching*, and Donald Walmsley, *Anton Mesmer* (London: Hale, 1967).

19. Benjamin Franklin, *Report of Dr. Benjamin Franklin, and other commissioners, charged by the King of France with the examination of animal magnetism, as now practised at Paris*, 28.

20. William Stone, an American observer, noted that "as a general rule, the female system is more susceptible of [magnetism's] mysterious influence than the male." Stone, *Letter to Doctor A. Brigham on Animal Magnetism: being an account of a remarkable interview between the author and Miss Loraina Brackett while in a state of somnambulism*, 63.

21. *Journal de Toulouse* (September 21, 1846), in Charles LaFontaine, *L'Art de magnétiser*, 300.

22. LaFontaine, *L'Art de magnétiser,* 6.

23. *Thought Reader* (London, 1885).

24. Ince, *Franz Anton Mesmer,* 30.

25. "[T]out les deux jours des Musiciens jouent dans l'anti-chambre des airs propres à exiter la gaité chez les malades." Photo and caption are reproduced in Robert Darnton, *Mesmerism and the End of the Enlightenment in France.*

26. Benjamin Franklin, *France. Commission chargé de l'examen du magnétisme animal,* 23.

27. Ibid., 24.

28. LaFontaine, *L'Art de magnétiser,* 300.

29. Ibid., 137.

30. Ibid., 51.

31. Ibid.

32. Ibid.

33. Barbier and Carré, *Les Contes d'Hoffmann,* Act III, scene 13, pp. 54–55.

34. J.J.A. Ancessy, Incidental Music for *Les Contes d'Hoffmann* (1851), no. 28.

35. Ibid., measures 74–82. The words "chanter encore et puis mourir" appear only in the vocal part; the published text has "un seul moment de bonheur et mourir." Barbier and Carré, *Les Contes d'Hoffmann* (1851), Act III, scene 13, p. 57.

36. Ancessy used measures 1–40 and 69–120 of Schubert's song. He transposed it down from D minor to B minor and orchestrated the piano accompaniment; bass, cello, viola, and violin play the harmonies, while a solo violin plays the "spinning" figure.

37. Barbier and Carré, *Les Contes d'Hoffmann* (1851), Act III, scene 13, p. 57.

38. I borrow Carolyn Abbate's very useful distinction between music that functions as a singing character's "unconscious" and external music that is audible to the character as she sings. See Abbate, *Unsung Voices: Opera and Musical Narrative in the Nineteenth Century.*

39. Review of *Le Violon du Diable, Revue et Gazette Musicale* (January 21, 1849). The prominence of violins in French *Hoffmannisme* was created and reinforced by numerous translations of "Rat Krespel" as "Le Violon du Cremone" and of another violin story, "Der Baron von B—" (1819). This story first appeared in French as "L'Archet de Baron von B—" in Hoffmann, "Opuscules rélatifs a la musique," *Revue Musicale de Paris* 9 (November 13, 1830): 1–12. Loève-Weimars included it in his translation of Hoffmann's *Œuvres complètes* as "La Leçon du Violon."

40. The music by Cesare Pugni has not been preserved, although several *morceaux* were published (not including the "magnetic" scene). The ballet played at the Opéra from January 19 to April 2, 1849.

41. Saint-Léon, *Le Violon du Diable,* 4.

42. William Pinchbeck, *The Expositor, or Many Mysteries Unravelled,* 29.

43. Ibid.

44. Offenbach, *Les Contes d'Hoffmann, Act IV* [orig. numbered act 3, no. 4.] Partial autograph, June 10, 1880. F-Po Res 1055.

45. Stone, "Letter," 35.

46. *Journal de Toulouse,* September 21, 1846, cited in LaFontaine, *L'Art de magnétiser,* 300.

47. Ibid., 243.

48. Ibid., 300.

49. Stone, "Letter," 37.

50. "Vois sous l'archet frémissant" is presumed to have been cut early in the revision of the opera for the opéra-comique because Mlle. Ugalde, the first Nicklausse, couldn't sing it. Fritz Oeser orchestrated Offenbach's piano-vocal version and included it in his edition as Act III, number 13 (Alkor: Edition-Kassel, 1978).

51. In the partial-autograph manuscript of this trio, the vocal parts, piano accompaniment, and orchestral solos in this middle section are in Offenbach's hand; therefore it is not incorrect to attribute the "instrumentalization" of Antonia in this scene to Offenbach rather than to Ernest Guiraud, who completed the orchestration. See Offenbach, *Les Contes d'Hoffmann Act IV* [orig. Act III, no. 4], pp 75-105, F-Po Res. 1055.

52. *Vocal and Optical Deceptions.*

53. Jean-Eugène Robert-Houdin, *Confidences d'un prestidigitateur,* in *King of the Conjurers, Memoirs of Robert-Houdin,* trans. Lascelles Wraxall, ed. Milbourne Christopher, 127. Robert-Houdin also left two other memoirs, *Album de soirées fantastiques* (Paris, 1851) and *Confidences et révélations* (Paris, 1868).

54. Robert-Houdin, *Confidences,* 127.

55. Ibid.

56. Ibid., 45.

57. See for example John Scheidler, *Art of Conjuring Simplified; Zamara: Explanatory Remarks;* Signor T. Somerfeld, *Modern Magic and Mystery Made Easy;* Howe and Howe, *World's Greatest Mind-readers* (Chicago: Wm. Franks, 1912); David J. Lustig ("La Vellma"), *Vaudeville Mind Reading and Kindred Phenomena.*

58. Nina Auerbach explores late-Victorian literary fantasies about young women's repressed desire making them vulnerable to both monsters and mesmerizers in "Magi and Maidens: The Romance of the Victorian Freud," *Critical Inquiry* 8, no. 2 (1981): 281-300, and in *Woman and the Demon: The Life of a Victorian Myth* (Cambridge, MA: Harvard University Press, 1982). Her reading of Stoker's *Dracula* and duMaurier's *Trilby* (two very late examples of the mesmerist/vampire tradition) concludes that the power of the entranced and apparently passive woman exceeds that of the "monster."

Chapter Three
Song as Symptom: Antonia, Olympia, and the Prima Donna Mother

1. Catherine Clément, *Opera, or, The Undoing of Women,* trans. Betsy Wing, 32–33, 78–82; Susan McClary, "Excess and Frame: The Musical Representation of Madwomen," in *Feminine Endings,* 80–111.

2. For a summary of French medical discourse on hysteria, see the Introduction and first two chapters of Janet Beizer's *Ventriloquized Bodies: Narratives of Hysteria in Nineteenth-Century France,* 1–54. On the production and dissemination of images of hysteria in this period, see Georges Didi-Huberman, *L'Invention de l'hystérie: Charcot et l'iconographie photographique de la Salpêtrière.*

The essays in *In Dora's Case: Freud—Hysteria—Feminism,* 2nd ed., ed. Charles Bernheimer and Claire Kahane have shaped my reading of the Antonia act, particularly the discussions of the mother-daughter relation in Maria Ramas, "Freud's

Dora, Dora's Hysteria" (149–80), Toril Moi, "Representation of Patriarchy: Sexuality and Epistemology in Freud's Dora" (181–99); and "Questioning the Unconscious: The Dora Archive" by Jerre Collins, J. Ray Green, Mary Lydon, Mark Sachner, and Eleanor Honig Skoller (243–53). On hysteria as a mode of feminist protest, see Elaine Showalter, *The Female Malady*, 145–66.

3. E.T.A. Hoffmann, "Rat Krespel," trans. J. T. Bealby, in *The Best Tales of Hoffmann*, ed. E. F. Bleiler, 229–30.

4. Hoffmann, "The Poet and the Composer," trans. Martyn Clarke, in *E.T.A. Hoffmann's Musical Writings*, ed. David Charlton, 190.

5. Charlton, "Introduction to *Kreisleriana*," in *E.T.A. Hoffmann's Musical Writings*, 37.

6. Hoffmann, "Johannes Kreisler's Certificate of Apprenticeship," in Charlton, ed., *E.T.A. Hoffmann's Musical Writings*, 162.

7. Ibid., 161.

8. Hoffmann, "Rat Krespel," in *Best Tales*, ed. Bleiler, 232.

9. Klaus Hortschansky cites this text from the unpublished Hamburg score of *Die Rhein-nixen* in "Offenbach's 'Grosse romantische Oper,'" in *Jacques Offenbach: Komponist und Weltburger*, ed. Winfried Kirsch and Ronny Dietrich (Mainz, 1985) 229–230. Anton Henseler discusses the opera in some detail in *Jakob Offenbach* (Berlin, 1930) 354–368.

10. Hoffmann, "Don Juan," 64.

11. Barbier and Carré, *Les Contes d'Hoffmann* (1851), Act III, scene 8, p. 48.

12. Ibid., p. 56.

13. Offenbach, *Les Contes d'Hoffmann*, piano-vocal score (Paris: Choudens, 1907), Act IV, no. 20.

14. Ibid.

15. Eduard Hanslick, "Hoffmanns Erzählungen, Phantastische Oper von Offenbach: Erste Aufführung in Wien 1881," in *Hoffmanns Erzählungen: Texte, Materialien, Kommentare*, ed. Attila Csampai and Dietmar Holland, 241.

16. Diana Fuss's discussion of hysteria as a discourse of repressed and *contagious* female desire, in *Identification Papers*, 107–40, is also germane to my reading of the relation between Antonia, her mother, and music.

17. Michel Poizat, *The Angel's Cry: Beyond the Pleasure Principle in Opera*, trans. Arthur Denner.

18. Hoffmann, "The Sand-Man," in *Best Tales of Hoffmann*, 205.

19. Alexander Faris, *Jacques Offenbach*, 205.

20. J.J.A. Ancessy, incidental music for *Les Contes d'Hoffmann* (1851), no. 15. F-PBn Vms 803.

21. Barbier and Carré, *Les Contes d'Hoffmann* (1851), Act I, scene 7, p. 29.

22. In this respect, the Antonia act is less an adaptation of "Rat Krespel" than it is a gender-reversed version of Hoffmann's novella *Der Goldene Topf*, in which a young male artist, the Student Anselmus, must choose between the fantastical world represented by an eccentric old man and the conventional bourgeois life represented by his fiancée. See "The Golden Flower Pot," trans. Thomas Carlyle, in *Best Tales of Hoffmann*, 1–70.

23. See Beizer, *Ventriloquized Bodies*, 43.

24. Théophile Gautier, "La Cafetière," in *Contes fantastiques*, ed. Hervé Alvado,

21. On the gender anxieties attendant on Romantic concepts of genius, see Christine Battersby, *Gender and Genius: Towards a Feminist Aesthetics,* 103–23 and 134–45.

25. Gautier, "Onuphrius, ou les vexations fantastiques d'un admirateur d'Hoffmann," in *Contes fantastiques,* 59. "La Morte Amoureuse" is translated as "The Dead in Love" in *Demons of the Night,* trans. and ed. Joan C. Kessler (Chicago: University of Chicago Press, 1995), 91–147.

26. A celebration of the opera-lover's hysteric pleasure may be found in Wayne Koestenbaum's *The Queen's Throat: Opera, Homosexuality, and the Mystery of Desire.* See my "Peering into *The Queen's Throat,*" *Cambridge Opera Journal* 5, no. 3 (November 1993): 265–75.

27. See Barbier, "Faksimile der Akte IV und V des Pariser Zensurlibretto vom Januar 1881 der *Contes d'Hoffmann,*" in Brandstetter, *Jacques Offenbachs Hoffmanns Erzählungen,* 462-63. Guiraud's completion of the Epilogue, found in *Les Contes d'Hoffmann,* Act IV, tableau 2 (F-Po Rés. 1055) also included a silent entrance and exit for Stella.

28. Barbier, *Les Contes d'Hoffmann,* ed. and rev. Fritz Oeser, in *Hoffmanns Erzählungen: Texte, Materialien, Kommentare,* 186–93.

29. Clément, *Opera, or, The Undoing of Women,* 31.

30. Edward T. Cone, "The World of Opera and Its Inhabitants," in *Music: A View from Delft,* 127.

31. Stella did sing in the Opéra-Comique premiere; see Offenbach, *Les Contes d'Hoffmann,* 1st ed. (Paris: Choudens, 1881), Act IV, no. 21. Having cut the Venetian act, Carvalho gave the *Duo de Reflet,* with new text, to Hoffmann and Stella. This decision had no basis in Barbier's play, the libretto, or Offenbach's manuscripts, and Guiraud's restoration of the Venetian act in 1882 returned the duet to its original place.

Chapter Four
Offenbach, for Posterity

1. "Premières Représentations/Opéra Comique," Auguste Vitu, *Le Figaro* (11 February 1881): 3.

2. Eduard Hanslick, "*Hoffmanns Erzählungen,* Phantastische Oper von Offenbach: Erste Aufführrung in Wien 1881," in *Hoffmanns Erzählungen: Texte, Materialien, Kommentare,* 243.

3. Siegfried Kracauer, *Jacques Offenbach und das Paris seiner Zeit* (1937).

4. H. L., "Audition de *Contes d'Hoffmann* d'Offenbach," *Revue et Gazette musicale de Paris* 46, no. 21 (May 25, 1879): 173.

5. Ibid., 173.

6. Frits Noske, *French Song From Berlioz to Duparc: The Origin and Development of the Mélodie,* 2nd edition, trans. Rita Benton.

7. The critic exaggerated, however, in declaring it an "absolute departure," for Offenbach had used the same style for similar affective moments in the earlier opéra-comiques *Fantasio* (1872) and *Le Voyage dans la lune* (1875), in which farce was either absent altogether or secondary to a melancholy-sentimental tone. While neither of these works precisely failed, neither one gained a place in the repertoire

or altered popular perceptions of its composer as a *farceur*. See for example Elspeth's Romance, "Pourquoi ne puis-je voir," in *Fantasio*, Act I, no. 3; and Caprice's Romance, "O reine de la nuit," in *Le Voyage dans la lune*, Act I. The assessment of Antonia's Romance as an entirely new mode for Offenbach reveals less about *Les Contes d'Hoffmann*'s novelty than about how little an impression the composer's earlier attempts at sincerity had made. For a brief discussion of Offenbach's virtually unknown opéra-comiques, see Laurent Fraison, "Exception? Non: continuité!," *L'Avant-Scène Opéra* 25 (October 1993): 126–30.

8. "Musique/Opéra-Comique: *Les Contes d'Hoffmann*," Simon Boubée, *La Gazette de France* (February 14, 1881): 2.

9. Offenbach, cited in Schneider, *Les Maîtres de l'opérette française: Offenbach*, 245. Pages from this edition are cited in the text.

10. Fabrizio Della Seta, *Italia e Francia nell'Ottocento*, vol. 9 of *Storia della musica* (Turin: Edizioni di Torino, 1993), 265.

11. Jacques Herman, "Feuilleton du Constitutionnel, 15 *Février.*/Musique / *Les Contes d'Hoffmann*," *Le Constitutionnel* (February 15, 1881): 2.

12. Vitu, *Le Figaro* (February 11, 1881): 3.

13. Philbert Joslé, "Gazette de la Musique/Théâtre de l'Opéra-Comique," *L'Événement* (February 13, 1881): 3.

14. Léon Kerst, "Premières Représentations. Opéra-Comique. *Les Contes d'Hoffmann*," *La Presse* (February 12, 1881): 2–3.

15. Gustave Chouquet, "Wagner et Offenbach," *L'Art musicale* 12, no. 9 (February 27, 1873): 66. Excerpted from Chouquet, *L'Histoire de la musique dramatique en France depuis ses origines jusqu'à nos jours* (Paris, 1873).

16. Ibid., 66. The "Uhlans" were Prussian cavalrymen armed with lances.

17. Ironically, later critics would embrace this reading, making Offenbach into a subtle moralist whose satires passed judgment on that very weakness and decadence. See Anton Henseler, *Jakob Offenbach*, and Siegfried Kracauer, *Offenbach und das Paris der seiner Zeit* (Amsterdam, 1937).

18. M. E., review of *Le Carnaval des Revues* in *La France Musicale* 24, no. 8 (February 19, 1860): 90.

19. Herman, *Le Constitutionnel* (February 15, 1881): 2.

20. Un Monsieur de l'Orchestre, "La Soirée Théâtrale: *Les Contes d'Hoffmann*," *Le Figaro* (February 11, 1881): 3.

21. Oscar Comettant, "Revue Musicale/Opéra-Comique: *Les Contes d'Hoffmann*," *Le Siècle* (February 14, 1881): 2.

22. Ibid., 2.

23. Richard Wagner, *Opera and Drama*, in *Richard Wagner's Prose Works*, vol. 2, trans. W. A. Ellis, 188.

24. Wagner, *Opera and Drama*, 163.

25. Ibid., 189.

26. Ibid.

27. Émile Zola, *Nana*, trans. with an introduction by Douglas Parmée, 13–14.

28. Ibid., 190. Wagner's remark is cited in *Jacques Offenbach: Schauplätze eines Musiker*, Ausstellung des Historischen Archives der Stadt Köln (Bad Ems, June 8–17, 1980): 169.

29. Zola, *Nana*, 415.

30. Ibid.

31. Léon de Froidmont, "Musique/Opéra-Comique: *Les Contes d'Hoffmann*," *Le Voltaire* (February 12, 1881): 3.

32. Kerst, "Feuilleton de la Presse. *Les Contes d'Hoffmann*," *La Presse* (February 15, 1881): 3, 120.

33. This trio was cut before the 1881 premiere and has been restored in Oeser's and Kaye's critical editions. See Fritz Oeser, "Vorwort," in *Hoffmanns Erzählungen/Les Contes d'Hoffmann*, ed. Oeser, i–xiii.

34. E. Durranc, "Feuilleton de la 'Justice' du 15 Février. Courrier dramatique. Opéra-Comique. *Les Contes d'Hoffmann*," *La Justice* (February 15, 1881): 1.

35. Offenbach, *Les Contes d'Hoffmann* Act III [*sic*], no. 2, pp. 12–16. MS score, June 26, 1880. F-Po Rés 1055. This *couplets* is Act IV, no. 27 in the traditional version (Choudens, 1907) and Act III, no. 27 in the critical edition by Michael Kaye (Mainz: Schott, 1988).

36. Chouquet, "Wagner et Offenbach," 66.

37. Camille Saint-Saëns, *Harmonie et mélodie*, 257–66. The claim that Offenbach's German origins made him incompetent to set French verse, and that he caused the decline of French prosody, persists in Frits Noske's *French Song*.

38. Jacques Offenbach, cited in Schneider, *Les Maîtres de l'opérette française: Offenbach*, 247.

39. Ibid.

40. "La Soirée Théâtrale," *Le Figaro*, 3.

Chapter Five
Reflections on the Venetian Act

1. While it is difficult to see the gentle Antonia as "degenerate," her abandonment of her promise to be Hoffmann's silent inspiration, and her subsequent yielding to the pleasure of music, constitute the fall into "the crime of those French and Italian sisters" that Wagner predicted for his German "prude." Wagner, *Opera and Drama*, 189.

2. Offenbach, *Les Contes d'Hoffmann* (Choudens, 1907), Act IV, scene 2, no. 27.

3. See for example Alice A. Kuzniar, "'Spurlos. . .verschwunden': Peter Schlemiel und sein Schatten als der verschobene Signifikant," *Aurora: Jahrbuch der Eichendorff Gesellschaft*, no. 45 (1985): 189–204. Oddly, only one version connects the lack of a reflection with traditional vampire lore, and that only in passing: in the finale of Barbier's 1881 libretto, Hoffmann curses Giulietta as a "Démon! Vampire!"

4. Barbier and Carré, *Les Contes d'Hoffmann*, Act IV, p. 65. Throughout this chapter the French spelling "Schlemil" designates Giulietta's lover in the play and libretto by Barbier, and the German "Schlemiel" designates the protagonist of Adelbert von Chamisso's in *Peter Schlemiels wundersame Geschichte*.

5. E.T.A. Hoffmann, "A New Year's Eve Adventure," trans. Alfred Packer, in *The Best Tales of Hoffmann*, ed. Bleiler, 104–29. Subsequent references are to this edition.

6. Adelbert von Chamisso, *Peter Schlemiel: The Man Who Sold His Shadow*, trans. with an introduction by Peter Wortsman. Subsequent references are to this edition.

7. von Chamisso, cited by Peter Wortsman in "The Displaced Person's Guide to Nowhere," introduction to *Peter Schlemiel*, xiv.

8. Roland Barthes, *S/Z*, trans. Richard Miller, 195.

9. Sigmund Freud, *Dora: An Analysis of a Case of Hysteria*, ed. and trans. Philip Rieff, 65. Jane Gallop remarks of this passage, "At the very moment [Freud] defines nonprurient language as direct and noneuphemistic, he takes a French detour into a figurative expression." See Gallop, "Keys to Dora," in *In Dora's Case: Freud—Hysteria—Feminism*, ed. Charles Bernheimer and Claire Kahane, 209.

10. E.T.A. Hoffmann, "Signor Formica," trans. J. T. Bealby, in *The Best Tales of Hoffmann*, ed. E. F. Bleiler, 325. The first French translation of this novella was *Salvator Rosa*, trans. and ed. Loève-Weimars in *Œuvres complètes d'Hoffmann*, Vol. 2 (Paris: Renduel, 1830).

11. Barbier and Carré, *Les Contes d'Hoffmann*, Act IV, scene 1, p. 63.

12. Friedrich Dürrenmatt, *The Visit*, trans. Patrick Bowles (New York: Grove Press, Inc., 1962).

13. See Sander Gilman, "Strauss and the Pervert," in *Reading Opera*, ed. Roger Parker and Arthur Groos (Princeton, NJ: Princeton University Press, 1991), especially pp. 316–24; and *Jewish Self-Hatred: Anti-Semitism and the Hidden Language of the Jews*.

14. On *charivari* as a cultural space for managing gender and family relations, see Natalie Zemon Davis, *Society and Culture in Early Modern France* (Stanford: Stanford University Press, 1975), and "Women on Top: Symbolic Sexual Inversion and Political Disorder in Early Modern Europe," in *The Reversible World: Sexual Inversion in Art and Society*, ed. Barbara A. Babcock (Ithaca, NY: Cornell University Press, 1978), 147–90.

15. von Chamisso's Peter Schlemiel is at least allowed to sublimate his loss: while remaining shadowless and exiled from human society, he acquires "seven-league boots" in which he travels the world and becomes a botanist of superhuman skill.

16. Oeser's libretto for the Venetian act is in *Hoffmanns Erzählungen: Texte, Materialien, Kommentare*, 145–81. For Barbier's 1881 version, see the facsimile of Acts IV and V in *Jacques Offenbachs Hoffmanns Erzählungen*, ed. Brandstetter, 456–59. Schott published a facsimile of Offenbach's setting of this finale in 1998.

17. The "Reflection Duet" was finished by May 18, 1879. "Tournez, miroir" was completed on July 19, 1880, according to a signed and dated skeleton score in the collection of François Cusset, Saint-Mandé. See the table of musical numbers and manuscript sources in Robert Didion's "A la recherche des *Contes* perdus. Zur Quellenproblematik von Offenbachs Oper," in *Jacques Offenbachs Hoffmanns Erzählungen*, ed. Brandstetter, 182.

18. Raoul Gunsbourg, *Cent ans de souvenirs: Ou presque*, 2.

19. Oeser describes the sources and editorial decisions that shaped his version of the Venetian act in his foreword to Jacques Offenbach, *Hoffmanns Erzählungen/Les Contes d'Hoffmann*, new source-critical edition by Fritz Oeser, xvii–xx.

20. "Tournez, miroir" appeared in the earliest score containing the Venetian act and in the *opéra-comique* version of 1882. See Offenbach, *Hoffmanns Erzählungen/I Racconti di Hoffmann*; and *Les Contes d'Hoffmann: Chants et Paroles*, Act III, no. 15.

21. Egon Voss, "'L'alouette ou la femme . . . l'une y laisse la vie, y l'autre perd son âme': Zur Bedeutung von Dapertuttos es-Moll-Chanson," in *Jacques Offenbachs Hoffmanns Erzählungen,* ed. Brandstetter, 325.

22. Offenbach, *Hoffmanns Erzählungen/Les Contes d'Hoffmann,* ed. Fritz Oeser, Act IV, no. 18–19, pp. 276–92.

23. Reception of Oeser's Venetian act has been decidedly mixed: Robert Didion goes so far as to declare it "eine verfälschende hybride Wucherung" [a falsified hybrid excrescence] in "A la recherche des *Contes* perdus," 244.

24. Heinzelmann reported his discovery of this libretto in the Archives Nationales de Paris, F 18 I 45 ("Enregistrement des avis, après examen, des ouvrages dramatiques") in "*Hoffmanns Erzählungen:* Eine Oper, ihre Autoren, ihre Bedeutungen," *Österreichische Musikzeitschrift* 42 (1987): 337–50. See also his "Offenbachs Hoffmann: Dokumente anstelle von Erzählungen," and the facsimile of Acts IV and V, in *Jacques Offenbachs Hoffmanns Erzählungen,* ed. Brandstetter, 421–64.

25. Offenbach, *Les Contes d'Hoffmann.* Musical MS (359 pgs). Frederick R. Koch Foundation Collection, no. 345, NY-Pm. The most concise and up-to-date comparison of editions is by Jean-Christophe Keck, "*Les Contes d'Hoffmann:* sept versions," in *L'Avant-Scène Opéra* 25 (October 1993): 19–23; see also his variorum edition of the libretto, "*Les Contes d'Hoffmann:* Commentaire littéraire et musical," ibid., 27–124. For a more exhaustive documentation that does not, however, include the sources edited by Michael Kaye, see Didion, "A la recherche des *Contes* perdus," 131–292.

26. E.T.A. Hoffmann, *Don Juan* (Stuttgart: Reclam, 1964), 61.

27. On Orientalist sirens, see Ralph Locke, "Constructing the Oriental 'Other': Saint-Saëns's *Samson et Dalila,*" in *Cambridge Opera Journal* 3 (1991): 261–302; and Susan McClary, *Georges Bizet: Carmen,* 56–58 and 87–89.

28. Barbier, "Faksimile der Akte IV und V des Pariser Zensurlibrettos vom Januar 1881 der *Contes d'Hoffmann,*" 449–51.

29. The full text of Giulietta's first verse, from the *livret de la censure,* is as follows: "L'amour lui dit: la belle / Vos yeux étaient fermés! / Puis, la touchant de l'aile: / Voyez le jour, aimez! / Voulez-vous dans la joie / Que votre âme se noie / Par des routes en fleurs? / Non! je veux la tristesse / D'une amère tendresse / Qui s'enivre de pleurs. / Ah! Voyez le jour! / Aimez! aimez! / Puis, la touchant de l'aile: / Voyez le jour, aimez!" See Barbier, "Faksimile," 451.

30. Barbier, *Les Contes,* Act II, no. 7.

31. At the risk of holding the prima donna responsible for "empty" virtuosity, I will observe that the coloratura passages were added to Giulietta's aria at the request of Adèle Isaac, who had also commissioned Olympia's Doll Song and presumably wanted a second show-stopper. See Keck, "*Les Contes d'Hoffmann:* Commentaire littéraire et musical," 105.

32. Hanslick, "Hoffmanns Erzählungen," 242.

33. Carl Dahlhaus, *Nineteenth-Century Music,* trans. J. Bradford Robinson, 283.

34. E.T.A. Hoffmann, "Don Juan," 61.

35. The earliest sketches date from 1876–1878: see the table of musical numbers and manuscript sources in Didion, "A la recherche des *Contes* perdus," 180–82.

36. The MSS in the Koch Collection, no. 345, NY-Pm include five "melodramas" that reprise the melodies of Hoffmann's *couplets* (MS 24); the "villain-motif" (MS 30); "Tournez, miroir" (MS 31); "Tournez, miroir" and "L'amour lui dit: La belle!" (MS 34); and the refrain of the *Duo de Reflet* (MS 36). Both the CD by Staatskapelle Dresden, cond. Jeffrey Tate (Philips 422 374-2, 1992) and the video recording by Opéra de Lyon, cond. Kent Nagano (Home Vision TAL 080, 1993), use these melodramas under spoken passages in the Venetian act.

37. The Venetian act suffers especially from proximity to the Antonia act. Even conductor Richard Bonynge, who declared severely in 1972, "I find no excuse for performing any more the unidiomatic version which has become known as Offenbach's *Tales of Hoffmann* but is full of music that he did not write," rationalized his decision to retain the incorrect order of the acts with the remark that the Antonia act "is of staggering musical inspiration and needs to be last." He also left Dapertutto's "Scintille, diamant" and Coppélius's "J'ai des yeux" where the 1907 arrangers placed them, as "the opera gains nothing by removing them and the ear is used to them." Bonynge, "This Recording," liner note to Jacques Offenbach, *Les Contes d'Hoffmann,* L'Orchestre de la Suisse Romande/Richard Bonynge (London 417 363-2, 1972): 19, 21.

38. Robert Pourvoyeur, "In search of the 'true' Tales," liner note to the recording by Orchestre Symphonique et Choeurs de l'Opéra National du Théâtre Royal de la Monnaie, Bruxelles, cond. Sylvain Cambreling (EMI CDS 7 49641 1/2/4, 1988).

39. Jean-Jacques Nattiez, *Music and Discourse: Toward a Semiology of Music,* trans. Carolyn Abbate, 16–37.

40. The theory of identity as imitative and performative is developed most cogently in Butler's "Imitation and Gender Insubordination," in *Inside/Out,* ed. Diana Fuss, 13–31.

41. Butler's somewhat opaque formulation of gender performativity in *Gender Trouble* came alive in Jennie Livingston's 1991 documentary film *Paris Is Burning,* an exploration of Harlem drag-ball culture and the quest for "Realness," defined as the most nearly perfect impersonation not only of glamorous women (old-style drag), but of visual icons of both genders. Butler in turn reads Livingston's film in "Gender Is Burning," in *Bodies that Matter* (New York: Routledge, 1994).

42. Suzanne Cusick, "Gender and the Cultural Work of a Classical Music Performance," *Repercussions* 3, no. 1 (spring 1994): 99.

43. It is worth noting that the hegemonic "original" in Cusick's discussion is not the music itself, but a prior rendition of it; it is unclear whether the thing-to-be-resisted in *Frauenliebe und -leben* resides in Schumann's score or in the "famous and oft-emulated performances" of Lotte Lehmann (Cusick, "Gender," 105).

44. Richard Taruskin has argued that nostalgia for authentic versions and performance styles is always a screen for what the present wants. See "Authenticity and Early Music" and "Resisting the Ninth" in *Text and Act: Essays on Music and Performance.*

Bibliography

Abbate, Carolyn. *Unsung Voices: Opera and Musical Narrative in the Nineteenth Century.* Princeton: Princeton University Press, 1991.

Auerbach, Nina. "Magi and Maidens: The Romance of the Victorian Freud." *Critical Inquiry* 8, no. 2 (1981): 281–300.

Babbington, Bruce and Peter Evans. "Matters of Life and Death in Powell and Pressburger's *The Tales of Hoffmann.*" In *A Night in at the Opera: Media Representations of Opera,* ed. Jeremy Tambling, 145–68. London: J. Libbey, 1994.

Barthes, Roland. *S/Z.* Translated by Richard Miller. New York: Farrar, Straus & Giroux, 1974.

Battersby, Christine. *Gender and Genius: Towards a Feminist Aesthetics.* Indianapolis. IN: Indiana University Press, 1990.

Beizer, Janet. *Ventriloquized Bodies: Narratives of Hysteria in Nineteenth-Century France.* Ithaca, NY: Cornell University Press, 1994.

Bernard, Paul. "Richard Wagner et la musique de l'avenir" (parts 1 and 2). *Le Ménestrel* 27, no. 9 (January 29, 1860): 65–66 and no. 10 (February 5, 1860): 78–79.

Bernheimer, Charles and Claire Kahane, eds. *In Dora's Case: Freud—Hysteria—Feminism.* 2nd ed. Gender and Culture series, ed. Carolyn G. Heilbrun and Nancy K. Miller. New York: Columbia University Press, 1990.

Bloch, Ernst. "Über Hoffmanns Erzählungen, Klemperers Kroll-Oper, Berlin 1930." In *Hoffmanns Erzählungen: Texte, Materialien, Kommentare,* ed. Attila Csampai and Dietmar Holland, 246–52. Rororo Opernbücher 7642. Reinbek bei Hamburg: Rowohlt Taschenbuch Verlag GmbH, 1984.

Brandstetter, Gabriele, ed. *Jacques Offenbachs Hoffmanns Erzählungen: Konzeption, Rezeption, Dokumentation.* Laaber: Laaber-Verlag, 1988.

Brewster, Sir David. *Letters on Natural Magic.* New York: J. & J. Harper, 1832.

Bronfen, Elisabeth. *Over Her Dead Body: Death, Femininity, and the Aesthetic.* New York and London: Routledge, 1992.

———. *The Knotted Subject: Hysteria and Its Discontents.* Princeton: Princeton University Press, 1998.

Brooks, Peter. *Reading for the Plot: Desire and Intention in Narrative.* Cambridge, MA, and London: Harvard University Press, 1984.

Buranelli, Vincent. *The Wizard from Vienna.* New York: Coward, McCann and Geoghegan, Inc., 1975.

Butler, Judith. *Gender Trouble: Feminism and the Subversion of Identity.* New York and London: Routledge, 1990.

———. "Imitation and Gender Insubordination." In *Inside/Out: Lesbian Theories, Gay Theories,* ed. Diana Fuss, 13–31. New York: Routledge, 1991.

Case, Sue-Ellen. "Toward a Butch-Femme Aesthetic." *Discourse* 11, no. 1 (1988/1989): 55–73.

Castarède, Marie-France. *La Voix et ses sortilèges*. Paris: Société d'édition Les Belles Lettres, 1987.

von Chamisso, Adelbert. *Peter Schlemiel: The Man Who Sold His Shadow*. Translated with an introduction by Peter Wortsman. New York: Fromm International Publishing Co., 1993.

Charlton, David, ed. *E.T.A. Hoffmann's Musical Writings*. Translated by Martyn Green with annotations and an introduction by David Charlton. Cambridge: Cambridge University Press, 1989.

Charpignon, M. *Physiologie, médecine et métaphysique du magnétisme*. Paris: Germer-Baillière, 1841.

Chouquet, Gustave. *L'Histoire de la musique dramatique en France depuis ses origines jusqu'à nos jours*. Paris, 1873.

Clément, Catherine. *Opera, or, The Undoing of Women*. Translated by Betsy Wing with an introduction by Susan McClary. Minneapolis: University of Minnesota Press, 1988.

Combarieu, Jules. *La Musique et la Magie*. Études Philologie Musicale, vol. III. Paris: Alphonse Picard et Fils, 1909.

"Concerts et Soirées." *Le Ménestrel* 45, no. 25 (May 18, 1879): 199.

Cone, Edward T. *Music: A View from Delft*. Chicago: University of Chicago Press, 1989.

Conradi. *Die Musik im Dienste der Magie*. Berlin: Horsterscher Verlag, 1927.

Cooke, Conrad William. *Automata Old and New*. London: Chiswick Press, 1893.

Crabtree, Adam. *Animal Magnetism, Early Hypnotism, and Psychical Research, 1766–1925: An Annotated Bibliography*. White Plains, NY: Kraus, 1988.

Csampai, Attila and Dietmar Holland, eds. *Hoffmanns Erzählungen: Texte, Materialien, Kommentare*. Rororo Opernbücher 7642. Reinbek bei Hamburg: Rowohlt Taschenbuch Verlag GmbH, 1984.

Cusick, Suzanne. "Gender and the Cultural Work of a Classical Music Performance." *Repercussions* 3, no. 1 (spring 1994): 77–110.

Dahlhaus, Carl. *Nineteenth-Century Music*. Translated by J. Bradford Robinson. Berkeley, CA: University of California Press, 1989.

Darnton, Robert. *Mesmerism and the End of the Enlightenment in France*. Cambridge, MA: Harvard University Press, 1968.

Davey, William. *The Illustrated Practical Mesmerist*. London: J. Burns, 1889.

de Francesco, Grete. *The Power of the Charlatan*. Translated by Miriam Beard. New Haven: Yale University Press, 1939.

Deleuze, Joseph Phillipe François. *Histoire critique du magnétisme animal*. 2nd ed. 2 vols. Paris: Germer-Baillière, 1819.

———. *Instruction pratique sur le magnétisme*. Paris: Germer-Baillière, 1825.

———. "Lettre à M. M. . . de la Marne, l'un de redacteurs de l'Éclair . . . " *L'Hermès, Journal du Magnétisme* 32 (October 1828).

———. *Practical Instruction in Animal Magnetism*. Translated and edited by Thomas C. Hartshorn. New York: Fowler and Wells Co., 1879.

Didi-Huberman, Georges. *L'Invention de l'hystérie: Charcot et l'iconographie photographique de la Salpêtrière*. Paris: Macula, 1982.

Didion, Robert. "A la recherche des *Contes* perdus. Zur Quellenproblematik von Offenbachs Oper." In *Jacques Offenbachs Hoffmanns Erzählungen: Konzeption,*

Rezeption, Dokumentation, ed. Gabriele Brandstetter, 131–292. Laaber: Laaber-Verlag, 1988.

Dobat, Klaus-Dieter. *Musik als romantische Illusion: Eine Untersuchung zur Bedeutung der Musikvorstellung E.T.A. Hoffmanns für seine literarisches Werk.* Studien zur Deutschen Literatur series, no. 77. Tübingen: Niemeyer Verlag, 1984.

Dumas, Alexandre. *La Femme au colliers de velours.* Paris: Calmann-Lévy, 1850.

———. *Joseph Balsamo.* Paris: Calmann-Lévy, 1888.

DuPotet. *Manuel de l'étudiant magnétiseur, ou nouvelle instruction pratique sur le magnétisme, fondée sur trente années d'observations, et suivie de la 4e édition des expériences faites en 1820 à l'Hôtel-Dieu de Paris.* Paris: Germer-Baillière, 1846.

Durville, Henri. *L'Hypnotisme théâtral.* Paris, 1921.

Erdan, Alexandre. *La France mistique*[sic]: *tableau des excentricités religieuses de ce temps.* Paris: 1855.

Escudier, Léon. "La Musique de l'Avenir à Paris." *La France Musicale* 24, no. 5 (January 29, 1860): 49–50.

Esdaile, James. *Mesmerism in India, and Its Practical Application in Surgery and Medicine.* Hartford: Silas Andrus and Son, 1850.

Evans, Henry Ridgely. *Cagliostro, a Sorcerer of the Eighteenth Century.* New York: The Masonic Bibliophiles, 1931.

Faris, Alexander. *Jacques Offenbach.* London: Faber and Faber, 1980.

Fétis, F. J. "Hoffmann." *Revue et Gazette Musicale de Paris* 6, no. 41 (1839): 324–27.

Fraison, Laurent. "Exception? Non: continuité!" *L'Avant-Scène Opéra* 25, 2nd ed. (October 1993): 126–30.

Franklin, Benjamin. *Report of Dr. Benjamin Franklin, and other commissioners, charged by the King of France with the examination of animal magnetism, as now practised at Paris.* (translated from the French). London: J. Johnson, 1785.

Freud, Sigmund. "The Uncanny." In *The Standard Edition of the Complete Psychological Works of Sigmund Freud.* 24 vols., ed. James Strachey. London: Hogarth Press, 1953–1974. Vol. 17, 244–53.

———. *Dora: An Analysis of a Case of Hysteria.* Edited and translated by Philip Rieff. New York: Collier Books, 1963.

Fulcher, Jane. *The Nation's Image: French Grand Opera as Politics and Politicized Art.* Cambridge: Cambridge University Press, 1987.

Fuss, Diana. *Identification Papers.* New York: Routledge, 1995.

Gallop, Jane. "Keys to Dora." In *In Dora's Case: Freud—Hysteria—Feminism,* ed. Charles Bernheimer and Claire Kahane, 200–220. Gender and Culture Series, ed. Carolyn G. Heilbrun and Nancy K. Miller. New York: Columbia University Press, 1990.

Garber, Marjorie. *Vested Interests: Cross-Dressing and Cultural Anxiety.* New York and London: Routledge, 1992.

Garofola, Lynn. "The Travesty Dancer in Nineteenth-Century Ballet." *Dance Research Journal* 17, no. 1 (1985): 35–40.

Gauthier, Aubin. *Le Magnétisme catholique, ou introduction à la vraie pratique, et réfutation des opinions de la médecine sur le magnétisme. Ses principes, ses procédés et ses effets.* Paris: Germer-Baillière, 1844.

———. *Traité pratique du magnétisme et du somnambulisme, ou Résumé de tous les principes et procédés du magnétisme, avec la théorie et la définition du somnam-bulisme, la description du caractère et des facultés des somnambules, et les règles de leur direction.* Paris: Germer-Baillière, 1845.

Gautier, Théophile. "Hoffmann." *Chronique de Paris* (August 14, 1836). Re-printed as "Étude sur les contes fantastiques d'Hoffmann." In E.T.A. Hoffmann, *Contes fantastiques,* translated by X. Marmier. Paris, 1843; repr. Geneva: Slatkine Reprints, 1979.

———. *Histoire de l'art dramatique en France depuis vingt-cinq ans.* Paris: Édi-tions Hetzel, 1858. Vol. 6 (Oct 1848–April 1852).

———. *Contes fantastiques,* ed. Hervé Alvado. Paris: Classiques Hachette, 1992.

Genty, Christian. *Histoire du Théâtre Nationale de L'Odéon, 1782–1982.* Paris: Fis-chbacher, 1982.

Ghio, Antonio Marcello. *La Prestidigitation pédagogique musicale.* Paris: Con-férence faite à la Chambre Syndicale de la prestidigitation à Paris par M.A.G., 1900.

Gilman, Sander. *Jewish Self-Hatred: Anti-Semitism and the Hidden Language of the Jews.* Baltimore and London: The Johns Hopkins University Press, 1986.

Guest, Leslie. *Melo-Dy-Namo, the Calostro System.* Summit, NJ: 1948.

Gunsbourg, Raoul. *Cent ans de souvenirs: Ou presque.* Monaco: Editions du Rocher, 1959.

H. L. "Audition des Contes d'Hoffmann d'Offenbach." *Revue et Gazette Musicale de Paris* 46, no. 21 (May 25, 1879): 173.

Hadlock, Heather. "Peering into *The Queen's Throat*." *Cambridge Opera Journal* 5, no. 3 (November 1993): 265–75.

———. "Returns of the Repressed: The Prima Donna from Hoffmann's Tales to Offenbach's *Les Contes.*" *Cambridge Opera Journal* 6, no. 3 (1994): 221–44.

Hanslick, Eduard. "*Hoffmanns Erzählungen:* Phantastische Oper von Offenbach: Erste Aufführung in Wien 1881." In *Hoffmanns Erzählungen: Texte, Materi-alien, Kommentare,* ed. Attila Csampai and Dietmar Holland, 238–45. Rororo Opernbücher. Reinbek bei Hamburg: Rowohlt Taschenbuch Verlag GmbH, 1984.

Harter, Deborah. *Bodies in Pieces: Fantastic Narrative and the Poetics of the Frag-ment.* Stanford: Stanford University Press, 1996.

Haven, Marc. *Le Maître inconnu Cagliostro, étude historique et critique.* Paris: Dor-bon-Ainé, 1912.

Hayward, Margaret. "Supercherie et Hallucination: La Peau de Chagrin: Balzac orientaliste et mesmérien." *Revue de Littérature Comparée* 56, no. 4 (October–December 1982).

Heinzelmann, Josef. "*Hoffmanns Erzählungen:* Eine Oper, ihre Autoren, ihre Be-deutungen." *Österreichische Musikzeitschrift* 42 (1987): 337–50.

———. "Offenbachs Hoffmann: Dokumente anstelle von Erzählungen." In *Jacques Offenbachs Hoffmanns Erzählungen: Konzeption, Rezeption, Dokumen-tation,* ed. Gabriele Brandstetter, 421–38. Laaber: Laaber-Verlag, 1988.

Henseler, Anton. *Jakob Offenbach.* Berlin: Max Hesses Verlag, 1930.

Higgins, Paula. "Women in Music, Feminist Criticism, and Guerilla Musicology: Reflections on Recent Polemics." *Nineteenth-Century Music* 17, no. 2 (fall 1993): 174–92.

Hoffmann, Freia. *Instrument und Körper: Die musizierende Frau in der bürgerlichen Kultur.* Frankfurt am Main and Leipzig: Insel Verlag, 1991.

Hoffmann, E.T.A. "Gedänken bei dem Erscheinen dieser Blätter." *Caecilia* 3, no. 9 (June 1825): 1–12.

———. "Les Aventures de la Nuit de la St.-Sylvestre." *Œuvres Complètes,* vols. 4–8. Translated by Mme E. Bulos. Paris, 1830.

———. *Œuvres complètes.* 18 vols. Translated by Loève-Weimars. Paris: Renduel, 1830–32.

———. "Opuscules relatifs a la musique" series in *Revue musicale de Paris* 9–10 (November 13, 1830–January 15, 1831). Translators not acknowledged.

———. "L'Archet de Baron von B—." *Revue musicale de Paris* 9 (November 13, 1830): 1–12. [Short story "Der Baron von Bagge," 1819.]

———. "Le Chevalier Gluck." *Revue musicale de Paris* 9 (November 20, 1830): 33–43. [From *Fantasiestücke in Callots Manier.*]

———. "Tribulations musicales du maître de chapelle Jean Kreisler: Le Concert de société." *Revue musicale de Paris* 9 (November 27, 1830): 65–73. [*Kreisleriana.*]

———. "Kreisleriana: Sur la musique instrumentale de Beethoven." *Revue musicale de Paris* 9 (December 4, 1830): 97–104.

———. "Don Juan." *Revue musicale de Paris* 10 (December 18, 1831): 161–72.

———. "Biographie de Kreisler—Fragment." *Revue musicale de Paris* 10 (January 8, 1831): 249–57. [Excerpt from *Käter Murr.*]

———. "L'Ennemi de la musique." *Revue musicale de Paris* 10 (January 15, 1831): 281–89. [*Kreisleriana,* "Die Musik-Fiend."]

———. "Sur la musique sacrée." *Revue et Gazette musicale de Paris* 1 (June 29, 1834): 205–10. [From *Die Serapions-Brüder.* First publication in France.]

———. "Le Poète et le compositeur (Part I)." *Revue et Gazette musicale de Paris* 6, no. 58 (November 10, 1839): 457–60. [First publication in France.]

———. "Le Poète et le compositeur (Part II)." *Revue et Gazette musicale de Paris* 6, no. 59 (November 17, 1839): 465–69. [First publication in France.]

———. *Rat Krespel, Die Fermate, Don Juan.* Stuttgart: Reclam, 1964.

———. *Der Sandmann, Das öde Haus.* Stuttgart: Reclam, 1969.

———. *Contes fantastiques.* 2 vols. Translated by Loève-Weimars (1830–32). Intro., chronology, and notes by José Lambert. Paris: GF-Flammarion, 1979–80.

———. *The Best Tales of Hoffmann,* ed. E. F. Bleiler. New York: Dover Publications, 1967.

———. *Kreisleriana I and II.* In *E.T.A. Hoffmann's Musical Writings.* Translated by Martyn Clarke, edited by David Charlton. Cambridge: Cambridge University Press, 1989.

———. "Don Giovanni, A Strange Episode in the Life of a Music Fanatic." In Heinrich Von Kleist, Ludwig Tieck, and E.T.A. Hoffmann, *Six German Romantic Tales,* 104–17. Translated by Ronald Taylor. London: Angel Books, 1985.

Holtus, Gunter. "Die Rezeption E.T.A. Hoffmanns in Frankreich: Untersuchungen zu den Übersetzungen von A. V. Loève-Weimars." *Mitteilungen der E.T.A. Hoffmann-Gesellschaft-Bamberg* 27 (1981): 28–54.

Hortschansky, Klaus. "Offenbachs 'grosse romantische Oper': *Die Rhein-Nixen* (1864)." In *Jacques Offenbach: Komponist und Weltbürger—eine Symposion,* ed. Winfried Kirsch and Ronny Dietrich, 209–47. Mainz: Schott, 1985.

How to Be a Thought Reader. Manchester: Cartwright & Rattay Ltd., 1920.

Ince, R. B. *Franz Anton Mesmer, His Life and Teaching.* London: William Rider and Sons, Ltd., 1920.

Janin, Jules. "Hoffmann, conte fantastique." *Revue et Gazette musicale de Paris* 1, no. 14 (March 30, 1836 and April 6, 1836). Incorporates unacknowledged translation of Hoffmann, "Gedänken bei dem Erscheinen dieser Blätter," in *Caecilia* 3, no. 9 (June 1825).

Kahane, Martine and Nicole Wild. *Wagner et la France.* Paris: Bibliothèque Nationale, 1983.

Kamla, Thomas A. "E.T.A. Hoffmann's 'Der Sandmann': The Narcissistic Poet as Romantic Solipsist." *Germanic Review* 63, no. 2 (spring 1988): 94–102.

Keck, Jean-Christophe. "La Genèse et les légendes." *L'Avant-Scène Opéra* 25, 2nd ed. (October 1993): 8–17.

———. *"Les Contes d'Hoffmann:* Commentaire littéraire et musical." *L'Avant-Scène Opéra* 25, 2nd ed. (October 1993): 26–124.

Koestenbaum, Wayne. *The Queen's Throat: Opera, Homosexuality, and the Mystery of Desire.* New York: Poseidon Press, 1993.

Kofman, Sarah. *The Enigma of Woman.* Translated by Catherine Porter. Ithaca: Cornell University Press, 1985.

Kracauer, Siegfried. "Der Pakt mit dem Tod." In *Jacques Offenbachs Hoffmanns Erzählungen: Texte, Materiale, Kommentare,* ed. Attila Csampai and Dietmar Holland, 228–36. Rororo Opernbücher. Reinbek bei Hamburg: Rowohlt Taschenbuch Verlag GmbH, 1984.

———. *Jacques Offenbach und das Paris seiner Zeit.* Amsterdam: A. de Lange, 1938.

Lacoue-Labarthe, Phillipe. *Musica Ficta (Figures of Wagner).* Translated by Felicia McCarren. Meridian: Crossing Aesthetics series, ed. Werner Hamacher and David E. Wellbery. Stanford: Stanford University Press, 1994.

LaFontaine, Charles. *L'Art de magnétiser: ou le magnétisme animal considéré sous le point de vue théorique, pratique et thérapeutique.* Paris: G-Baillière, 1847.

La Vellma [Lustig, David J.]. *Vaudeville Mind Reading and Kindred Phenomena.* New York: R. W. Doidge (Caliostro Publications), 1929.

Le Parfait Physicien. Paris: Le Bailly Libraire, 1850.

Leask, Nigel. "Shelly's 'Magnetic Ladies': Romantic Mesmerism and the Politics of the Body." In *Beyond Romanticism: New Approaches to Texts and Contexts 1780–1832,* ed. Stephen Copley and John Whale, 53–78. London: Routledge, 1992.

Leonardi, Susan J. "To Have a Voice: The Politics of the Diva." *Perspectives on Contemporary Literature* 13 (1987): 65–72.

Locke, Ralph. "Constructing the Oriental 'Other': Saint-Saëns's *Samson et Dalila.*" *Cambridge Opera Journal* 3 (1991): 261–302.

Martin, Marietta. *Un aventurier intellectuel sous la Restauration et la Monarchie de Juillet: le docteur Koreff (1783–1851).* Paris: 1925.

Martinet, André. *Offenbach.* Paris: Dentu, 1887.

Maskelyne, J. N. *The Magnetic Lady, or A Human Magnet De-magnetized.* Bristol and London: Simpkin, Marshall, Hamilton, Kent & Co., 1892.

McClary, Susan. *Feminine Endings.* Minneapolis: University of Minnesota Press, 1991.

———. *George Bizet: Carmen.* Cambridge Opera Handbook. Cambridge: Cambridge University Press, 1993.

Mesmer, Franz Anton. *Mesmerism, a translation of the original scientific and medical writings.* Translated by George Bloch. Los Altos, CA: W. Kaufman, 1980.

Miller, J. Hillis. *Fiction and Repetition: Seven English Novels.* Cambridge, MA: Harvard University Press, 1982.

Miner, Margaret. *Resonant Gaps: Between Baudelaire and Wagner.* Athens, GA: University of Georgia Press, 1995.

Moss, Arthur and Evalyn Marvel. *Cancan and Barcarolle: The Life and Times of Jacques Offenbach.* New York: Exposition Press, 1952.

Nattiez, Jacques. *Music and Discourse: Toward a Semiology of Music.* Translated by Carolyn Abbate. Princeton: Princeton University Press, 1990.

———. *Wagner Androgyne.* Translated by Stewart Spencer. Princeton: Princeton University Press, 1993.

Noske, Frits. *French Song from Berlioz to Duparc: The Origin and Development of the Mélodie,* 2nd ed. Revised by Frits Noske and Rita Benton, translated by Rita Benton. New York: Dover Publications, 1988.

Oeser, Fritz. "*Hoffmanns Erzählungen* in kritischer Neuausgabe." In *Jacques Offenbachs Hoffmanns Erzählungen: Texte, Materiale, Kommentare,* ed. Attila Csampai and Dietmar Holland, 218–27. Rororo Opernbücher. Reinbek bei Hamburg: Rowohlt Taschenbuch Verlag GmbH, 1984.

———. "Vorwort." In Offenbach, *Hoffmanns Erzählungen/Les Contes d'Hoffmann, phantastische Oper in fünf Akten.* New source-critical edition by Fritz Oeser. Alkor: Edition-Kassel, 1977.

Offenbach, Jacques. *Les Contes d'Hoffmann: Dossier de presse parisienne (1881).* Ed. Arnold Jacobshagen. Paris: Musik-Edition Lucie Galland, 1995.

———. *Lettres à Meilhac et Halévy,* ed. Philippe Goninet. Paris: Séguier, 1994.

Le Petit physicien. Paris, Lille: Imprimerie de Blouquel, 1820.

Pinchbeck, William. *The Expositor, or Many Mysteries Unravelled.* Boston: Pinchbeck, 1805.

Poizat, Michel. *The Angel's Cry: Beyond the Pleasure Principle in Opera.* Translated by Arthur Denner. Ithaca: Cornell University Press, 1992.

Porel, Paul and Georges Monval. *L'Odéon: Histoire administrative, anecdotique et littéraire du Second Théâtre Français (1782–1853).* Paris: 1876, 1882.

Pourvoyeur, Robert. *Offenbach.* Paris: Seuil, 1994.

The Practical Magician and Ventriloquist's Guide. New York: L. Lipkind, 1976.

Price, David. *Magic: A Pictorial History of Conjurors in the Theater.* New York, London, and Toronto: Cornwall Books, 1985.

Professeur De Vere le fakir et sa fille enchantée Miss Lily Edith. Paris and London: Paris, Choumara; London, C. de Vere, 1873.

Putnam, Allen. *Mesmerism, spiritualism, witchcraft and miracle: a brief treatise showing that mesmerism is a key which will unlock many chambers of mystery.* Boston: Colby and Rich, 1890.

Reynolds, Charles and Regina. *100 Ans d'affiches de la magie*. Paris: 1976.

Ricard. *Traité théorique et pratique du magnétisme animal, ou méthode facile pour apprendre à magnétiser*. Paris: Germer-Baillière, 1841.

Rice, N. L. *Phrenology Examined . . . also an examination of the Claims of Mesmerism*. New York: Robert Carter & Bros., 1849.

Rissin, David. *Offenbach, ou le rire en musique*. Paris: Fayard, 1980.

Robert-Houdin, Jean-Eugène. *Confidences d'un prestidigitateur*. Paris, 1859.

———. *King of the Conjurers, Memoirs of Robert-Houdin*. Translated by Lascelles Wraxall, edited by Milbourne Christopher. New York: Dover, 1964.

———. *Les Secrets de la prestidigitation et de la magie*. London and New York: G. Routledge and Sons, 1881.

Rouff, Marcel and Thérèse Casevitz. *La Vie du fête sous le second empire*. Paris: Éditions Jules Tallandier, 1931.

Salmen, Walter. "Venedig und die Barkarole in Oper und Operette." In *Die 'Couleur locale' in der Oper des 19. Jahrhunderts,* ed. Heinz Becker, 257–68. Studien zur Musikgeschichte des 19. Jahrhunderts XLII. Regensburg: Bosse, 1976.

Saint-Léon. *Le Violon du Diable, ballet fantastique en 2 actes*. Music by Cesar Pugni. Paris: Librairie de l'Opéra, 1849.

Saint-Saëns, Camille. *Harmonie et mélodie*. Paris, 1885.

Scheidler, John G. *Art of Conjuring Simplified*. Cleveland: John G. Scheidler Enterprises, 1876.

Schneider, Louis. *Les Maîtres de l'opérette français: Offenbach*. Paris, 1923.

Scott, Sir Walter. "Sur Hoffmann et les compositions fantastiques." Introduction to E.T.A. Hoffmann, *Œuvres complètes*. 18 vols. Translated by Loève-Weimars. Paris: Renduel, 1830–32.

Showalter, Elaine. *The Female Malady: Women, Madness, and English Culture, 1830–1980*. New York: Penguin Books, 1985.

Silverman, Kaja. *The Acoustic Mirror: The Female Voice in Psychoanalysis and Cinema*. Bloomington, IN: Indiana University Press, 1988.

Sinnett, Alfred Percy. *The Rationale of Mesmerism*. Boston and New York: Houghton, Mifflin and Co., 1892.

Solie, Ruth, ed. *Musicology and Difference*. Berkeley, CA: University of California Press, 1993.

Somerfield, Signor T. *Modern Magic and Mystery made easy*. Wolverhampton: Paulton Bros., 1890.

Stone, William L. *Letter to Dr. A. Brigham on Animal Magnetism: being an account of a remarkable interview between the author and Miss Loraina Brackett while in a state of somnambulism*. New York: George Dearborn & Co., 1837.

Taruskin, Richard. *Text and Act: Essays on Music and Performance*. New York: Oxford University Press, 1995.

Tatar, Maria M. *Spellbound: Studies on Mesmerism and Literature*. Princeton: Princeton University Press, 1978.

Thought Reader. London: Griffith, Farran & Co. Ltd., 1885.

van der Tuin, H. *L'Évolution psychologique, esthétique et littéraire de Théophile Gautier*. Paris and Amsterdam: 1933.

Le Véritable escamoteur. Paris: L. Baudot, 1865.

Vocal and Optical Deceptions. London: J. & R. Maxwell, 1885.

Voss, Egon. "'L'alouette ou la femme . . . l'une y laisse la vie, et l'autre y perd son âme': Zur Bedeutung von Dapertuttos es-Moll-Chanson." In *Jacques Offenbachs Hoffmanns Erzählungen: Konzeption, Rezeption, Dokumentation,* ed. Gabriele Brandstetter, 317–38. Laaber: Laaber-Verlag, 1988.

Wagner, Richard. *Opera and Drama.* Vol. 2, *Richard Wagner's Prose Works,* translated by W. A. Ellis. New York: Broude Brothers, 1966. Reprint, London: Routledge & Kegan Paul, 1892–1899.

Weiner, Marc. *Richard Wagner and the Anti-Semitic Imagination.* Omaha: University of Nebraska Press, 1995.

Wessling, Berndt. *Wagners Beute, Heines Geisel.* Dusseldorf: Droste, 1984.

Woolf, B. "Letter from Kater Murr." *Berliner allgemeine musikalische Zeitung* 2, no.11 (March 16 1825): 81–83.

Zamara: Explanatory Remarks. Leicester: W. Willson, 1889.

Zola, Émile. *Nana.* Translated and with an introduction by Douglas Parmée. Oxford: Oxford University Press, 1992.

Musical and Theatrical Works

Adam, Adolphe. *Cagliostro.* Opéra-comique. Paris: Bureau Central de Musique, 1844.

Ancessy, Joseph-Jacques-Augustin. Incidental music for *Les Contes d'Hoffmann.* Score. 1851. F-PBn Vms 803.

Antony, Béraud and Léopold Chandezon. *Cagliostro.* Melodrama. Paris: Bezou, 1825.

Barbier, Jules and Michel Carré. *Les Contes d'Hoffmann, drame fantastique en 3 actes.* Paris: Michel Lévy, 1851.

Barbier, Jules. "Faksimile der Akte IV und V des Pariser Zensurlibrettos vom Januar 1881 der *Contes d'Hoffmann.*" In *Jacques Offenbachs Hoffmanns Erzählungen: Konzeption, Rezeption, Dokumentation,* ed. Gabriele Brandstetter, 439–64. Laaber: Laaber-Verlag, 1988.

Dumanoir, Anicet. *La Fiole de Cagliostro.* Vaudeville. Paris: 1835.

Dumersan, Théophile Marion, Jules-Joseph Gabriel (pseud. Lurieu), and Charles Desire Dupeuty. *Victorine, ou, La Nuit porte conseil.* Paris: 1831.

Dupaty, Alphonse and de Reveroni. *Cagliostro ou les Illuminés.* Opéra-comique. Paris: Chez Barba, Libraire, Palais-Royal, 1810.

Grangé, Phillipe Gille, and Ludovic Halévy. *Le Carnaval des Revues.* Paris: Heugel, 1860.

Offenbach, Jacques. *Les Contes d'Hoffmann,* "Duo de troisième act" [C'est une chanson d'amour]. Autograph MS, May 29, 1877. F-PBn Ms 5923.

———. Sketchbook. 1879. F-PBn Ms 20649.

———. *Les Contes d'Hoffmann,* "3ème Acte, nos. 1–5" [Antonia act and Epilogue]. Partial autograph score completed by Ernest Guiraud et al., 1879–1881. F-PBo Ms Res 1055.

———. *Les Contes d'Hoffmann,* "No. 23. Finale du quatrième act" [Giulietta]. Facsimile of the autograph score. Mainz: Schott, 1998.

———. *Les Contes d'Hoffmann; opéra fantastique en 4 actes,* 1st edn. Piano-vocal score. Paris: Choudens, 1881. Plate no. A.C. 5100.

————. *I Racconti di Hoffmann/Hoffmanns Erzählungen; opéra fantastique en 4 actes.* Piano-vocal score. Paris: Choudens, 1881.

————. *Les Contes d'Hoffmann; opéra fantastique en 4 actes: Chants et Paroles.* Paris: Choudens, 1882.

————. *Les Contes d'Hoffmann; opéra fantastique en 4 actes,* 5th edn. Paris: Choudens, 1907. Plate no. A.C. 5303.

————. *Hoffmanns Erzählungen/Les Contes d'Hoffmann: phantastische Oper in fünf Akten.* Piano-vocal score. New source-critical edition by Fritz Oeser. Alkor: Edition-Kassel, 1977.

————. *Hoffmanns Erzählungen.* Text by Jules Barbier after the play of the same name by Jules Barbier and Michel Carré; German text by Joseph Heinzelmann. Edited by Michael Kaye. Mainz: Schott, 1988.

————. *Fantasio.* Paris: Choudens, 1872.

————. *La Symphonie de l'avenir.* Paris: Heugel, 1860.

————. *Le Voyage dans la lune.* Paris: Choudens, 1875.

Palianti, Louis. *Cagliostro ou les Illuminés.* Livret de *mise en scène.* 1810. F-Pn Rés. Th-B0138, vols. 1 and 5.

Scribe, Eugène. *Cagliostro, opéra-comique en 3 actes.* Music by Adolphe Adam. Paris: La France Dramatique, 1843.

Select Discography

Offenbach, Jacques. *Les Contes d'Hoffmann.* Choeur et Orchestre du Théâtre National de L'Opéra-comique/André Cluytens. EMI Classics CD5-65260-2, 1948. This recording follows the Choudens 1907 score, except that "Scintille, diamant" is transposed down for Charles Soix (Dapertutto). Bourvil gives the most distinctive performance available of Andres/Cochenille/Pitichinaccio/Frantz.

————. *Les Contes d'Hoffmann.* Choeur René Duclos et Orchestre de la Société du Conservatoire / André Cluytens. EMI Classics CMS 7-63222-2, 1965. This recording follows the Choudens 1907 score, except that Nicklausse is played by baritone Jean-Christophe Benoit.

————. *Les Contes d'Hoffmann.* L'Orchestre de la Suisse Romande / Richard Bonynge. London 417 363-2, 1972. Bonynge's performing edition, with spoken dialogue in place of Guiraud's recitatives and the ensemble "Hélas! mon coeur" reworked as a quartet in the Epilogue.

————. *Hoffmanns Erzählungen/Les Contes d'Hoffmann.* L'Orchestre Symphonique et Choeurs de l'Opéra National du Théâtre Royal de la Monnaie, Brussels / Sylvain Cambreling. EMI Records CDS 7 49641 1/2/4, 1988. This recording follows Oeser's 1976 edition, but includes Nicklausse's "Une poupée aux yeux d'émail," Dappertutto's "Scintille, diamant," and the ensemble "Hélas! mon coeur" (all rejected by Oeser) in an appendix.

————. *Les Contes d'Hoffmann.* Staatskapelle Dresden/Jeffrey Tate. Philips 422-374-2, 1992. This recording follows a modified version of Kaye's 1988 edition.

————. *Les Contes d'Hoffmann.* Chorus and Orchestra of the Opéra de Lyon / Kent Nagano. Erato 14330, 1996. This recording follows Kaye's 1988 edition.

Videography

The Tales of Hoffmann. Produced, directed, and written by Michael Powell and Emeric Pressburger. Music by Jacques Offenbach. Choreography by Frederick Ashton. 125 min. Janus Films, 1951; reissued Home Vision TAL 060. Videocassette. Sung in English. A fantastical, if uneven, interpretation. The filmmakers take Offenbach's opera as the point of departure for exploring their own concerns with sexuality, identity, and performance. They translate many of the opera's musical motifs into balletic ones; the Olympia act, starring Moira Shearer, is the most famous and most successful. See Ian Christie, *Arrows of Desire: The Films of Michael Powell and Emeric Pressburger* (London: Faber, 1994); and Bruce Babbington and Peter Evans, "Matters of Life and Death in Powell and Pressburger's *The Tales of Hoffmann*" in *A Night in at the Opera: Media Representations of Opera,* ed. Jeremy Tambling (London: J. Libbey, 1994), 145–68.

Jacques Offenbach: Des Contes d'Hoffmann. Opéra de Lyon, directed by Louis Erlo, cond. Kent Nagano. 150 min. Home Vision TAL 080. Videocassette. Sung in French. This video records the May 1993 Opéra de Lyon production based on Michael Kaye's edition. See my review in *Notes* (September 1995): 158–59.

Index

Adam, Adolphe, 72, 78
Aeolian harp, 64
allegory, *Les Contes* as, 94
de Almeida, Antonio, 3–4
"Amis l'amour tendre," 122, 36
"A New Year's Eve Adventure," 22, 32, 45, 115
animal magnetism, 51, 67; and hysteria, 67
Antonia act, 7, 99–108; association with Offenbach's life, 87; and Carvalho revision, 11; death scene, 40–41, 54, 56; synopsis, 5
Antonia character, 4, 145n.1; as Hoffmann's alter ego, 65–66; and compulsion to sing, 68; and forbidden music, 66; as mesmerized woman, 52; as prima donna, 73; relation to Olympia character, 79; in "The Tales of Hoffmann" (1951 film), 18; voice of, 21
Auber, D.F.E., 7, 75, 113

ballad. *See* narrative ballad
Ballo in Maschera, Un (Verdi), 121
Barbier, Pierre, and 1907 libretto, 11
Barbier, Jules: 1881 libretto as basis for Kaye edition (1995), 12. *See also* Barbier and Carré
Barbier and Carré, 4; and Giulietta character, 126–27; literary values of, 17; and Pitichinaccio character, 119–20; and Schlemiel character, 116; as source for Venetian act, 115
"Barcarolle": in Carvalho revision, 11; in Guiraud revision, 11; as siren song, 127–28, 133
baritone voice, and diabolical characters, 28
Bat-a-clan (Offenbach), 95
"Belle nuit, o nuit d'amour." *See* Barcarolle
Belle Hélène, La (Offenbach), 95
Bertram character (Meyerbeer), 31
Bizet, Georges. *See Carmen*
Bloch, André, 11
Bonynge, Richard, 148n.37
Bouffes Parisiens, Les, 6
Butler, Judith, 130–32

Carmen (Bizet), 14, 126; as model for *Les Contes*, 8; as modern opéra-comique, 9; performed song in, 36
Carré, Michel. *See* Barbier and Carré
Carvalho, Leon, 79, 90, 108; as first editor of *Les Contes*, 10–12; influence on *Les Contes* genesis, 8–10
castration, symbolic: linked to laughter and death, 121; and loss of reflection, 120
"C'est une chanson d'amour," 7
von Chamisso, Adelbert, 116; "Peter Schlemil's wundersame Geschichte," 120. *See also* Schlemiel character
Charcot, Jean-Michel, 52, 68
Chouquet, Gustave, 94–95
clairvoyant speech, 59. *See also* mesmerism
clarinet: in Dr. Miracle scene, 64; as female voice, 75. *See also* woodwinds
Clément, Cathérine, 67, 84
coloratura. *See* Doll Song
Comettant, Oscar, 96
Confidences d'un prestidigitateur (Houdin), 64
Contes d'Hoffmann, Les (Offenbach): as allegory about musical style, 94; libretto (*see also* Barbier and Carré), castration motif in, 120–21; libretto, Oeser's version, 124; premiere at Opéra-Comique (1881), 86; preview performance (1879), 89, 89; relation to *Don Giovanni*, 33–35; synopsis, 5–6
Contes d'Hoffmann, Les (1851 play), 4; Giulietta character in, 126 (*see also* "A New Year's Eve Adventure"); music in, 6, 54–56, 80; premiere at Théâtre de l'Odéon, 42; reception, 18, 42; as source for Venetian act, 115
Coppélia (Délibes), 78, 80
Coppélius character, 7, 78; as nemesis figure, 22; in 1907 version, 11
"Councilor Krespel" (E.T.A. Hoffmann), 44. *See also* "Rat Krespel"
couplet structure, 8; and French operetta style, 93–94; and Hoffmann character, 28
Crespel character, 65, 66